Towards a Theatrical Jurisprudence

This book brings the insights of theatre theory to law, legal interpretation and the jurisprudential to reshape law as a practice of response and responsibility.

Confronting a Baconian antitheatrical legality embedded in its jurisprudences and interpretative practices, Marett Leiboff turns to theatre theory and practice to ground a theatrical jurisprudence, taking its cues from Han-Thies Lehmann's conception of the post-dramatic theatre and the early work of theatre visionary Jerzy Grotowski. She asks law to move beyond an imagined ideal grounded in Aristotelian drama and tragedy, and turns to the formation of the legal interpreter – lawyer, judge, jurisprudent – as fundamental to understanding what's "noticed" or not noticed in law. We "notice" most easily through that which is written into the body of the legal interpreter, in a way that can't be replicated through law's standard practices of thinking and reasoning. Without more, thinking and reasoning are the epitome of antitheatricality legality; a set of theatrical antonyms, including transgression and instinct, offer instead a set of possibilities through which to reconceive assumptions and foundational concepts etched into the legal imaginary. And by turning to critical dramaturgy, the book reveals that the liveliness that sits behind theatrical jurisprudence isn't a new concept in law at all, but has a long pedigree and lineage that had been lost and hidden. Theatrical jurisprudence, which demands an awareness of self and beyond self, grounds a responsiveness that can't be found within doctrine, principle, or the technocratic, but also challenges us to notice what it is we think we know as well as what we know of lives in law that aren't our own.

The book will be of interest to scholars and students in the field of jurisprudence, legal theory, theatre and performance studies, cultural studies and philosophy.

Marett Leiboff is Associate Professor of Law at the University of Wollongong, Australia.

Space, Materiality and the Normative
Series Editors: Andreas Philippopoulos-Mihalopoulos and Christian Borch

Space, Materiality and the Normative presents new ways of thinking about the connections between space and materiality from a normative perspective. At the interface of law, social theory, politics, architecture, geography and urban studies, the series is concerned with addressing the use, regulation and experience of space and materiality, broadly understood, and in particular with exploring their links and the challenges they raise for law, politics and normativity.

Books in this series:

Border Security
Shores of Politics, Horizons of Justice
Peter Chambers

Towards a Theatrical Jurisprudence
Marett Leiboff

Forthcoming:

Placing International Law
Authority, Jurisdiction, Technique
Fleur Johns, Shaun McVeigh, Sundhya Pahuja, Thomas Skouteris, and Robert Wai

Controlling Urban Events
Law, Ethics and the Material
Andrea Pavoni

Spatial Justice in the City
Sophie Watson

https://www.routledge.com/Space-Materiality-and-the-Normative/book-series/SMNORM

Towards a Theatrical Jurisprudence

Marett Leiboff

Routledge
Taylor & Francis Group
LONDON AND NEW YORK

First published 2020 by Routledge

2 Park Square, Milton Park, Abingdon, Oxon, OX14 4RN
605 Third Avenue, New York, NY 10017

Routledge is an imprint of the Taylor & Francis Group, an informa business

First issued in paperback 2020

British Library Cataloguing in Publication Data
A catalogue record for this book is available from the British Library

Library of Congress Cataloging-in-Publication Data
Names: Leiboff, Marett, author.
Title: Towards a theatrical jurisprudence / Marett Leiboff.
Description: Abingdon, Oxon ; New York, NY : Routledge, 2020. |
Series: Space, materiality and the normative
Identifiers: LCCN 2019015168 (print) | LCCN 2019018276 (ebook) | ISBN 9781315562346 (ebk) | ISBN 9781138672789 (hbk)
Subjects: LCSH: Jurisprudence. | Sociological jurisprudence. |
Law--Psychological aspects.
Classification: LCC K240 (ebook) | LCC K240 .L45 2020 (print) |
DDC 340/.11--dc23
LC record available at https://lccn.loc.gov/2019015168

ISBN: 978-1-138-67278-9 (hbk)
ISBN: 978-0-367-78469-0 (pbk)

Typeset in Galliard
by Taylor & Francis Books

This book is dedicated to my mother, Elizabeth Leiboff (1929–2018), with love.

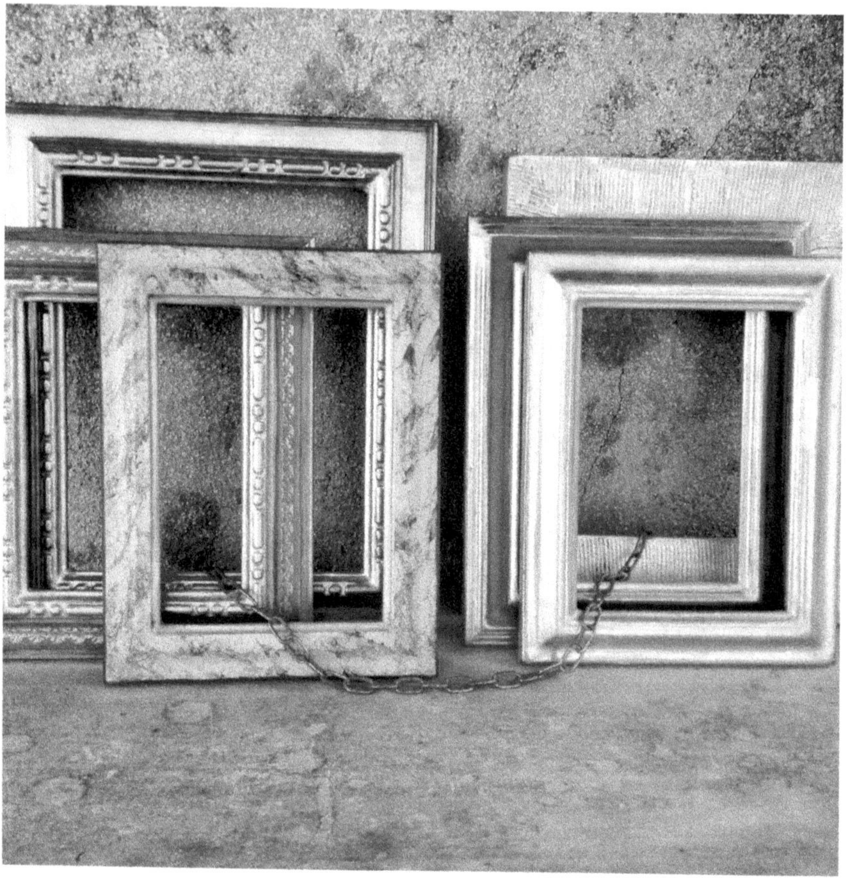

http://picpoet.net

Contents

Illustrations

Figures

Table

Preface

It is odd to contemplate what this book would have looked like if I had managed to complete it years ago, when I first began to conceive of a theatrical jurisprudence. The book, as finally proposed in 2015, has changed. Most of the differences are largely inchoate, though some of the case examples I use have changed because of their potency as exemplars of the theatrical, and through the inevitable developments in the broader field since I first proposed the book, including the availability in English of Hans-Thies Lehmann's extraordinary, magisterial volume *Tragedy and Dramatic Theatre*, published in 2016, which has now done so much of the work accounting for philosophy and theory's antipathy towards theatre (and by extension jurisprudence and critical legal thinking) that has saved me reinventing this position and authorises my position from within theatre. Yet none of these instances explain why the book is different.

What drives the difference is a recognition, not noticed in happier times, of just how much the theatrical, and by extension theatrical jurisprudence, is shaped by and responds to the challenges and dangers thrown out through and by time and place. It has always been thus, but the pull to the jurisprudential and law somehow obscured the theatrical's activation in times of strife. The circumstances surrounding the completion of this book in 2018 are exemplary in this respect, giving theatrical jurisprudence an urgency and piquancy unimaginable even two years before. This, then, is what makes the book different, taking further its original task of asking us as lawyers to notice and be aware beyond our own selves, to understand just how much of ourselves is deployed in undertaking the most minute practices of law, and to be aware of the material conditions of existence as an essential and fundamental facet of our engagement with law and its texts. What this reminds us, too, is that law is inevitably bound up in each of our lives and in the time and place from which we experience and imagine it, and it reminds us too that there is something extra that we need as lawyers to hear the signals and warnings of law that might, and could, go wrong.

In a sense, this book needed to wait until the time was right, though it wasn't clear, ever, that this time would come. That its time did come is not a cause for celebration, though, but regardless, the book would have been finished, but it would have lacked the thing that it needed to make it do its work. So spending a few years on ice, in large part through circumstances that forced an unwanted hiatus, revealed a silver lining that was to provide the conditions that the theatrical needs, or at least a theatrical that is imbued with something to do or say – a world that is out of shape, that is tilted off course, when there is something pressing that demands a response. That is not to say that others haven't noticed other times where law has gone wrong by drawing on the lens of theatre and performance. Rather, this book, in thinking of a theatrical jurisprudence, interrogates the foundational conditions that have shaped law, which, at some point after 2015 or 2016, seemed to unravel. So this book holds the shape and content it was always going to contain, but it has been given its dramaturgical trigger, the thing that takes it into an active practice, a living jurisprudence that responds to the here and now through images – imagination – and experience, as well as the deeply imbricated stories and concepts. What the theatrical asks of us, too, is to notice and connect law and its pasts to law in the present, and by necessity its future, as a work in progress with an eye to the easiness with which foundational stories are lost and in doing so, how law can repeat mistakes and injustices as a result.

Theatrical jurisprudence, too, is driven by something else that is largely considered an irrelevancy for law, grounded as it is in a Kantian ideal and the hope of rationality, impartiality, and an unbounded belief in the liberal self. For the theatrical reminds us just how much those ideals begin to unravel at the moment we are confronted with the liveness of an encounter forced upon us but also that it affords the depth of that moral imagination that reveals how law needs more than technocrats and automatons to do its work. Given the fundamental importance of law and its role in shaping and regulating the lives of the polity, society and individuals, it is striking that we pay such little attention to *what we bring* to law, a mark of how we do our law, while theatre, which has no actual consequence of the kind law has, expects its participants, actors, directors and dramaturgs, to be deeply inured in forms of training that expect them to be both self-aware and aware beyond the self. Law, by and large, doesn't care, meaning that whilst we are expected to be technically capable, there is next to no consideration of self-awareness or awareness of worlds beyond the self. Thus, limited ethics training and training in the rules of professional responsibility aside, mean that law is able to be left in the hands of the careful and careless, the selfish and the selfless, and aware and unaware, largely because we hold onto the belief that law is activated through and by the ideal, that the text itself embeds and imbricates all that is needed. But scratch the surface just a little and we find that there is an invisible hand at play, the ghost in the machine that animates the ideal is bound up in worlds beyond the limits of the law. Genovese and McVeigh's jurisographic has provided the most significant move towards understanding what this means for reading, interpreting, and practising law. Inspired by the work of Pierre Hadot, jurisography also points in the direction of a mistrust of conventional philosophy and theory as the prime and best means by which thinking is shaped, and the best outcomes created. For Hadot is impatient with philosophy and the dissonance between what it says it does, and what it does, ideals that do not match up with practice and the activating self, holding ideals that fail to match with their practices This, too, is the concern of theatrical jurisprudence, which does not pretend or suggest that it is a jurisprudence in the tradition of philosophy or of theory, but as a practice that guides and shapes understanding of foundational concepts and ideals in law. As a living jurisprudence, thus, theatrical jurisprudence sits within the conflicting images of the minor jurisprudence, so perfectly shaped by Peter Goodrich and Panu Minkkinen, and taken forward by others, in particular Olivia Barr's moving jurisprudence, but it is far less jurisprudential, in the sense of jurisprudence conceived as theory or philosophy, for the reasons that Hans-Thies Lehmann makes plain. So even as theatre and its related fields of performance draw upon the philosophical and the theoretical, theatrical jurisprudence, like theatre itself, is a jurisprudence that is meant to be done and acted upon, as a practice and a form of conduct that shapes through the formation of the self as aware and noticing, and imbricated through practice, into the consciousness and hence the body of the lawyer. But it is not just any conduct or any form of behaviour, but a deeply conscientious and historically aware body, of the kind that Jerzy Grotowski demanded of his actors and of his audiences.

Theatrical jurisprudence, then, is concerned with the conduct of law through the legal self, which brings an awareness of the world beyond the margins as expressed in law, which has, in any case, been part and parcel of the conditions and practice of law regardless of what we might tell ourselves. What theatrical jurisprudence does, though, is to make this plain, and through careful attention to the cases, we find that the law is replete with instances of the world beyond its imagined boundaries, theatricalised. What the theatrical points to is that law is a curated practice, and that lawyers, and by extension the courts, are its curators, its custodians, who need to take care of and be responsible for law, giving form to the promise of Scott Veitch's reminder of law's irresponsibility, in the terms shaped by the Melbourne School, in particular through the custodianship of Shaun McVeigh, Ann Genovese, and Olivia Barr. Theatrical jurisprudence, asks us, too, to notice the world beyond the pages of law, to pay attention to the times and places of law, and to notice the ghost in the machine of law, the legal self who is aware or not, alert or not, or hostile or not to the circumstances which inevitably ground the law. Without McVeigh and Genovese's creation of jurisography, I am not quite sure that I would ever have been able to make these claims, for Shaun McVeigh is right in saying that I write small, not large things, and I am also beyond hesitant in making claims, far preferring to write stories that will then force responses, as acts of theatrical jurisprudence. So in making claims at all, this book is to remind us that we ought to pay attention to those small stories and the lives embedded in them, as a practice of reminding each of us how our lives shape our reading of law.

Acknowledgments

I have so many people to thank, acknowledge and recognise for their role in helping me think through theatrical jurisprudence and in getting this book from a set of ideas into a proposal and beyond – people who have been central in the writing of this book. They are legion for so many reasons. To Andreas Philippopoulos-Mihalopoulos, for his excitement and encouragement, and he and Christian Borch for their patience in the delays in finishing the book. To Colin Perrin, and the Routledge editorial assistants Laura Muir, Hannah Lovelock, and Nicola Sharpe, who have patiently waited for the book to be finished, extending deadlines with good humour. I can't thank Shaun McVeigh enough, for his friendship and encouragement, for his awareness that going into the unknown and unchartered is a terrifying prospect. His early understanding of this project and encouragement is something I can't ever repay. Peter Goodrich has championed and made me pay attention to the theatrical beyond my first forays into my pre-law field, and in his own inimitable style forced my hand into claiming a theatrical jurisprudence, through his commission, along with Marco Wan, of the first Critical Terrain piece, "Theatricalizing Law" in the journal *Law and Literature*. Ann Genovese has been cheering on from the sidelines, as a real historian and jurisprudent, noticing how I would use histories to force responses and seeking more from me, along with Peter Rush, one of the first scholars to actively contribute the theatrical to legal scholarship, and so too Les Moran, whose guidance and friendship I cherish and whose performances are legendary. My thanks and gratitude to them all.

There are so many more people to thank, for giving me places and spaces in which to ply nascent ideas, for their interest and curiosity about this work, and for their friendship. Daniela Carpi, Jeanne Gaakeer and Greta Olson have been the most wonderful friends and supporters. The young and brilliant scholars who began their careers at Melbourne Law School who have been excited by this work and taken it into their orbit: Connal Parsley, Olivia Barr, Laura Petersen, Adil Khan and Marc Trabsky, just to scratch the surface, and the young scholars also trained in both law and theatre/performance at Warwick and Monash Sean Mulcahy, and Markéta Štěpáníková (née Klusoňová) at Masaryk are taking performance, theatre and law into new and exciting places. My colleagues for their support, questions, challenges and curiosity – Luis Gómez Romero, Macarena Iribarne, Cassandra Sharp, Nan Seuffert, and Karina Murray have been closest to the book, along with my students and colleagues Yvonne Apolo and Ryan Kernaghan. There are so many other people who in their questions and comments, observations and remarks, conversations and more, and who have trusted my work, many of whom are friends, to whom I owe immense debts of gratitude and thanks: Rick Mohr, Des Manderson, Hanne Petersen, Scott Veitch, Chris Tomlins, Alison Young, Alessandro Pelizzon, Anne Wagner, Arild Linneberg, Martin Kayman, Ruth Herz, Karin van Marle, Carl Stychin, Mark Thomas, Simon Stern, Maks Del Mar, Bernadette Meyler, Linda Mulcahy, Jonathan Crowe, Justine Poon, Leif Dahlberg, Gary Watt, Felicity Bell, Katherine Biber, Honni van Rijswijk and Penny Crofts, Karen Crawley, Steven Howe, Sidia Fiorato, Chiara Battisti, Martin Škop, Tim Peters, Kieran Tranter, Julen Etxabe, Mónica López Lerma, Karen Crawley, Doris Pichler, Richard Sherwin and Bill MacNeil.

I'm indebted to Margaret Hamilton, my theatre and performance colleague at Wollongong, who had been one of Hans-Thies Lehmann's postgraduate students, for confirming my instincts about this new theatre scholarship and Hans-Thies Lehmann's work, and for her support and friendship. Likewise Alan Read, whose investigations into law through theatre and performance has ignited the field, along with Sophie Nield, who co-edited "Law's Theatrical Presence" with me through *Law Text Culture*. The contributors to that issue invigorated what was already becoming an exciting field. It's been a pleasure to engage with aspects of Nicole Rogers' 2008 Ph.D. in performance and law that weren't subsequently published, in particular her grandmother's story that revealed how the self manifests as an agent in law. I came across this aspect of her work belatedly. My discussions with Frans-Willem Korsten and Tessa de Zeeuw have produced some challenging engagements between law and theatre and theatricality. There are so many other people who've brought theatre and performance to law whose work has been pathbreaking, including Julie Stone Peters and Gillian Calder.

My thanks too to participants who commented, responded, challenged, and listened with care and attention to ideas that were both foreign and more, at seminars and conference panels and as visitor at Melbourne, Copenhagen, Lugano, Erasmus Rotterdam, Masaryk, Westminster, Wellington, Otago, Karl-Franzens University Graz, John Jay New York, Kent at Canterbury, Giessen, Hong Kong, Luzern, City, University of London, Verona, and Queen Mary, University of London, as well as the Law Literature and Humanities Conference of Australasia in its various places of meeting, and all the informal discussions and challenges that have inevitably helped shape and clarify my thinking. There are so many other people whose discussions I value and who I have inevitably have left out of this list. Thank you! I'm also conscious that new work is appearing all the time in this field – the scholarship used in this book doesn't generally extend further than early 2017, though some examples slip into 2018. This new and exciting work will shape the field in extraordinary ways.

I also express my thanks and acknowledge the assistance and support of the Grotowski Institute, Wrocław, Poland and Aneta Kurek and the Director, Jarosław Fret, who were so supportive, and curious, about why a law scholar would want to work with Grotowski. I thank them too for arranging permissions for the wonderful images from Grotowski's work that appear in Chapter 4. And to my classmates and the scholars who ran the Drama major at the University of Queensland in the 1970s, the first secondary school drama teaching course made up of three of us, and those who were in my classes and the scholars who participated in the first year of the M.A. in Theatre Studies at UNSW in the mid-1980s – and the denizens of the pre-NIDA course run at East Sydney Tech under the name of Community Theatre Arts – you played a part in an as unlikely as possible conjunction of theatre that could be, that appears in the pages that follow.

There are other people to thank and for whose care and skill I am eternally grateful and who would, I know, be abashed if I were to include them here – thank you for making that happen. I don't know what would have happened without your interventions. And to my father Morrie (Moses) Leiboff and siblings Jillian Leiboff and Andrew Leiboff. And to my mother, Elizabeth Leiboff (née Goldflam), who was formidable and fiercely protective of all of us, as a mother and unusually for her lifetime, a medical practitioner. She died before this book was finished, and I hoped she knew that this would be a book for her. I express my thanks and gratitude for their support, forbearance, patience and care during difficult times. And as always, I remember my late brother, Jonathan Leiboff.

. . .

Jack (Jacob) Goldflam and Eda (Estera) Kolska were my maternal grandparents. I remember them in this book, along with my mother and brother. Something of Jack and Eda's life is traced in this book. Jack and his cousin, Mark Younger, and friend Max Kolski left Poland in the 1920s. Secular Bundist Polish speaking Jews, the men made their way to Australia, and Eda, Max's sister, followed to Melbourne in Australia, where she and Jack married and where my mother, named Betty, was born. This book is indebted to a place Jack, Eda, Mark and Max had to leave, and who knew they had to leave long before we imagine this had to happen, and who, in leaving, were brave in ways I can't ever imagine. Their foresight and courage, and the reasons for them leaving the land of their birth, shouldn't be forgotten.

Marett Leiboff
Wollongong, March 2019

Before you turn the page ...

This book moves across unlikely fields and its terrain might be unfamiliar in different ways. So a few brief words about law, jurisprudence and theatre ...

Law

The law referred to in this book is common law, which originated in England and spread to its former colonies, including Australia, my home country. Common law is not just codes or legislation. It is made up of a complex of elements that were shaped through case law – judge made law – over the centuries, and continue to develop as new cases come before the courts. Law is contained in these cases, or judgments, and each significant case adds to the body of the common law. These are more than simply a decision or verdict. The cases contain an explanation of the circumstances of a case, and depending on the stage of the decision, might account for evidence and "facts", in order to work out what the law means in any given case. Cases that account for the findings in a trial will look very different from cases that are dealing with an appeal. Once an appeal case is decided, particularly at the highest level of the judicial ladder, its logic will be adopted as law, as well as deciding whether the case has been won or lost. These cases add to the body of judge made law.

Some cases explain what legislation means, because legislation is made up of words, and words are not always clear cut and so the meaning of the legislation isn't always straightforward. Legislation sits against the existing common law, which means that words that might seem obvious are pinned against law that doesn't appear in the legislation. Law adopts a raft of interpretative methods, techniques and principles to assist in finding the meaning of legislation, including whether it is actually lawful itself, by drawing on constitutions, as applicable, and existing legal principles drawn from the case law that form the longstanding, foundational concepts that operate, ghost in the machine like, as a continuing presence in law, such as the rule of law, the limits of governmental power, and what have been termed fundamental common law rights and freedoms that are protected by a concept that has been developed by the courts called the "principle of legality". What might seem surprising is that through a principle known as the doctrine of the separation of powers, the courts are meant to check on the lawmakers or legislature as well as the government, so that power isn't held in the hands of one entity alone. This means that governments might be told that what they want to do might not be lawful, or might be beyond the limits of their power.

Cases come to us from trials, and though law is most visible in its trial mode, trials are rare in common law systems, except in criminal cases. Most law is not visible or on display, with disputes being handled privately or cases being settled or worked out before going to trial, while most other law swirls around us, affecting every aspect of our lives through what Andreas Phillipopoulous-Mihapopoulos aptly calls the lawscape.[1] Law is left in the hands of individuals, by and large, though the move towards the courts usually happens through the intervention of lawyers, who shape the cases that appear before the courts. How those cases are shaped, and what the arguments they deploy depend on the lawyers themselves, based in the law that exists already. One of the most difficult tasks for a lawyer is to try to open up existing law for reconsideration, and how the lawyer goes about that task depends on their approach to law, or the jurisprudence they deploy.

Jurisprudence

This bifurcated word is a highly contested term used to refer, generally, to philosophical and theoretical considerations about law, including techniques of legal interpretation. It is concerned with asking foundational questions about law, from the nature of law itself to obligations that individuals have towards law. There are deep divisions between different types of jurisprudence when asking these basic questions, from those grounded in morality on the one hand, to bare questions of legal authorisation on the other. What tends to typify those theories is their abstract nature and ideal character, from theories of natural law on the one hand, that are traced to Socrates, Plato and Aristotle, and then through Augustine and Aquinas, to theories grounded in the early modern move to rationality and political liberalism that presaged analytical and positivist jurisprudences that instantiated bare forms of abstraction from the nineteenth century onwards. Added into the mix are critical jurisprudences that range from the material and social to the abstract and ideal, some of which took shape in the nineteenth century but were largely ignored by conventional forms of law until the late twentieth century. The deep divisions between the different jurisprudences are multivalenced, but they play a part in guiding the courts when faced with difficult legal questions, and though often not overtly visible, are able to be seen in the reasoning found in cases if you know what to look for. On occasion, jurisprudence is expressly invoked by the courts.

In this book, all of these different forms of jurisprudence will appear, but the work of theatrical jurisprudence is grounded in the posterior part of the word. Juris, clearly, invokes law, but it is "prudence" and its invocation of wisdom, good

1 Andreas Philippopoulos-Mihalopoulos, *Spatial Justice: Body, Lawscape, Atmosphere* (Abingdon: Routledge, 2015).

sense, care and judgment that is the concern of theatrical jurisprudence – and what it comprehends – will be rethought in the book. So too a related term, jurisography, coined by Shaun McVeigh, Ann Genovese and Peter Rush,[2] that asks us to think of how law is shaped through the lives, times and places of its bearers, and through that the adoption of the term "jurisprudent" as an individual who bears that responsibility well.

Theatre

Theatre is a place and activity that is known to most humans, but the term theatre as used in this book is not to be confused with the literary form, drama and the acting in or "playing" in plays. The invocation of the literary has been inherited as a mark of higher modes of thinking through tragedy as philosophy, through Aristotle's *Poetics*, or having a didactic or moral purpose to play. For this reason, tragedy, in particular has been used in order to shape thinking jurisprudentially, such as Hegel's engagement with *Antigone* in order to consider the scope and obligation of law. That is starkly different from theatre's purpose. Theatre requires nothing other than bodies and space in order to manifest itself; in 1968, the esteemed English director Peter Brook remarked: "A man [sic] walks across this empty space whilst someone else is watching him, and this is all that is needed for an act of theatre to be engaged."[3] This brief aphorism, however, leaves out just how that occurs, and the rich and deep work that occurs to make that walk one where that engagement happens. In this book, the work of one of the most influential theatre theorists of the twentieth century, Jerzy Grotowski, will be drawn upon. His work was so influential that it reshaped the grammar and vocabulary of theatre practice profoundly, so much so that ten years after he died (on the cusp of the millennium in 1999), a UNESCO year was devoted to his legacy in 2009. His creation of a "poor theatre", as part of the first period of his work that he called Theatre of Productions, radically reshaped what theatre would expect of its participants – actors and spectators – and this book draws on part of that legacy in the book called *Towards a Poor Theatre*. The book quite consciously draws on theatre, rather than the more radically inscribed performance, inspired it must be said, by Grotowski's work. The terminology of theatre is adopted not least because the term performance is weighed down by a distracting overabundance of meanings, definitions and scope.

2 Ann Genovese, Shaun McVeigh and Peter D Rush, 'Introduction', *Law Text Culture* 20 (2016) 1–13.

3 Peter Brook, *The Empty Space* [orig. McGibbon & Kee, 1968] (Harmondsworth: Penguin Books, 1968), 11.

1 The theatrical as jurisprudence

Taking aim

The theatrical – theatre – must seem the most unlikely candidate as a potential jurisprudence. Plays or drama as a literary genre might seem more appropriate a site of consideration as text holding within it accounts of law and of displays of morality apposite to the ideals of being,[1] or the burgeoning field of law and performance, with its accounts of the visibility and display of law and its practices as political praxis.[2] Theatre, and the place and the form of action that it entails, is popularly imagined as nothing but ersatz entertainment, and of attention seeking and display. For much of its history, theatre has been the subject of law's attention, to be controlled and resisted as abject and untrustworthy, and potentially treacherous and destructive, precisely because it was – and is – a practice of the body and of the senses, and thus unruly and uncontainable. Bound up in what Jonas Barish has termed the antitheatrical prejudice,[3] theatre has through history been maligned as subaltern and marginal, as the evil antithesis of the philosophical as the preferred and ideal form through which existence ought be shaped. Hans-Thies Lehmann recalibrates the problem of this antonymic within theatre, in terms that are profoundly useful for considering the assumptions of the jurisprudential and law:

> To put matters somewhat starkly: for European theatrical discourse, the sensory is admitted only as the double – the inherently deficient double, at that – of *logos* … Hatred of the theatre forms a red thread running through the history of European philosophy and theology (as well as theatre theory). The anti-theatrical prejudice reaches from ancient philosophy and Plato's contempt

1 For example, Julen Etxabe, *The Experience of Tragic Judgment* (Abingdon: Routledge, 2013); Maria Aristodemou, *Law and Literature: Journeys From Her to Eternity* (Oxford: Oxford University Press, 2000).

2 Julie Stone Peters, 'Legal Performance Good and Bad' (2008) 4.2 *Law, Culture and the Humanities* 179–200.

3 For example, Jonas Barish, *The Antitheatrical Prejudice* (Berkeley: University of California Press, 1981); Martin Puchner, *Stage Fright: Modernism, Anti-Theatricality, and Drama* (Baltimore, MD: Johns Hopkins University Press, 2002).

> for *theatrokratia*, over to the Church Fathers, up to Rousseau, and into the present day. Philosophy and theology behold their own distorted image in the theatre, which they must chase out of the polis of *logos* (or out of the Church) in order to save thinking, order, morality, ethics, propriety and/or belief.[4]

Lehmann could have added, by extension, law and jurisprudence as embodying an *antitheatrical legality*. The irritation and disappointment that lies within his words might surprise on a number of levels, for as well as the charge against philosophy and theory they contain, they also reveal an image of theatre that seems to hold the very opposite of its denunciation.[5] Lehmann captures precisely the mood that sits behind theatrical jurisprudence, a practice, as it will be seen, that is impatient with the presumption that the philosophical and abstract ought be conceived as jurisprudential perfection. Also manifest in its social mode,[6] and critical forms of jurisprudence that ignore and discard the sensory and the material in favour of new variations of abstraction, the philosophical functions against which everything else must justify or offer as exception. The material, and that which is lived and is present that the theatrical embodies, is conceived as secondary at best and subaltern at worst. Those alternative and critical jurisprudences that engage with the sensory and material, in Andreas Phillipopoulous-Mihapopoulos' spatiality,[7] and from Olivia Barr's jurisprudence of movement to James Parker's auditory jurisprudence,[8] are among the jurisprudential exceptions that show just what the theatrical can reveal of law and its interpreters. That is not to say that there isn't extraordinary jurisprudential scholarship that draws on themes and concepts analogous to the theatrical,[9] and theatre has produced an extraordinary set of insights into law in return, in particular through Alan Read's exploration of law and performance.[10] But when pressed, jurisprudence, and through it law, turns back into the philosophical and theoretical. This wouldn't matter except that rather than do

4 Hans-Thies Lehmann, *Tragedy and Dramatic Theatre*, trans. Erik Butler (Abingdon: Routledge, 2016), 28.

5 Jacques Rancière, *The Emancipated Spectator* [trans. Gregory Elliott] (London and New York: Verso, 2009).

6 Brian Tamanaha, 'The Third Pillar of Jurisprudence: Social Legal Theory' (2015) 56 *William and Mary Law Review* 2235–2277, in particular at 2271–2277.

7 Andreas Philippopoulos-Mihalopoulos, *Spatial Justice: Body, Lawscape, Atmosphere* (Abingdon: Routledge, 2015).

8 Olivia Barr, *A Jurisprudence of Movement: Common Law, Walking, Unsettling Place* (Abingdon: Routledge, 2016); James EK Parker, *Acoustic Jurisprudence: Listening to the Trial of Simon Bikindi* (Oxford: Oxford University Press, 2015); and Peter Rush's antecedent work: Peter Rush, 'Killing Me Softly with His Words: Hunting the Law Student' (1990) 1 *Law and Critique* 21–37.

9 Especially scholarship drawing on music and improvisation: Desmond Manderson, 'Fission and Fusion: From Improvisation to Formalism in Law and Music' (2010) 6.1 *Critical Studies in Improvisation* 1–10; Desmond Manderson, *Songs without Music: Aesthetic Dimensions of Law and Justice* (Berkeley: University of California Press, 2000); Sara Ramshaw, *Justice as Improvisation: The Law of the Extempore* (Abingdon: Routledge, 2013).

10 Alan Read, *Theatre and Law* (Basingstoke: Palgrave Macmillan, 2016).

what jurisprudence ought, as a *prudence* through which the jurisprudent deploys wisdom and good sense, and through that, takes care of law, it is as likely to become a game, a conceptual straightjacket, a set of rules without more. Moreover, the jurisprudent, as the legal self responsible for law, is rarely asked to consider who they are and the conditions of their responsiveness towards law, for the imbrication of philosophy within jurisprudence (and through it, law) makes an assumption that doctrine and principle embed wisdom, and thus its practitioners will hold within them without more the mark of responsibility needed to work with and be responsible for law. It might, but as Lehmann shows us, the imprint of *logos* is no guarantee of anything other than doctrine and dogma.

What it does guarantee, however, is the negation of the 'sensory as double', the physical and material, the visual and auditory, and its bamboozling and disorienting effects and interruption of the conditions that ground law's presumptive orientation, that of reason and rationality. This is the theatrical in all of its disrupting and responsive modes found in theatre practice that took shape in the late nineteenth- before erupting in the twentieth century. Its practices are now grammatical and commonplace, but this theatrical *avant-garde* forced a move away from the image of theatre as drama (that is largely embedded within law's logics and expectations, to be considered in the next chapter). Turning away from the inherited position that theatre was the basely artisanal presentation and representation of a literary drama created by an intellectual, author as playwright, in whom higher ideals would be generated, theatre practitioners created theatre that needed nothing more than body, space, and the responsiveness demanded through the presence of being created in a unique time and space.[11] This theatre requires no script, no drama, no words, no literature, no *logos*, no silly costumes or dress-ups, no characters in the ordinary sense, no 'playing', but it makes intense demands on anyone with its purview, through the challenges it creates and the responsiveness it demands. Its characteristics are encapsulated in a now famous concept coined by Lehmann – postdramatic theatre:[12]

> Theatre is not to be defined as a dramatic process, but as one that is corporeal, scenic, musical, auditory and visual – in space and time: a material process that implies its own being – seen or participation, even as it displays a certain opacity that resists full perceptive penetration [*wahrnehmende Durchdringung*] just as much as it refuses complete rationalization.[13]

And there is the rub. Postdramatic theatre challenges, confronts, and forces us, as spectators (and as actors/performers/interpreters) to respond to that confrontation as a bodily response first; intellectual responses matter and move from this

11 Hans-Thies Lehmann, *Postdramatic Theatre* [trans. Karen Jürs-Munby] (Abingdon: Routledge, 2006).

12 That isn't to say that text has no role in this theatre. It is one of a complex of elements and the engagement with the text rather than slavery to the text. This will be explored more in the next chapter.

13 Lehmann, *Tragedy*, 424.

initial confrontation, disruption, and rattling of expectations, constituting the concept of 'response' embedded in theatrical jurisprudence. As Peter Brook remarks, theatre: 'always asserts itself in the present. This is what can make it more real than the normal stream of consciousness. This is also what can make it so disturbing'.[14] To disturb reveals, and it forces us to pay attention, usually to something most of us would prefer to avoid. Of a new 2016 production of *A Midsummer Night's Dream*, the artistic director of the Sydney Theatre Company reminds us that repetition for the sake of it is pointless: 'For us to do the umpteenth production of it in Sydney, we had to have something new to say.'[15] It said lots – of power in the hands of a megalomaniac, and the vacuousness of fame for fame's sake – bound up in text centuries old but brought directly into the present through a hint of a then US Presidential candidate dressed in a gold sequinned jacket in the form of Theseus/Oberon, and a Kim Kardashian-like vision in gold as a reimagined Hippolyta/Titania. And it forced its audience to pay attention, to notice the double through sound, its weight oppressing and suffocating in its demand to realise just what is at stake when power does the same.[16] To 'chase [theatre] out of the polis of *logos* ... to save thinking, order, morality, ethics, propriety and/or belief',[17] is to understand why theatre and its practices were subject to restriction and regulation for millennia, because it has at its disposal the tools that help us to notice and respond, to injustice, to power, and to histories that hold within them messages for the present, and to test and challenge our own presumptions and preconceptions, where it matters in the most profound way: *through our bodies, prior to the trigger of reason and rationality.*

Theatre, rather than operating *contra* what is good, seeks to achieve what is good as a form of practised humanity. If our bodies are responsive then our minds will be too. Think of the form of practised conduct that was learnt in childhood: to give up seats for those in need registers throughout our lives as a pattern of response to people in need in general as a practice of the body, as an embodied morality. The opposite is true as well, in the negative, as a practice of the mind that is unable to register in the body. It would be a mistake to think that theatre or the theatrical dismisses or discards those things that Lehmann attributes to *logos*. For theatre is bound up in thinking, order, morality, ethics and propriety/belief through different registers. The sensory as double plays on our bodies, and what our bodies draw upon through these responses are antonymic of those things to be 'saved' from theatre: instinct (as opposed to thinking), disruption (as opposed to order), liveliness and courage (morality), transgression (ethics), and/or imagination (propriety/belief).[18] The sensory as double as enmeshed in these *theatrical antonyms* is a threat to *logos*, but not in the ways it might seem, for the

14 Peter Brook, *The Empty Space*, [orig. McGibbon & Kee, 1968] (Harmondsworth: Penguin Books, 1968), 11.

15 Andrew Upton, 'A Message from Andrew Upton' *Program: A Midsummer Night's Dream* (Sydney, Sydney Theatre Company, 2016).

16 I attended this production in September 2016.

17 Lehmann, *Tragedy*, 28.

18 This isn't to be conflated with Jung's concept of the shadow.

items on this list alert us to what philosophy insists on suppressing – *our* selves and their limitations, and the dangers that nest within us through our presumptions, expectations, limitations, and carelessness that we choose to blinker, at our peril.[19]

To best understand the basis of this otherwise subordinated double, it is worth briefly turning to its source – Antonin Artaud's anguished response to the state of life, society and culture he observed in the 1920s and 1930s. The cause of this anguish boils down to the irredeemably harmful conditions, and the negative consequences for a fully lived life. Artaud's solution was to restore it through theatre, out of the shadow or the double that was otherwise sublimated it would be restored, up to a point.[20] But this in turn meant reviving theatre, rescuing it from the dead hand of repetition, and from the conventions through which 'dramas' would be staged. In the preface to his collection of writings published in 1938 as *Le théâtre et son double* (*The Theatre and Its Double*), Artaud began by turning his attention to a barely relevant means by which life is guided – philosophy. Not only did no one read it, and hence didn't use it as a guide to live one's life,[21] it was incapable of offering what was needed to manifest life. Only theatre had that capacity to move and stir up those shadows 'around which assembles the true spectacle of life'.[22] Life itself is ineffable, that 'fragile fluttering center which forms never reach'.[23] Forms stultify, and drama as language stultified; instead, 'to break through language in order to touch life is to create or recreate theater … the essential thing to believe is that not just anyone can create it, and there must be a preparation'.[24] He tells actors to be like 'victims burnt at the stake, signaling through the flames';[25] far from being an image (the burning of heretics, and so on), Artaud was prescribing something to actors, for this was how they had to stir up that 'true spectacle of life'. Artaud was also present and prescient, his reputation as visionary being operative in more ways than one. The year the book was published, *Kristallnacht*, with its burnings and looting and murders and deportations to concentration camps, was unleashed just across the border in Nazi Germany.

Artaud's insistence that theatre can't be created by 'just anyone', and requires preparation must seem perplexing, even more so when it is understood that preparation is not just learning lines or being told where to stand or what to wear or

19 I intentionally avoid speaking in terms of bias or prejudice except when there's no other possibility.

20 Artaud's deployment of the unconscious, drawing on Freud and Jung but reframed through Balinese shadow theatre and theatre rituals from Mexico.

21 Antonin Artaud, *The Theater and Its Double* [trans. Mary Caroline Richards] (New York: Grove Press, 1958), 7–9.

22 Ibid., 12.

23 Ibid., 13.

24 Ibid.; also Antonin Artaud, *Antonin Artaud: Collected Works* [trans. Victor Corti] (London: Calder & Boyars, 1974); Jacques Derrida, 'The Theater of Cruelty and the Closure of Representation' (1978) 9.3 *Theater* 6–19.

25 Artaud, *Double*, 13; Jerzy Grotowski uses the following translation: 'Actors should be like martyrs burnt alive, still signalling to us from their stakes', in Jerzy Grotowski, *Towards a Poor Theatre* (New York: Simon and Schuster, 1968), 125.

when to frown or smile. This is superficial and careless: 'I have to look happy', 'I have to look determined'. A spectator will see someone who is 'showing myself looking happy', will see a body registering no commitment, and no responsibility. Instead, Artaud is demanding something else entirely, a depth of engagement *with* the self and *beyond* the self. The body is trained to be responsive beyond a bare *theasthai*,[26] out of which the theatrical antonyms are discovered through cultivation and commitment, in order to be responsive and aware beyond the self. Law's equivalent superficiality and carelessness appears in these terms: 'I can repeat what the law says without understanding how it affects life and lifeworlds of and beyond law'. Law in those terms makes its practitioners human algorithms, practising a law of calculability absent consequences, or to calculate if it is worth bothering to comply with law at all. This is not just law without morality, but it is a law without life. Law really has no purpose other than guiding and manifesting the conditions of existence of all of us; for law to ignore life by drawing on algorithmic certainty is to take *logos* into a place where law becomes a game, and one of chance at that. Theatre expects its practitioners to display awareness beyond the self;[27] it would seem to be the most basic expectation of law for its practitioners to be aware of the self and the lifeworlds which law holds in its hands. This extends across the board, from situations where the individual is imagined as holding certain traits and characteristics regardless of the reality, where *logos* is unable to function without requiring the mind of the lawyer to leak into their own reality, whether they are aware of doing this or not.

Let me illustrate with one example how wrong we get it if we presume that *logos* will achieve a better outcome than the theatrical antonyms: instinct (as opposed to thinking), disruption (as opposed to order), liveliness and courage (morality), transgression (ethics), and/or imagination (propriety/belief). Moreover, this illustration reveals how the philosophical, as embedded into law, can distort and cause harm rather than help. In a notorious 1993 decision, a judge in Victoria, an Australian state, decided that because a 16- year-old-girl was unconscious at the time of her rape (her attacker slit her throat first, leaving her in this state), the impact was lessened because she couldn't have been traumatised by the rape, and so a lighter sentence was imposed.[28] Drawing on psychiatric evidence and ignoring the victim's impact statement which had recounted her trauma, the empirical and abstract categories of will and knowledge overriding what she experienced as a result of what happened to her. The appeal court read the

26 Lehmann, *Tragedy*, 27.

27 For example, even a conventional degree such as the BA Acting at the Royal Central School of Speech and Drama, University of London, asks this of its students: '**Self-discovery** – we encourage you to investigate and interrogate your world, challenging your own habits and preconceptions … and making curiosity, originality and artistic courage the cornerstones of your professional and artistic life'. https://www.cssd.ac.uk/course/acting-ba

28 Rae Kaspiew, 'Rape Law: Legal Narrative and Sexual Violence' (1995) 20 *Melbourne University Law Review* 350–392, 362–366; *R v Stanbrook* (Supreme Court of Victoria, O'Bryan J, 10 November 1992).

situation in vastly different terms, and drawing on a deeply theatrical response to the young woman's situation:

> [t]hese are very difficult matters on which persons such as judges who have not had the experience and who cannot be thought to be fully empathetic with it, should pass judgment without hearing from the victim herself and other relevant evidence.[29]

The appeal judgment takes us into the theatrical antonyms, for if the inherited concepts in the form of precedent were followed, it would be hard to rupture the logic drawn upon by the trial judge. We see instinct, disruption, liveliness and courage, transgression, and imagination on display through the response of the appellate court that *feels* the cry of the victim burning through the flames and demands a correction. The theatrical antonyms ground wisdom that is in the body and is bodily,[30] as a deeply theatrical response grounded in the body, and that is bodily, in the hands of an Appellate Justice and Bench *aware beyond the self.* What this means is that the court was able respond in law beyond the limit of *logos*, and as the book proceeds, more of these examples will show that there is no other way for law to respond in order to correct error, to notice problems, and to realise when the conditions of inheritance imbricated into precedent contain injustice and more. This bodily response triggers what is otherwise discarded – experiences, situations, lives, pasts, presents and more – out of which the intellectual response follows, as a secondary conduct of reason and rationality.

The sensory as double functions beyond the limits of that which is cognisable: 'it is not that the body remembers, but that the *body itself is memory*',[31] in which the 'active search for knowledge is closely linked to work with memory and the rediscovery of something lost or forgotten'.[32] These latter remarks are of or about the work of Polish theatre practitioner and theorist, Jerzy Grotowski, whose work radically reoriented theatre in the most fundamental of ways, and whose work

29 Marks J, *R v Stanbrook* (Court of Criminal Appeal, Marks, Southwell and Harper JJ, 16 March 1993) cited in Kaspiew, 'Rape Law', 366.

30 'Bodily' or 'body' as deployed here seeks to register the interactions of mind and body that the theatrical manifests. It operates in a different register from work on the significant feminist and critical scholarship including: Pheng Cheah, David Fraser and Judith Grbich, *Thinking Through The Body Of Law* (St. Leonards, Australia: Allen & Unwin, 1996); Alan Hyde, *Bodies of Law* (Princeton, NJ: Princeton University Press, 1997); Judith Grbich, 'The Body in Legal Theory' (1992) 11 *University of Tasmania Law Review* 26–58; and on corporeality and affect: Greta Olson, 'The Turn to Passion: Has Law and Literature become Law and Affect?' (2016) 28.3 *Law and Literature* 335–353.; Martin A. Kayman, 'Corpus Juris, Habeas Corpus, and the 'Corporeal Turn' in the Humanities' (2016) 28.3 *Law and Literature* 355–378.

31 Richard Cieślak, cited in Dominika Laster, 'Embodied Memory: Body-Memory in the Performance Research of Jerzy Grotowski' (2012) 28.3 *New Theatre Quarterly* 211–229, 214. Richard Cieślak was one of the core members of Grotowski's Laboratory Theatre and was considered to be the epitome of the Grotowskian actor. Images of him appear in Chapter 4.

32 Laster, 'Embodied Memory', 222.

offers the forms of training that imbue the responsiveness of the theatrical antonyms. And though Artaud might be the trigger that asks us to notice, it is Grotowski whose work grounds theatrical jurisprudence. His 1968 book, *Towards a Poor Theatre*,[33] which is echoed in the title of this book, is a collection of interviews, some of his writing, and articles about his work that record an almost jurisprudential account of response and responsibility that is shaped through the actor and spectator. A record of the experiments and discoveries carried out in the first phase of his work from 1957 to 1969, 'The Theatre of Productions', carried out in his Laboratory Theatre,[34] reveals that what Grotowski asked of theatre was nothing less than a reconceptualisation of life:

> Theatre – through the actor's technique, his art in which the living organism strives for higher motives … [is] … a totality of physical and mental reactions. This opportunity must be treated in a disciplined manner, with a full awareness of the responsibilities it involves. It is true that the actor accomplishes this act, but he can only do so through an encounter with the spectator … in direct confrontation with him, and somehow 'instead of' him. The actor's act – discarding half measures, revealing, opening up, emerging from himself as opposed to closing up – is an invitation to the spectator.[35]

This is the theatre that shapes theatrical jurisprudence, as preparation of the self to engage with law *beyond* the self, as a deeply human experience, through the demands that Grotowski makes of his spectator and his actors. His practices capture the self as a whole so that something deep within the human psyche and humanity is brought from within the self to be brought to the surface to bring that experience to spectators as theatre. Grotowski gives life to the promise of Artaud, and through Grotowski's forms of training and the demands of his practice, offers a means by which law can be alerted to its limitations, in order for law to bring something back into life itself. I return to his work later in this book, but its presence suffuses everything to come.

Theasthai

Theatrical jurisprudence asks the legal self to do more than simply engage as *thea*, an act of seeing, but instead to ask to realise that we respond through our bodies, as *theasthai*. As neurobiology has confirmed, long after Grotowski or Artaud

33 Grotowski, *Poor Theatre*.

34 In the period known as the Theatre of Productions, the term refers to his original theatre space called the Theatre of 13 Rows in Opole, where the term 'Laboratory Theatre' was added to the name in 1962 before moving to Wrocław in 1965, where it was renamed the Institute for the Study of Acting Methods, and later still taking the name of the Actors' Institute – Laboratory Theatre in 1971, during the period of research known as the Theatre of Sources: Culture Poland, *Artists: Jerzy Grotowski* 'Laboratory Theatre'. https://culture.pl/en/artist/jerzy-grotowski

35 Grotowski, *Poor Theatre*, 255–256.

intuitively understood it, minds and bodies are not distinct but are interacting agents.[36] This means legal bodies are also responsive in both positive and negative ways, to law, to facts, to circumstances, to irritations, to dislikes, likes, that are more likely to attenuate the intellectual premises that we think are operative than we would want to believe: politics, gender, sexuality, race, ethnicity and so on.[37] We respond through our bodies before our minds are even engaged, but the idea that we are inscribed through our bodies as practice or training,[38] is nothing new, as Peter Goodrich reminds us:

> Just as the soul is inscribed through the training of the body, through the institutional and everyday routines that give the body affect and speech, so too the body – its attitudes, tones, deportment and dress – is in turn the expression of the qualities of the soul … In the same vein, the body is in classical terms an image, a mode of transport between words and things, a site of passage that exists according to the various chimerical temporalities of memory and hope.[39]

Once imbricated, the body's memory sends shivers down our spines, the physical reaction of taste and distaste, the movement towards catching a ball by a rugby player even before knowing why, the automatic response when driving to put the foot on the brake even before we begin to reason why, and having the awareness to notice when harms are done that will be dismissed by someone without that memory.[40]

36 Antonio Damasio, *Descartes' Error: Emotion, Reason and the Human Brain* (London: Vintage, 2006); Antonio Damasio, *The Feeling of What Happens: Body, Emotion and the Making of Consciousness* (London: Vintage, 2000); Antonio Damasio, *Looking for Spinoza: Joy, Sorrow and the Feeling Brain* (London: Vintage, 2004); Mark Johnson, 'Mind Incarnate: from Dewey to Damasio' (2006) 135 *Daedalus* 46–54. For an examination in theatre: Rhonda Blair, *The Actor, Image, and Action: Acting and Cognitive Neuroscience* (New York: Routledge, 2008); Rhonda Blair, 'Cognitive Neuroscience and Acting: Imagination, Conceptual Blending, and Empathy' (2009) 53.4 *TDR* 92–103; Rhonda Blair and Amy Cook (eds), *Theatre, Performance and Cognition: Languages, Bodies and Ecologies* (London: Methuen, 2016); Clelia Falletti, Gabriele Sofia, and Victor Jacono (eds), *Theatre and Cognitive Neuroscience* (London: Bloomsbury Methuen, 2016); Pil Hansen and Bettina Bläsing, *Performing the Remembered Present: The Cognition of Memory in Dance, Theatre and Music* (London: Methuen, 2017).

37 Greta Olson, 'Law Is not Turgid and Literature not Soft and Fleshy: Gendering and Heteronormativity in Law and Literature Scholarship' (2012) 36 *Australian Feminist Law Journal* 65–86.

38 I avoid making any reference to the overly invested binary of emotion and reason that has been spawned by Antonio Damasio's work. The scientific basis of the amygdala as the source of emotion as a neurobiological, physiological response is too often reshaped as carelessness and thoughtlessness *qua* reason and rationality.

39 Peter Goodrich, 'Rhetoric and Somatics: Training the Body to Do the Work of Law' (2001) 5 *Law Text Culture* 241–70, 250.

40 See for example, David Seymour, *Law, Antisemitism and the Holocaust* (London: Routledge Cavendish, 2007); Didi Herman, '"I Do not Attach Great Significance to it": Taking Note of "The Holocaust" in English Case Law' (2008) 17 *Social and Legal Studies* 427–452; Didi Herman, 'David Seymour, Law, Antisemitism and the Holocaust' (2009) 18 *Social and*

Even in the absence of memory, it is possible to create bodily responses that help us notice,[41] out of which sympathetic responses are triggered that will help us notice what we were otherwise unable to register before.[42]

Nothing that I have posed up to this point could be more antithetical to law's expected practices,[43] for to learn to think like a lawyer involves discouraging extraneous or sloppy thinking. For most lawyers, this is an easy task, the mathematical techniques used to create forms of legal problem solving and reasoning being altogether easier than being asked to consider multiple facets of life. Desmond Manderson has vividly described these techniques as the discursive strip-mining of case law,[44] where bare rules are extracted from the complex of stories and reasoning built into judgment. Over time, they are stripped again and again, leaving intact a single line or two recounting the principles held in the case. It is assumed that the bare unadorned rules will function with clarity and certainty because they are uncluttered by irrelevancies, but what happens instead is that legal interpreters fill the voids left behind with their own assumptions and presumptions (rather than going back to the case, for instance to reveal what actually happened). However, these interpretative lacunae are filled in *sub auditio*,[45] as Peter Goodrich has so acutely observed,[46] through 'theatrical arrangements that precede appearance and audition'.[47] Law is revealed as far more friable and fragile than countenanced, and its reasons far more surprising than imagined.[48]

For most lawyers are Jungian introverts, whose adopt a systolic form of engaging with knowledge, in which they bring 'objects' to themselves.[49] This means that whatever is already imbricated in the individual is operative in new or unknown

Legal Studies 423–425; Didi Herman, *An Unfortunate Coincidence: Jews, Jewishness and English Law* (Oxford: Oxford University Press, 2011).

41 Marett Leiboff, 'Law, Muteness and the Theatrical' (2010) 14 *Law Text Culture* 384–39; Marett Leiboff, 'Towards a Jurisprudence of the Embodied Mind – Sarah Lund, *Forbrydelsen* and the Mindful Body' (2015) 6.2 *Naveiñ Reet: Nordic Journal of Law and Social Research* 77–91; Marett Leiboff, 'Theatricalizing Law' (2018) *Law and Literature*, DOI: 10.1080/1535685X.2017.1415051

42 Martha C. Nussbaum, *Political Emotions: Why Love Matters for Justice* (Cambridge, MA: Belknap Press, 2013); Martha C. Nussbaum, *Cultivating Humanity: A Classical Defense of Reform in Liberal Education* (Cambridge, MA: Harvard University Press, 1997); Martha C. Nussbaum, *Poetic Justice: The Literary Imagination and Public Life* (Boston: Beacon, 1995).

43 Jeanne Gaakeer, '"*Sua cuique persona*?"A Note on the Fiction of Legal Personhood and a Reflection on Interdisciplinary Consequences' (2016) 28.3 *Law and Literature* 287–317.

44 Desmond Manderson, 'Statuta v. Acts: Interpretation, Music, and Early English Legislation' (1995) 7.2 *Yale Journal of Law and the Humanities* 317–366, 317–318.

45 Marett Leiboff, 'Cultural Legal Studies as Law's Extraversion', in Cassandra Sharp and Marett Leiboff (eds), *Cultural Legal Studies: Law's Popular Cultures and the Metamorphosis of Law* (Abingdon: Routledge, 2016), 29–49, 45–46.

46 Peter Goodrich, 'The New Casuistry' (2007) 33 *Critical Inquiry* 673–709, 682 and 707.

47 Peter Goodrich, 'Specters of Law: Why the History of the Legal Spectacle Has not Been Written' (2011) 1.3 *UC Irvine Law Review* 773–812, 808.

48 Marett Leiboff, '"DITTO": Law, Pop Culture and Humanities and the Impact of Intergenerational Interpretative Dissonance' (2012) 36 *The Australian Feminist Law Journal* 145–163.

49 Leiboff, 'Law's Extraversion', 41–43.

situations. This is law's preferred standpoint, because it appears to lock interpreters into known legal patterns. But this breaks down the moment a lacuna appears and the interpreter draws on existing *non-legal* knowledge to fill in gaps that fall *within* the expectations of the interpreter. The relatively rare extravert lawyers, who as Jungian diastolics are oriented towards moving 'objects' away from the self are more likely to draw on external material or knowledge when faced with new or unknown situations. But without a grounding in the field, what the legal interpreter draws on is as likely to be amiss as it is appropriate.[50] For whatever law might have assumed of its interpreters once,[51] it has been rent asunder in an age of digital legalities, where the crowd seeks its law shared through wiki, blog, and the app *de jour*, preferring versions of law that suit the priorities of the day, through opinion, feeling and belief. So if the crowd has agreed that a case was decided a particular way, the chances of dislodging that interpretation are next to impossible, even as this militates against legal method and technique. And this matters, for if first-line lawyers draw on this as law, the consequences are dire not only for the individuals affected by poor legal advice, but it begins to chip away from the entire edifice on which law is grounded.

But I hear a rumble of discontent. Critical jurisprudence has, for significant reasons, sought to expose problems embedded within conventional practices of legal interpretation and the prejudices of its interpreters, as we have already seen. So in accounting for these new legal practices, surely this is political action on the part of digital legal natives seeking to uncover embedded prejudices and preconceptions in law that will reveal a significant problem in existing principle. I will ask you to pause and think about this alternative response, and what it entails, as I add in some of the missing text from the earlier paragraph, provoked in part by a handful of real cases (which I am merging into one).[52] The case was argued on two bases, a constitutional claim and a claim grounded in a government decision that was made without power and authority. The constitutional claim didn't succeed, but the case was successful on the latter point. The headnote makes reference to the constitutional point first, and the latter issue uses some words that are similar to the constitutional principle. The crowd has it that the case was won on the constitutional point. That error is significant, because the point that succeeded contained a significant update on the scope of a fundamental concept within the common law, explaining the limitations that governments must adhere to. But the crowd, when this was pointed out, was unimpressed, and decided that the court concerned was wrong. The preferred position? That governments ought to have unfettered power and that courts had no right to intervene in the decisions of government. Centuries of legal principle involving the obligation of governments to conduct themselves according to law obliterated in one fell swoop, grounded in an image of 9/11.[53]

50 Leiboff, '"DITTO"'.

51 Goodrich, 'Specters of Law'; Jeanne Gaakeer, 'Reverent Rites of Legal Theory: Unity-Diversity-Interdisciplinarity' (2012) 36 *Australian Feminist Law Journal* 19–43; Marett Leiboff, 'Ghosts of Law and Humanities (Past, Present, Future)' (2012) 36 *Australian Feminist Law Journal* 3–17.

52 To protect the anonymity of contributors to a range of discussions.

53 To be considered further in Chapter 5. In the *Law's Generations Project*, a baseline question asked participants to name the World War II Axis countries (Germany, Italy

If by chance you steamed up on any of these counts, it doesn't take much to understand that this response is bodily and systolic first, before any intellectual response occurs. There are, too, more than one bases on which a bodily response will be triggered, from an irritation at what looks like a trick, to a gasping surprise that lawyers would even think that foundational legal concepts ought be discarded. For in assuming all lawyers share a deeply held commitment to law and its principles, we have brought the 'object' to our ourselves and our dramatic expectations of law (to be considered in the next chapter), grounded in expected stories and conventions. This experience and everything it revealed ought, now, to register as memory now inscribed in the body, meaning that we are now alert to and should begin to notice when we hear or see these insults to law's integrity on display.[54] It also reveals that the sensory as double, the short, sharp shock that forces us to pay attention is not rhetorical but is real, is lived and has consequences. We need to notice not only the 'signalling through the flames' and what they don't reveal on their face as end result, but to also notice and be alert to the conditions and forces that kindled them in the first place. Without memories bound deeply into the body of lawyers, we simply don't notice when law starts to go wrong. Law's preferred mode, to shoehorn what is new into what already exists, is its temperamental orientation, and is exemplary of the antitheatrical legality.

The workshop

At the beginning of the millennium, jurisprudence found theatre, or more particularly it found performance and performatives. And in return, theatre and performance found law.[55] Plays and dramas, drawing on Shakespeare to Antigone and beyond, as literary forms that could be used to ground morality or function didactically (as already grounded in philosophy), or to reveal previously ignored textual engagements with law as a social and cultural function, have been drawn upon since at least the inception of the Law and Literature movement.[56] The

and Japan). Fewer than 50 per cent of those born after 1966 were able to answer this question. Of those born after 1986, significant numbers interpolated the 'Axis of Evil', i.e. Iran, North Korea and Iraq. University of Wollongong Human Research Ethics Approval HE10/206, *Talkin''bout law's generations: an empirical and jurisprudential investigation into the reading of legal cases by different generations of lawyers*, approval 10 June 2010. All results are held on file with the author. The surveys have no identifying information about individuals and interviews are anonymised.

54 Rianna Croxford, 'Exeter University Suspends Five Law Students in Racism Scandal', *The Financial Times* 21 March 2018. https://www.ft.com/content/807db2b0-2c42-11e8-a34a-7e7563b0b0f4; Katie King, 'Racism at Exeter Law School: Students Expelled and Suspended as Investigation Concludes', *Legal Cheek* 1 May 2018. https://www.legalcheek.com/2018/05/racism-at-exeter-law-school-students-expelled-and-suspended-as-investigation-concludes/. At time of writing, one of the students had their traineeship offer revoked, and students had been expelled, suspended or had other sanctions applied by the university.

55 Read, *Theatre and Law*.

56 Gary Watt and Paul Raffield (eds), *Shakespeare and the Law* (Oxford: Hart Publishing, 2008); Paul Raffield, *Shakespeare's Imaginary Constitution: Late-Elizabethan Politics and the Theatre of Law* (Oxford: Hart Publishing, 2010).

performative turn in law was directed towards law in its visible manifestation, the trial, and drama, along with philosophical inflected concepts of performance and the performative. So too concepts of play, theatre, and dramaturgy, brought into jurisprudence as a sociological concept grounded in the work of sociologist Erving Goffman,[57] have almost overwhelmed the image of theatre as sociological – rather than as *theatre*. What theatre existed was nearly exclusively confined to pedagogical activity.[58] But engaging with the existing jurisprudential logics of philosophy and sociology, or through the deployment of self-actualising performatives as a form of direct action, as didactics and politics,[59] law has barely engaged with theatre, and when it has done so largely it has been generally as *theatron*.

The theatrical as *theasthai* rarely appears in jurisprudential scholarship,[60] and when it does, it appears in guises that rarely recognise its own theatrical presence.[61] Thus critical rereadings of case law undertaken by McVeigh and Genovese, as reporting grounded in time and place reveal something of law shaped beyond the self,[62] the nature of the examination of self through work on the conduct of office in law,[63] along with jurisography, and legal biography, reveal something of the conditions that shape the legal self.[64] Judgments can be a surprising repository of insights into the judge, as legal self, through intentionally placed clues, or through details pieced together, which can reveal the judge who is aware both of self and beyond the self. But what is more likely is that commentary reveals a judge whose discomfiture with difference retreats to abstraction, as hyper-realising individuals who fall out of the ideal, and denying them their humanity in a single manoeuvre.[65] All of these factors come together under the

57 Erving Goffman, *The Presentation of Self in Everyday Life* (Harmondsworth: Penguin, 1990).

58 Maksymilian del Mar, 'The Education of Attention and Encounter in the Legal Academy', in Zenon Bańkowski and Maksymilian Del Mar (eds), *The Moral Imagination and the Legal Life: Beyond Text in Legal Education* (Farnham, Surrey: Ashgate, 2013), 33–63, 50–59; and generally Zenon Bańkowski and Maksymilian Del Mar (eds), *The Moral Imagination and the Legal Life: Beyond Text in Legal Education* (Farnham, Surrey: Ashgate, 2013); in comparison, Marett Leiboff and Sophie Nield, 'Law's Theatrical Presence: Special Issue' (2010) 14 *Law Text Culture* 1–2, reflected in indexing which has seen this preface retitled 'Law's *Theoretical* Presence', for law might be theoretical but presumably can't be theatrical.

59 Nicole Rogers, 'The Play of Law: Comparing Performance in Law and Theatre' (2008) 8.2 *QUT Law Review* 429–443.

60 Compare Leiboff, 'Muteness'; Leiboff, 'Sarah Lund', which are expressly concerned with the theatrical.

61 Jack L Sammons, 'The Law's Melody' (2011) 55 *Villanova Law Review* 1143–1160; Jack L Sammons, 'Justice as Play' (2010) 61 *Mercer Law Review* 517–550.

62 Ann Genovese and Shaun McVeigh, 'Nineteen Eighty Three: A Jurisographic Report on *Commonwealth v Tasmania*' (2015) 24.1 *Griffith Law Review*, 68–88.

63 Shaun McVeigh, 'Office and Persona of the Critical Jurist: Peripheral Legal Thought (Australia)', in Justin Desautels-Stein and Christopher Tomlins (eds), *Searching for Contemporary Legal Thought* (Cambridge: Cambridge University Press, 2017), 386–405.

64 Gary Watt, *Dress, Law and Naked Truth: A Cultural Study of Fashion and Form* (London: Bloomsbury, 2013).

65 Herman, *An Unfortunate Coincidence*.

mark of the theatrical through the feminist judgment projects, in particular the UK project of 2010 under the curatorship of Rosemary Hunter, Clare McGlynn and Erika Rackley.[66] Those projects were taken up in Australia,[67] and New Zealand (as a feminist and Māori project),[68] with Rosemary Hunter, and have extended into the US and India, and have ranged beyond the feminist into the Wild Law judgments projects,[69] projects that reconsider the circumstances of a single case,[70] and children's judgment projects.[71]

Rosemary Hunter and her collaborators have demonstrated in practised ways how different lives affect the reading, shaping and interpreting of law,[72] not only as commentary or argument, but through their reimaging based on the personal and through experience, as the New Zealand project expressly observes in its publication publicity:

> Feminist judging is an emerging critical legal approach that works within the confines of common law legal method to challenge the myth of judicial neutrality and illustrate how the personal experiences and perspectives of judges may influence the reasoning and outcome of their decisions. Uniquely, this book includes a set of cases employing an approach based on mana wahine, the use of Maori values that recognise the complex realities of Maori women's lives. Through these feminist and mana wahine judgments, it opens possibilities of more inclusive judicial decision making for the future.[73]

This broader remit of feminist judging as an embodied critical practice reveals *theasthai* at work in its response to lifeworlds beyond the self; Nicole Rogers takes this one step further in the Wild Law judgment project as performance, and through it an act of subversion, of playing at judging as a form of political action,[74] through the lawyer as political and activist self.

66 Rosemary Hunter, Clare McGlynn and Erika Rackley (eds), *Feminist Judgments: From Theory to Practice* (Oxford: Hart Publishing, 2010).
67 Heather Douglas, Francesca Bartlett, Trish Luker and Rosemary Hunter (eds), *Australian Feminist Judgments: Righting and Rewriting Law* (Oxford: Hart Publishing, 2015).
68 Elisabeth McDonald, Rhonda Powell, Māmari Stephens and Rosemary Hunter (eds), *Feminist Judgments of Aotearoa New Zealand – Te Rino: A Two-Stranded Rope* (Oxford: Hart Publishing, 2017).
69 Nicole Rogers and Michelle Maloney (eds), *Law as if Earth Really Mattered: The Wild Law Judgment Project* (Abingdon: Routledge, 2017).
70 Gabrielle Appleby and Rosalind Dixon (eds), *The Critical Judgments Project: Rereading Monis v The Queen* (Leichhardt, Sydney: Federation Press, 2016).
71 Helen Stalford, Kathryn Hollingsworth and Stephen Gilmore (eds), *Rewriting Children's Rights Judgments: From Academic Vision to New Practice* (Oxford: Hart Publishing, 2017).
72 Rosemary Hunter, 'More than Just a Different Face? Judicial Diversity and Decision-making' (2015) 68.1 *Current Legal Problems* 119–141.
73 *About Feminist Judgments of Aotearoa New Zealand.* https://www.bloomsburyprofessional.com/uk/feminist-judgments-of-aotearoa-new-zealand-9781509909759/
74 Nicole Rogers, 'Performance and Pedagogy in the Wild Law Judgment Project' (2017) 27 *Legal Education Review* Article 3, 8–11.

The projects commence from the starting point of a participant who is *aware of the self*, and through that aware *beyond* the self. What is less obvious is what triggers the rewriting judge to notice the 'victim as the stake', to see something different in the texts of law. So the decision of the Scottish Feminist Judgments Project in 2017 to hold a theatre workshop was an intriguing move. However, the theatre praxis used, Augusto Boal's (1931–2009) *Theatre of the Oppressed*,[75] would take the workshop in a different direction. Designed to empower the disempowered and disadvantaged as a Marxist act of political engagement to help ground actual political change in the Brazilian favelas,[76] Boal's work has the pull of the immediacy of action, and the desire to achieve 'something'. The theatre group running the workshop guided the participants through a series of physical exercises, out of which they workshopped a legal problem and its move into judgment, and then concluded with a discussion:

> At the end, we reflected on lessons learned from the process – key questions came up about being mindful of *who the judgment is being written for; what voices are and are not present and listened to as part of the process (and why);* and what changes in process or substance will make a feminist contribution even if not a distinctive feminist outcome. The theme of discomfort with the process of judging (in all senses of the word) came up again, as did our ability to explicitly acknowledge that *discomfort and its emotional impact* on us as judges.[77]
>
> (My emphasis)

This was an exciting intervention but one that fell back into the expectation in law that activities must 'pay up' practically, and achieve a recognisable outcome. I have highlighted the reference to excluded 'voices' in the part of the report to which I have referred, because there is nothing (obvious) in it that reveals how participants would be helped to notice those voices. Boal draws on concepts that law already understands – the political, questions of power and so on – and there is little scope for the legal self to move from these as abstract categories to see the excluded voice as 'the victim at the stake' in law's texts, and what might alert lawyers in re-reading and re-writing judgments to the 'flames'. But maybe it is there after all, implicit in the reactions of participants to the 'emotional' impact of judging, for to judge in law presumes reasoning that distances through abstraction. The theatrical

75 Scottish Feminist Judgments Project, *Theatre Workshop*. www.sfjp.law.ed.ac.uk/2017/10/16/hello-world/.

76 Augusto Boal, *Theatre of the Oppressed* [trans. Charles A. McBride, Maria-Odilia Leal McBride and Emily Fryer, updated edition] (London: Pluto Press, 2008); Augusto Boal, *Legislative Theatre: Using Performance to Make Politics* [trans. Adrian Jackson] (London: Routledge, 1999); Gillian Calder, 'Embodied Law: Theatre of the Oppressed in the Law School Classroom' (2009) 1 *Masks: An Online Journal for Law and Theatre* 11–35; Augusto Boal, *Games For Actors and Non-Actors*, 2nd edn [trans. Adrian Jackson] (London: Routledge, 2002).

77 Scottish Feminist Judgments Project, *Theatre Workshop*.

has to be suppressed, and the body as memory discarded, along with the wisdom of the theatrical antonyms. These judgments projects insist on engaging in judgment within expected conventions, leaving the judgment writers conflicted between the self as feminist judge, and the activity of judging within convention. Law, on its face, demands effacement seemingly as a condition of fairness. The feminist judges seek to conform, and then find they are conflicted between what is already embedded in law's texts and methods and what the self notices through their lifeworld, as etched into the body, which is treated as noise, extraneous and irrelevant and having no place within law, and which bears the same characteristics as theatre, and its challenges to norms and expectations, as Lehmann observes:

> The combination of heterogeneous matter (body, language, space, rhythm) and sensory– mental reality – which is 'illogical' according to the standards of reason yet displays a structure all the same – offers the deceptive appearance of thinking; at the same time, it calls for one to think about the deception it practices.[78]

This sensory disruption of the theatrical interferes with law's ontologies, including a spectral normativity that has its origins in a deep hostility towards theatre, out of which legal antitheatricality was shaped. For theatre is able to challenge, if it really gets under the skin through the Artaudian ructions it creates. From there we are a heartbeat away from breaking cover as reasoning, rational creatures,[79] to reveal an uncontained self, and that is something that legal antitheatricality is unable to abide.

The idol of the theatre

It is not hard to see how this fear of the uncontained self is fed by the Platonic mistrust of the mimetic and the communal, and the Aristotelean prioritising of the poetry of drama over staging, as text to be best consumed through reading and thought.[80] Theatre's practices were denied by the philosophers, and so too through the early Christian Church fathers' negation of the body as immature and imperfect, in contradistinction to the mind and soul as mature and perfect,[81] as we find in Tertullian's condemnation of 'theatre, games, spectacles and "public shows" … [as] excessive in a religious tradition that demanded silent, and above all, serious worship, both quietude of the body and composure of the mind'.[82] Without more, there is nothing uniquely legal about this antitheatricality, other

78 Lehmann, *Tragedy*, 25.

79 Leiboff, 'Muteness', 386.

80 Lehmann, *Tragedy*, 20, 34–35. Lehmann also quips that philosophy has 'exhibited an Aristotelian prejudice and not attended the theatre', 32.

81 Henry Chadwick, *Augustine: A Very Short Introduction* (Oxford: Oxford University Press 2001), 120.

82 Peter Goodrich, 'Theatres of the Book: Covering, Flaunting, Marketing, Author and Text' (2010) 14 *Law Text Culture* 357–383, 377.

than the integration of condemnatory gestures combined with control and limitation. How this religious and moral disapprobation developed into a distinctively *legal* antitheatricality can be traced to the multivalenced strands of writing on fields ranging from philosophy, natural science, learning, morality, and law in hands of the sixteenth- and seventeenth-century polymath lawyer,[83] Sir Francis Bacon (1561–1626).[84] Through a range of manoeuvres, law would adopt Bacon's logics to construct doctrines and principles, practices and attitudes to construct law as a field devoid of lifeworlds, negating the factors that speak to the theatrical. This position was shaped, in part, through Bacon's own antipathetic attitude to theatre (echoing Plato).[85] Despite this, Bacon's writing reveals that despite creating a method of science and knowledge creation and making claims for law based on an *absence* of self, he actively cultivated the self, creating masques at the Inns of Court, writing allegories; and saw in poetry a practice of morality that spoke against his own position, at least as inherited and hardened into a legal commonsense.

Our received position of Bacon in law is as a moderniser and discarder of verities, as an absolute disrupter of the old. But as Kristen Poole points out, Bacon was as much a product of a medieval world as a product of the early modern, and continued to hold on to inherited epistemes as much as he shaped and advocated for new forms of knowledge and its creation.[86] For instance, in revealing a marked disjuncture between his claims that language must meet the object of its attention directly through the *idola fori* (and *vice versa*),[87] and his own allegorical writing,[88] a form that could not have been more different, Poole demonstrates that his claims and the realities of his own practices were paradoxical at best, and contrary at worst. And of Bacon's claims for law, to which I will turn in a moment, the

83 Barbara J Shapiro, *A Culture of Fact: England, 1550–1720* (Ithaca, NY: Cornell University Press, 2000); Barbara J Shapiro, 'Law and Science in Seventeenth-Century England' (1969) 4 *Stanford Law Review* 727–766.

84 Marett Leiboff, '"Stir Up the Australian Youth to Merriment": A Midsummer Night's Dream, Summer 1989–1990 (Sydney, Australia) and the Theatrical Transmutability of Law's Texts', in Daniela Carpi and François Ost (eds), *As You Law It: Negotiating Shakespeare* (Berlin: De Gruyter, 2018), 247–268, 249–253.

85 Allison P Hobgood, *Passionate Playgoing in Early Modern England* (Cambridge: Cambridge University Press, 2014), 188–189. Bacon's own involvement in masques at the Inns of Court concerned private events in the hands of an 'appropriate' audience, distinguishing it from common theatre going.

86 Kristen Poole, 'God's Game of Hide-and-Seek: Bacon and Allegory', in Howard Marchitello and Evelyn Tribble (eds), *The Palgrave Handbook of Early Modern Literature and Science* (London: Palgrave Macmillan, 2017), 115–138, 118.

87 Roy Porter, *Enlightenment: Britain and the Creation of the Modern World* (London: Penguin, 2000), 54 reveals the influence of Bacon's position perfectly on the demands of language: 'Setting reality about verbality, the coming English empiricism … looked favourably on quantification. Were not numbers, at least, unambiguous and trustworthy? "Instead of using only comparative and superlative Words and intellectual Arguments", explained Sir William Petty, a founder fellow of the Royal Society, "I have taken the course … to express myself in Terms *of Number, Weight,* or *Measure*"'.

88 Poole, 'Bacon and Allegory'.

same contradictions are in place. Richard Ross reminds us that for Bacon and his contemporaries, there could never have been a clear bifurcation between *law* and arts and sciences:

> Lawyers also invoked the 'golden chain' of Homer that connected the various arts and sciences 'horizontally' with each other and 'vertically' with the divine mind Taken at its highest cosmological level of abstraction, the golden chain preserved divinely ordered and mutually dependent harmony among the arts, as the closely related concept of the 'great chain of being' did for the angels and corporeal creatures in God's plenitude of creation All things 'above and below, formed one system', argued a favorite text of Bacon and other lawyers, Cicero's *De Oratore* ... Was the common law a disorganized heap of writs, cases, and pleading tricks, a thing of shreds and patches, as unfriendly clients, civilians, university scholars, and divines claimed? No, for like any other body of knowledge, it stood connected to the other arts and sciences, and thence to God.[89]
>
> (References omitted)

Whatever it is that Bacon advocates, it is one shaped through a coterminous discursive universe that is bound into a logic that is unable to contemplate, or at least to effect, a marked separation of knowledge and law.[90] The belief that he instituted and formalised distinct ruptures as a clear bifurcation is a product of Bacon's advocacy rather than his own formation. Regardless, his new science informed his claims for law and *vice versa*.[91] So common law and statute should be reduced, digested, and recompiled,[92] as a form of proto-legal science that would be taken up with vigour in later centuries. First, a book would need to be prepared that accounted for the origins of doctrine (and in the process removed complexity and complication); second, the medieval year books, and their digesting practices, would be reinstituted,[93] replacing the then still new law reports; and third, a textbook for the study of the 'science of law', as a treatise with authorities, would be written.[94] Although the project never came to fruition, its desiderata are found in law's practices of strip-mining and of using summarised accounts of law and the preference for textbooks (or now blogs and slide presentations). Bacon established a set of attitudes that are reiterated as the spectral normativity to which I have

89 Richard J Ross, 'The Memorial Culture of Early Modern English Lawyers: Memory as Keyword, Shelter, and Identity, 1560–1640' (1998) 10 *Yale Journal of Law and the Humanities* 229–326, 293–294.

90 Peter Goodrich, 'Poor Illiterate Reason: History, Nationalism and Common Law' (1992) 1.1 *Social and Legal Studies* 7–28.

91 Francis Bacon, *Elements of the Common Lawes of England* (London: J. More Esq., 1636).

92 Perez Zagorin, *Francis Bacon* (Princeton, NJ: Princeton University Press, 1999), 175–182.

93 Ibid., 195.

94 Ibid., 185.

referred, though its origins are largely unknown in law. The normative dimension of Bacon's inheritance occurred through the establishment of doctrines and practices that took shape in the eighteenth and nineteenth centuries, drawing on Bacon's legal desiderata, in combination with his natural philosophy and practices of logic created in the *Novum Organum*.[95]

But his law project, for all of its modernising force, is riven with contradictions, including the continued presence of Bacon's own 'post-medievalism'.[96] His desire to return to the superseded year books, which had existed from 1268 to1535, on the one hand seem to constitute a claim for modernity, because on the surface they operate as a digest. But the year books were not digests. Instead they contained accounts of pleadings with a bare decision.[97] Manderson makes it clear that reasoning was superfluous, because what mattered instead was the authority, that is who reached the decision in the case, and not how they decided,[98] that conformed with Bacon's view of the courts as, in effect, agents of the king.[99] Because they were incomplete in so many respects, the year books had to be supplemented – through the handing down of the logics of the case through memory and the sharing of commonplace books,[100] notebooks and annotations made by lawyers to explain the reasons behind the judgments that were needed in order to understand the law itself. The new law reports were created in the first place by lawyers whose commonplace books were sought after by others because of their quality and the depth of coverage of the case and the reasons of the courts. Judgments now are issued in written form, but in these courts, judgments were uttered orally. Though their creation has been explained as a move towards reason and objectivity,[101] the reports were popularised by happenstance and then quickly moved to become an authoritative record of the law.

The first and most influential of the new reports of Edmund Plowden (1515–1585) were published under his name initially as a corrective.[102] Plowden's notes and commonplace books were shared around by other lawyers and through a

95 Robert A Yelle, 'Bentham's Fictions: Canon and Idolatry in the Genealogy of Law' (2005) 17 *Yale Journal of Law and the Humanities* 151–179: the connection to later projects such as Bentham's, on the creation of a science of law is clear.

96 Poole, 'Bacon and Allegory', 118.

97 Manderson, 'Statuta', 329: Manderson remarks that year books tended to jump from pleadings to the statement 'and so to judgment'.

98 Ibid.

99 Daniel Lee, 'Legal Science and Legal Reform in the Juridical Thought of Sir Francis Bacon' (Berkeley: University of California Press, 2014), 1–13, 2, 10, 13: http://rems.berkeley.edu/files/2012/03/Daniel-Lee-Legal-Science-and-Legal-Reform-in-the-Juridical-Thought-of-Sir-Francis-Bacon.pdf

100 Ross, 'Memorial Culture'. See also Pierre Nora, 'Between Memory and History: *Les Lieux de Mémoire*' (1989) 26 *Representations*, 7–24 for a consideration of collective memory and history, and the formation of the collectivity.

101 Paul Raffield, 'The Dramatic Imagination and the Dream of Law', in Marco Wan (ed.), *Reading The Legal Case: Cross-Currents between Law and the Humanities* (Abingdon: Routledge, 2012), 175–189, 178.

102 'Wherefore wishing the Reader to reap as much Profit by reading this Work as I did by composing it (which, I confess, was great), I commit him to God's Direction, desiring no other Reward for this my Trouble than his candid Reception hereof, and

range of factors, had been passed onto publishers. His notes were badly bowdlerised. Plowden published the correct version of the reports, created by his attending court, listening to the arguments of counsel and by noting down the remarks and reasons of the judges, coincident with and as part of the development of the newly formed doctrine of precedent, the binding authorities of law through principles created by the courts that connected the law through a practice of historical continuity from one case to the next.[103] Plowden did more than just listen to the judgments but arranged for his reports to be checked by the courts, so for the first time, lawyers and the courts themselves had an authoritative account of the law and its reasons;[104] as Penny Crofts notes, within a year of the publication of his reports, they were cited in judgments.[105] His reports now contained an account of the facts of the case as well as the principles of law, and unlike the year books, were contemporaneous accounts of what happened. They also read as play, and as play found their way into theatre.[106]

The brevity of the year books would superficially have met Bacon's preference for words to meet their objects, and his desire for knowledge to be stripped of superfluities; his own identification of the need for supplementary accounts of the law acknowledged that this form of digested law had limitations. Bacon held onto an old practice to shape law in the image of the new forms of knowledge he advocated, which demanded a mind stripped bare, to ground reason in order to work with verifiable sense-data (in the form of digested law). Law stripped down is more likely to meet its objects, in an abstract sense only, for law and its application is far from straightforward, however much Bacon (and his inheritors) would want it to be. Though unstated in any express way, the new reports spoke too much of forms of *poesie* as history and narrative, through the creation of detailed accounts of the facts, bringing the texts of law close to drama, along with the incidental problem of the reports being used to create plays,[107] thus bringing law into the despised theatre.

his good Report': Edmund Plowden, *The Commentaries, or Reports of Edmund Plowden* 176, viii.

103 Penny Crofts, *Wickedness and Crime: Laws of Homicide and Malice* (Abingdon: Routledge, 2013), 68.

104 Christopher W Brooks, 'Plowden, Edmund (c.1518–1585)' *Oxford Dictionary of National Biography* (Oxford: Oxford University Press, 2004–); Michael Widener, *Landmarks of Law Reporting 4 – Plowden: The First Modern Law Reports.* https://library.law.yale.edu/news/landmarks-law-reporting-4-plowden-first-modern-law-reports, 4 May 2009.

105 Crofts, *Wickedness*, 68.

106 Andrew Zurcher, *Shakespeare and Law*. Arden Critical Companions (London: Methuen, 2010); Paul Raffield, *The Art of Law in Shakespeare* (Oxford: Hart Publishing, 2017); Kevin Curran, *Shakespeare's Legal Ecologies: Law and Distributed Selfhood* (Evanston, IL: Northwestern University Press, 2017).

107 The terms play and drama haven't been defined as yet. They can be one and the same, but drama tends to denote serious subject matter, or material that seeks to instruct or provide guidance. Drama is etymologically tied to the word 'action' and is grounded in Aristotle's *Poetics,* which sets out rules for drama as tragedy in connection with subject matter and structure. Plays generally refer to a script or story to be displayed or 'played'. Further consideration of Aristotelian drama, and aspects of play as apposite to law will be taken up in the next chapter.

For Bacon, poetry or *poesie* was acceptable up to a point but not, as it is possible to deduce, for law. In the same way that Aristotle approved of drama as a literary form, it had a role in the moral formation of an individual, as Bacon remarked in the *Advancement of Learning* of 1605: 'In this third part of learning, which is poesy, I can report no deficience'.[108] But in *De Augmentis* of 1623, Bacon peeled apart three kinds of poesie – narrative, dramatic and allegorical – as a mark of discomfiture between those forms of which he approved and those which were less fit.[109] He appreciates the first, and is glowing of the last (to be expected as a writer and creator of allegories). Drama is complicated by its relationship with theatre, for theatre is a danger to reason. So in the *Advancement of Learning*, Bacon warns of drama, as well as theatre:

> For the expressing of affections, passions, corruptions, and customs, we are beholding to poets more than to the philosophers' works; and for wit and eloquence, not much less than to orators' harangues. But it is not good to stay too long in the theatre. Let us now pass on to the *judicial place* or palace of the mind, which we are to approach and view with more reverence and attention.[110]

Judgment is philosophy's ally, and the judicial palace, or reason, needs to be protected against *affection, passion, corruption and custom* and *orator's harangues.* These conceits are analogous to the theatrical antonyms, and that imperils morality, reason and rationality and order. But there was a problem that Bacon later realised, and in *De Augmentis* found a way to decouple drama from theatre, to save it from its evil twin, and to warn of the dangers that follow when the reason is corrupted by action, both on the stage and in the company of others:

> Dramatic poetry, *which has the theatre for its world*, would be of excellent use *if it were sound*; for the discipline and corruption of the theatre is of very great consequence … The *action of the theatre,* though modern states esteem it but ludicrous … *that the minds of men in company are more open to affections and impressions than when alone.*[111]
>
> (My emphases)

Theatre is action, and action is an inferior state of being, so it will inevitably corrupt minds, something which Bacon (echoing Plato) in his discussion of poetry in *De Augmentis*, reminded that the active world is inferior to the rational mind.[112]

108 Francis Bacon, *The Advancement of Learning* [1893], ed. Henry Morley (The Project Gutenberg ebook), Book 2, Aphorism V.

109 Francis Bacon, *The Works of Francis Bacon, Volume the Sixth Containing De Augmentis Scientiarum*, vol. 1 (London: M Jones, 1815), 36–37. This translation doesn't contain the Aphorism references.

110 Bacon, *Advancement of Learning*, Book 2, Aphorism V.

111 Bacon, *De Augmentis*, 40–41.

112 Ibid., 37–38.

That the inferior, active world might harm the rational mind through the base artisanal restates the position of the ancients and church fathers on the corrupting forces of the theatre. Yet Bacon, in the *Novum Organon* of 1620,[113] the treatise that set out his philosophy of knowledge in order to ground a new rational science, turns this around in order to find a way to attack philosophy – through theatre. Bacon insisted that minds had to be stripped of preconceptions and presumptions that existed in doctrine, pre-existing structures of the mind, language, and philosophy, in order to ground the formation of new, correctly calibrated knowledge. These impediments, the Idols of the Tribe, the Cave, the Marketplace and the Theatre, stand in for these conceptual impediments, and of theatre, it is philosophy and received forms of knowledge that he has in his sights. Theatre, already perfidious, is now a vehicle for other iniquities:

> Lastly, there are Idols which have immigrated into men's minds from the various dogmas of, and also from wrong laws of demonstration. These I call Idols of the Theater, because in my judgment all the received systems are but so many stage plays, representing worlds of their own creation after an unreal and scenic fashion. […] which by tradition, credulity, and negligence have come to be and received.[114] […] And in the plays of this philosophical theater you may observe the same thing which is found in the theater of the poets, that stories invented for the stage are more compact and elegant, and more as one would wish them to be, than true stories out of history.[115]

The demands of the *Novum Organon*, in combination Bacon's claims for law, created the conditions of an economy of sense-data with its politics of verification, logic, method and stripped down rationality that would later ground legal positivism and the presumptions of the analytical in law that in turn created the conditions that ground legal antitheatricality. Bacon's own uniquely grounded antitheatricality is literally and figuratively hostile to the world of action through the irrepressible *theasthai*, suggesting that Bacon was terrified of the possibility of the body and its response, and of theatre's ability to unmask through *theasthai* (in addition to its inversion of the proper forms, of intellect over the artisanal).

But it is how Bacon has been inherited that matters. His legal antitheatricality contains a series of features – that reason can function in isolation from life and the lifeworlds, that law ought to be a product of the post-medieval in combination with the proto-scientific, and that law is to disregard the active world and through that the insights of the theatrical. In combination, if Bacon's account of law is considered in the absence of the rest of his writing, we are left with a position that law has to be stripped of any extraneous knowledge in order to undertake the

113 Francis Bacon, *The New Organon, or True Directions Concerning the interpretation of Nature* (1863) [trans. James Spedding, Robert Leslie Ellis and Douglas Denon Heath] (eBooks@Adelaide, 2014). https://ebooks.adelaide.edu.au/b/bacon/francis/organon.html

114 Bacon, *New Organon*, Book 1, Aphorism XLIV.

115 Ibid., Aphorism LXII.

practice of reading and interpreting law. Or if Bacon's other writings are acknowledged, he is understood to demand the partitioning of the educated, formed self from the legal self. Either way, this is law's inheritance, and explains why the participants in the Scottish Feminist Judgments Project were so on edge about their role as judges, because Bacon, despite doing nothing of the sort himself, has left us with a legacy that insists on stripping the life out of law, and ourselves out of that life and law. It has left law and its practitioners engaging in contortions in order to meet demands that are both unattainable, and distorting of the lifeworlds of the law. Theatre would break the cover of this distortion, and so in Bacon's logic, everything associated with it had to be suppressed.

Bacon's legacy in law is far from anodyne. While he was on the losing side of the continuation of law reports and of the unfettered royal power, the structural alternations in the formation of knowledge he generated has had significant influence in the image of law as a scientific rather than a genre formed through the humanities. Bacon's method forces the compartmentalisation of human conduct, and in law, contributed to the construction of tests and steps and methods of rationalisation that turns law into a mathematical puzzle. But rather than improving law, these techniques distort by turning lifeworlds into tests that reconstruct rather than achieve the intended aim of ensuring that law is justifiable and its application fair. Put another way, law reconstructs existence through the deployment of sense-data in such a way that results in distortions of being and presence. Law, through the adoption of these techniques in judgment, has turned people into men (excluding women), a drawing into a painting, a painting into a signature, a right into a wrong, a fact into an opinion, all the while following legal techniques and reasoning. Along the way, Bacon's inheritance strips law of response (in both the bodily and intellectual sense referred to earlier), and responsibility (relying on Olivia Barr's conception of responsibility for law, and Shaun McVeigh's account of care, through office),[116] that is, the conditions through which we respond to law, and the concomitant characteristics that manifest care for law. This law is care*less* and creates the conditions for law absent responsibility.

To turn this around, it seems barely possible to argue against Bacon's influence and the significant role that legal sense-data plays, for the idea of being convicted without evidence, or for ownership to be transferred without proof, seems beyond comprehension. But there is a tipping point where it is rendered into nonsense and causes harm, from the judge who denies the rape victim a voice because she couldn't verify what happened to her; to the denial of rights to indigenous creativity in the absence of evidence of experts, despite the continued adherence in community to those creative forms; where evidence is used *against* particular groups; where concepts of property are organised against the wider good; where transactional law uses its components to the advantage of those with power over those without; to techniques of cross-examination designed to create doubt about

116 McVeigh, 'Office and Persona of the Critical Jurist'; Barr, *A Jurisprudence of Movement*, 33–37.

a witness's reliability and honesty and hence the reliability of their evidence, despite the truth of their account: if you can't remember the exact colour of the spot on your assailant's tie – how can the rest of your evidence be trusted if you can't remember that detail? These games of law brutalise as much as they ignore the actual conditions of existence, where law actively harms rather than helps. As Scott Veitch points out, creating the conditions of law as *irresponsibility* legitimates rather than corrects the conditions that lead to harm.[117]

Through these techniques, law has held onto the relics of Bacon's antipathy towards theatre, taken at its word by those who were unaware of or who chose to ignore that he held onto a highly developed complex of learning and morality that was tightly sedimented into his being. Lawyers soon began to ignore the need for this broader learning, and the effects of legal antitheatricality didn't take long to extend to their training. Of Bacon and his peers and contemporaries, Peter Goodrich was able to remark, in contradistinction to lawyers now, 'The early humanists were lawyers, they wrote the book, and they read the law. The contemporary humanist is a nonlawyer'.[118] Law would begin to imagine itself immune from the world around it, and in no need of training in anything other than law, to the dismay of Blackstone 130 or so years after Bacon wrote *De Augmentis*, when, in his inaugural lecture at Oxford in 1758 as first Vinerian Professor of Common Law, he warned of:

> a practice, which, if ever it had grown to be general, must have proved of extremely pernicious consequence. *I mean the custom by some so very warmly recommended, of dropping all liberal education, as of no use to students in the law* ... should this infatuation prevail to any considerable degree, we must rarely expect to see a gentleman of distinction or learning at the bar. *And what the consequence may be ... [that law will] fall wholly into the hands of obscure or illiterate men, is a matter of very public concern.*[119]
>
> (Emphasis added)

That liberal education is now largely lost from law. Management, accounting, IT, engineering, that which is useful, is considered helpful, is now law's helpmeet, but history, literature, the arts in general, have largely been jettisoned as unnecessary for law. As Goodrich has pointed out:

> Lawyers don't do much history now .... Law, pure law, nomocon jurisprudence is in practice an erasure of legal history, of the artistic reason of law, and we find in its place an inculcation of a finely honed and infinitely

117 Scott Veitch, *Law and Irresponsibility: On the Legitimation of Human Suffering* (London: Routledge Cavendish, 2007).

118 Peter Goodrich, 'The Theatre of Emblems: On the Optical Apparatus and the Investiture of Persons' (2012) 8 *Law, Culture and the Humanities* 47–67, 49.

119 William Blackstone, 'On the Study of Law', *Introduction to the First Volume of the Commentaries on the Laws of England*, 1765–1769. http://avalon.law.yale.edu/subject_menus/blackstone.asp

> abstracted training in virtual instrumentalities that pay no attention to philology, literature, or the interpretations that require attention to what is relayed *sub auditio* or through the text.[120]

What is left behind is a self who is able to turn to law, and read its words and play its games, but who has none of the resources at their disposal to deal with law beyond the self and hence the self-referential. And so law is recalibrated back into the self, as a systolic activity. Along the way, lawyers have been left without the techniques that will enable them to notice and use the texts of judgments which offer stories and explanations of law whose meaning and value is lost in the absence of a world beyond the self. And so the restoration of the theatrical, which now turns to the body as the first port of call over the rational mind, offers a technique, a jurisprudence that takes us back to law that is imbued with life.

Entr'acte

It is hard to imagine theatrical jurisprudence making even the slightest dent into the most arch forms of positivism and analytical jurisprudence. But what might be slightly disconcerting for these forms of jurisprudence is to be reminded that Bacon, whose science grounds the means by which law is split off from its life-worlds, was, in his law, pre-modern, or post-medieval. In this image of law, the doctrine of separation of powers never existed, and the authority of law rests solely in the hands of the holder of power. It is the theatrical that gives us the tools to notice, to look behind the assumptions, by turning back to the life and lifeworld of the creators of the image of law as much as it asks us to look at law and its interpreters and judges as well. So whatever it is that we imagine Francis Bacon to represent, at least since 9/11, a new image has taken hold in the early twenty-first century – that governments have power untrammelled by law. While this raises an entirely different jurisprudential question, the theatrical asks us to notice something of how these lawyers managed to step back into Bacon's post-medieval belief in a regnal authority. And here is a paradox. A legal self that has been trained in the presumptions of a Baconian legal antitheatricality has inherited an image of law that affords the legal self – not only the actual site of power – an untrammelled sense of self-authorisation. In the absence of a training *beyond* the self, and beyond law, contrary to the inheritance of Francis Bacon, law has the potential to move down the path of absolutism at best, and totalitarianism at worst because of those forces.

The theatrical insists that we do more than notice; it instead forces us to respond and react, to learn, to be traumatised, to be profoundly challenged, not intellectually or rationally (or solely so) but acquire something of that imagination and experience needed to notice when law or its interpreters, goes wrong, through other means, through the body. Without training, the sensory as double, the theatrical antonyms, and the self as aware and beyond the self are as likely to be

120 Goodrich, 'New Casuistry', 682 and 707.

problematic, in the same way as the abstract is problematic without an awareness beyond the self. All of the antonyms are as capable of being deployed for negative as well as positive purposes, in much the same way that an image of 9/11 becomes a reiterating device that narrates a particular account of power over law. To learn how to wrangle instinct (as opposed to thinking), disruption (as opposed to order), liveliness and courage (morality), transgression (ethics), and/or imagination (propriety/belief), requires something of the tenor of Francis Bacon's neglected double, and not just Artaud. Grotowski demands even more, as we shall see.

And this reminds us that to think of law in the abstract, or hold to a jurisprudence in the abstract absent the material, holds within it all the conditions for the development of law without responsibility and law grounded in injustice. As Olga Taxidou observes: 'the difference between philosophy and *theoria* is the body with all its senses. Possibly the difference between philosophy and *theoria* is that *theoria* needs to be experienced through the body – the senses, that is, the aesthetic'.[121] *Theoria* is another variation of the *theatrical*, theory shaped through experience and taught to respond through the body. It asks us to look up and pay attention beyond ourselves, and our expectations, partialities and presumptions. It asks us to pay attention to time and place, and through time and place. It has to burn into the body, in the same way that Grotowski, and the deeply grounded forms of training he required of his actors, and through them his spectators, will find new lines etched into the self through his work on and through the body. The theatrical can't be learnt (solely) as an intellectual endeavour, or law simply accounted for through the literary in the form of drama, a problem that will be taken up in the next chapter.

121 Olga Taxidou, *Tragedy, Modernity and Mourning* (Edinburgh: Edinburgh University Press, 2004), 35 cited in Lehmann, *Tragedy*, 27.

2 Law's dramatic pretence

Action

Law bears more than a few striking resemblances to drama, largely grounded in Aristotelian rules and prescriptions for drama and tragedy.[1] Aristotelian drama ('drama') shouldn't be mistaken for theatre, but is fundamentally a literary form that is antitheatrical. In its adoption into law, through law reports and judgment and its plethora of methods, principles, doctrines and rules, drama provides the means through which legal antitheatricality becomes operative. Law follows the rules of drama, as 'a representation of an action that is whole and complete and of a certain magnitude',[2] meaning that action that fails to meet the requirement of magnitude isn't drama.[3] Law, like drama, insists on plot, and where they exist, turns lives into characters or more correctly perhaps, imposes characterisation on lives. Law imposes or demands, like drama, a 'piece of action' that forms a whole,[4] made up of a beginning, middle, and end.[5] Drama has no ragged edges, and though it might have some twists and turns, has no ambiguities, and functions as causation through action, just like law. It's 'the natural result of something else but from which nothing else follows … well constructed plots must not therefore begin and end at random, but must embody the formulae we have stated',[6] just like law. Drama has other requirements: *catharsis*; responses, affects and feelings that are borne out a sense of pity or fear. Of all of the element of Aristotelian drama, it's the requirements of *action, causation, and magnitude* that have their closest connection with law, and as Rancière observes with acuity, reordering the unruliness of being into something that coheres, as action:

1 Compare Etxabe, *Tragic Judgement*, 110. The broader remit of the tragic offers a different examination and exploration of law and its possibilities.

2 Aristotle, *Aristotle in 23 Volumes, Vol. 23* [trans. W.H. Fyfe] (Cambridge, MA: Harvard University Press; London: Heinemann, 1932). Aristotle, *Poetics*, 1450b. www.perseus.tufts.edu/hopper/text?doc=Perseus%3Atext%3A1999.01.0056%3Asection%3D1450b

3 Aristotle, *Poetics*, 1450b.

4 Aristotle, *Poetics*, 1450a.

5 Ibid.

6 Aristotle, *Poetics*, 1450b.

> Action, as is well known, *is not simply the fact of doing something.* It is a *mode of thought*, a *structure of rationality* that defines both a norm of legitimate social behaviours and a norm of composition of fictions. Such was the Aristotelian arranging of actions linked through bonds of causality according to necessity or verisimilitude. The rationality of action corresponds to a certain form of the whole: that constituted by a denumerable and coherent set of relations — relations of coordination between causes and effects, of subordination between centre and periphery. *Action requires a finite world, circumscribed knowledge, calculable forms of causality and designated actors.*[7]
>
> (My emphases)

Law's reasoning, doctrines and principles, the tests it deploys, and the writing and structure of judgments and law reports: drama embeds a spectral normativity into law. Law demands magnitude, and is irritated with the inconsequential or minor, which will be reframed to become magisterial enough to warrant law's attention.[8] I don't mean, of course, the myriad disputes, and decisions dealt with on a daily basis, but law that warrants interpretation by the superior courts of a kind that creates new precedent and principle to be used by everyone. For this purpose, law craves certainty and completeness over uncertainty and the fragmentary, imposes order over chaos and perfection over unpredictability, rationality over intuition, causation over haphazardness, imposing confined logics over the unpredictable and uncontainable. Like Aristotelian drama, law delimits by creating finite and closed worlds and draws on circumscribed knowledge, made more so by its reliance on paper, because these cases are nearly always appellate where witnesses aren't called and facts aren't determined. But even in the very rare instances where law is litigated, where people appear in court, and arguments move between bench and bar table, the normalising practices of drama appear. Alan Dershowitz is irritated by how, in law, we work backwards to create narratives out of everyday chaos, and impose meaning on the chaotic.[9] We make up stories about the people and whose lives and affairs are to be assessed through law and its rules and turn the ineffable, through rules of evidence and procedure, into narratives that make sense. To reiterate Rancière, law creates through denumerability, calculable forms of causation, and reshapes the untamed into designated forms of existence.

7 Jacques Rancière, *The Lost Thread: The Democracy of Modern Fiction* [trans. Steven Corcoran] (London: Bloomsbury, 2017), 101.

8 And of major jurisprudences rather than those of a minor key: Panu Minkkinen, 'The Radiance of Justice: On the Minor Jurisprudence of Franz Kafka' (1994) 3 *Social and Legal Studies* 349–363; Peter Goodrich, *Law in the Courts of Love: Literature and Other Minor Jurisprudences* (Abingdon: Routledge, 1996); Olivia Barr calls the jurisprudence of movement a minor jurisprudence: Barr, *Jurisprudence of Movement*, 27–28.

9 Alan M Dershowitz, 'Life Is not a Dramatic Narrative', in Peter Brooks and Paul Gewirtz (eds), *Law's Stories: Narrative and Rhetoric in the Law* (New Haven, CT: Yale University Press, 1996), 99–105, 99–101.

These logics take the ordinary, insignificant, and accidental, and reshape them to give them a significance beyond their quotidian everydayness to make them worthy of attention. That's not to say that law doesn't deal with the everyday or ordinary. Rather, it's recast to bring it into the realm of tragedy, in much the same way that Lehmann observes of Aristotle's edict that tragedy (the abstract and ideal) is more philosophical than history (the material and quotidian):

> Tragedy … describes what always happens according to necessity or probability – that is, it is a matter of logical order, not empiricism. By seemingly elevating its status to philosophy, this gesture subordinates tragedy to the jurisdiction of the abstract concept; ultimately, it is conceptual thinking alone that determines the worth of tragedy. What is more, the distinction implies that tragedy has an obligation to its higher, 'more philosophical' nature.[10]

In this way, law 'describes what always happens according to necessity or probability'. Until this transformation occurs, law is blind to ordinariness; by reordering everydayness and liveliness into abstraction and ideal forms, law does more or less the same thing that Lehmann observes of tragedy *qua* philosophy. Lehmann remarks that, despite some nods to the (lesser) staging of drama:[11] 'Aristotle is not concerned with the senses, but with demonstrating that a *logos* can be read in, and abstracted from, tragedy'.[12]

Aristotle's prescriptions provide for a number of steps in the shaping of the drama. A *prologue* foreshadows what is to come, followed by a number of *episodes*, and then the *exode*, and a *choral song* broken down into two components, the *parode* and the *stamison.*[13] Judgment follows a similar pattern, from the overview as *prologue*, the accounts of fact and law as a series of *episodes*, the connection between law, fact, and the possibility of new legal principle as *exode*, and of the establishment of new principles or doctrine, *the choral song* its conclusion and consequence. Through plot, judgment negotiates discord and contradiction, the conditions of *anagnorisis*, and the struggle that culminates in *dénouement*,[14] where all the key facets of the judgment are brought together in the determination of the *ratio decidendi* where the law is established, before the decision affecting the parties is reached. Judgment functions as 'representation of an action that is whole and complete and of a certain magnitude',[15] and the end is 'the natural a result of something else but from which nothing else follows'.[16] Though judgment involves the narration of facts and law, its purpose is to move towards *dénouement* in the

10 Lehmann, *Tragedy*, 21.
11 I'll now generally refer to drama to include tragedy, though specific references to tragedy will appear from time to time.
12 Lehmann, *Tragedy*, 20: 'Given the general devaluation of sensory experience as 'mute', so to speak, the significance attached to voice in the *Poetics* carries little weight.'
13 Aristotle, *Poetics*, 1452b.
14 Aristotle, *Poetics*, 1455b.
15 Aristotle, *Poetics*, 1450b.
16 Ibid.

formulation and emergence of law as a probable or inevitable, as *catharsis*, though Aristotle points out that:

> Drama's object is not [only] to tell what actually happened but *what could and would happen either probably or inevitably.* The difference between a historian and a poet is not that one writes in prose and the other in verse.[17]

But judgment also involves this kind of deferral, where there is a possibility of 'would' or 'could'. It's not hard to see how a court functions as *chorus*, commentating on facts, law and the validity of arguments of counsel, or as *hupokrínomai*, the actor or player, the one who answers and responds to the *chorus*. The *hupokrínomai* was both interpreter and expounder and also a pretender, dissembler, a *hypocrite*. As poet, the court reaches into these contributions to create judgment, and a decision in the case, but effaced and resisting complete ownership of the judgment, just as *chorus* was effaced by mask.[18] Moving between fact, law, principle, and by stepping in and out of the position of *chorus* and *hupokrínomai*, the courts engage in that act of deferral that is bound up in the drama.[19]

These same Aristotelian dramatic prescriptions are found in law across the board and have attendant consequences for legal responsiveness beyond the boundaries of law's dramatic texts. They provide us with the tools of avoidance of the bodily presences and responses of law's interpreters that affect everything we do in law in the most unexpected ways. However much we imagine our bodies are secondary to the real task of working with our minds, because we have been trained to think within the logics of Aristotelian drama, all of us draw on the training embedded in our bodies in how we respond to lives, circumstances and events that come to us in law. Law's dramatic pretence attempts to protect the legal interpreter from the unruliness of the body. The lawyer's lifeworld is held in the body, through training that points us to notice, or fail to notice, what law holds within it.[20] What that training does is make us responsive or unresponsive, through law, in unexpected ways that I'll turn to now.

17 Aristotle, *Poetics*, 1450a.

18 Compare Connal Parsley, 'The Mask and Agamben: The Transitional Juridical Technics of Legal Relation' (2010) 14 *Law Text Culture* 12–39. See his observations of Hobbes' account of mask and persona, 13–15. Hobbes (1588–1679) is a rough contemporary of the figures of the early modern considered here.

19 In speaking of narrative and judgment, Simon Stern also points to this shift; that judges take on the role of either narrator or actor, depending on whether they claim that they are compelled by law or use another method in the move from evidence to narrative: Simon Stern, 'Narrative in the Legal Text: Judicial Opinions and their Narratives', in Michael Hanne and Robert Weisberg (eds), *Narrative and Metaphor in the Law* (Cambridge: Cambridge University Press, 2018), 121–139, 137.

20 See Damasio, Chapter 1, note 36.

Denying the body

Aristotelian dramatic presumptions embed the prime conditions of legal antitheatricality through the primacy of word. Aristotle presumes that drama is *writing*; performance or staging, and the body is unnecessary for drama to achieve its ends:

> The Spectacle has, indeed, an emotional attraction of its own, but, of all the parts, *it is the least artistic, and connected least with the art of poetry.* For the power of Tragedy, we may be sure, *is felt even apart from representation and actors.* Besides, the production of spectacular effects depends more on the art of the stage machinist than on that of the poet.[21]
>
> (My emphases)

Within this logic, artistry (or intellect) resides in the hands of poets or writers – and not the artisans, who work with their bodies – such as actors. Display or spectacle is secondary to the real function of drama as of the work of the mind. Treating spectacle as emotion, with its antonymic of reason, Aristotle reduces experience and *theasthai* to the margins, as subaltern and irrelevant. Thus law's interpreters are better off without their bodies, and by denying the bodily as a site of irrationality, ignores the possibility that legal interpreters might read, respond to and interpret law through their bodies. The *logos* of drama becomes a cloak of rationality which is assumed to keep the physical, visceral and corporeal at bay. But scratch the surface and it isn't hard to find the bodily on display in judgment, but mostly papered over in the language of doctrine and principle. As a range of different jurisprudences grounded in the material have observed, the cloak of doctrine will be used to obscure politics, prejudice and so on; psychoanalytic jurisprudences take us into the subconscious; theatre takes us back to our bodies and how they attenuate law. Drama allows us to avoid, using preordained plot bound up in an expected order of action. As Rancière observes of drama 'on display', the form of theatre Artaud railed against, law as drama distorts through its obverse:

> the theatre of well-constructed actions, of speech that sums up thought and leads it to act … was but itself a theatre of marionettes, *giving a bodily device to abstract ideas. It is dramatic action as the plot of knowledge that is a lie:* one about the nature of thought and the way in which it takes shape and is acted out; about the motivations and paths of action.[22]
>
> (My emphasis)

This kind of lifeless theatre that is bare display,[23] or what Peter Brook called the deadly theatre (the repetition of expected forms of display and stripped of

21 Aristotle, *Poetics* XXVI, 1–4. http://classics.mit.edu/Aristotle/poetics.1.1.html

22 Rancière, *Lost Thread*, 129.

23 The notion of marionette used by Rancière bears something of director and radical stage designer Edward Gordon Craig's manifesto on production, which was equivocal with respect to actors and the agency of their bodies based on practices that were self-

life),[24] is law's presumption too. But law wasn't always like this. Though the history of law tells us that medieval and early modern law were bound by the strictures of writ and practice, through procedure and formality, it was a lively law that grew out of and from its place. The story of modern law, though, plots out a movement towards modernity as the ultimate form of legality; this is when law takes on most of its Aristotelian dramatic presumptions, by the second part of the nineteenth century (a story that will be taken up later in this chapter), just as theatre had begun to disrupt the inheritance of Aristotelian drama and theatre. The theatrical avant-garde of late nineteenth and early twentieth century, including the famous Stanislavski and the far less known Meyerhold, began to lay bare how the presumption of action as thought was, as Rancière puts it of drama, a lie. As Lehmann observes, action as thought is only one part of a whole of theatre:

> as a component of (a) play, *a thought basically has no greater 'depth' than does a hand movement*, a pause in speech, or any other gesture – a stride or a blow. This circumstance *gives the lie to the arrogance of consciousness that deems itself free of physical determination*. Moreover – and this holds for all theatrical activity, not just for drama – thinking connects back to the speaker; the link to the actor's *physis* blurs its clarity.[25]
>
> (My italics, excluding *physis*)

Law, on the other hand, steadfastly holds to logics that presume that actions are *consciously preformed*. That's not to say that there aren't instances when action follows thought, but the pull of *logos* is so strong that it is next to impossible for law to find ways to accommodate the unanticipated, the ineffable, where the body functions first, and the mind second.[26] Regardless, popular examples abound showing how the body confounds logic. For example, an internet phenomenon known as the 'dress' shows that an apparently obvious physical property, that of the colour of a dress, wasn't able to be vouchsafed through thought, or determinable through reason. Person A would see the dress as one colour and Person B as another, as white and gold or blue and black (it was the latter).[27] Science explains how these differences in perception are unrelated to logic and thought. The dress confounds rationality, and the presumption that thinking will produce a perfected and correct outcome. It can happen to all of us. I mention to a colleague that the colour of a footpath is silver-grey. She said it's charcoal. She's right, so long as you're standing upright and looking down at the footpath. I'd seen the footpath from a very different angle, having torn a ligament and ending up on the

serving and worked against the ensemble as a whole: Edward Gordon Craig, 'The Actor and the Übermarionette' (1908) 1.2 *Mask* 3–15.

24 Brook, *Empty Space*, 1–17; The term deadly is used by indigenous Australians in an entirely different way.

25 Lehmann, *Tragedy*, 35.

26 Leiboff, 'Sarah Lund'.

27 *The dress* https://en.wikipedia.org/wiki/The_dress

ground; from that angle, combined with bright sunlight and the effects of the injury, the footpath looked silver-grey, just as light affected how the dress was viewed.

The conditions of rationality in law have no place for experiences and accounts that break the bonds of causality. An incongruence like this one is produced by the body that *precedes* thought, and is an irrational *failure of action as thought* because it functions pre-logically and bodily, just like the events accounted in a story that follows.[28] This is a story of bodies, in which training, responsiveness and irrationality produces circumstances of *responsibility*, as theatre, that confounds the presumptions in law that the mind, abstraction, ethic and rationality that would have produced *irresponsibility*, as drama, in law.

The irrational/pre-logical account of an event on a highway

It is halfway through 2008, and I am an hour or so into a nearly 1,000-km drive that I will take over two days from my home city to a place I will be moving to within a few weeks. I'm on a highway I've driven on a handful of times, and not too far from a medium sized town, but the surroundings are countryside. I'd been happily following a car for some time on the drive. It was doing the speed limit at an even pace, and I like that I am having an easy run on this dual lane highway. We have to slow to 60 kph as we go through a hamlet, and the highway moves into a single lane, not unusual in Australia, even on a major highway. The hamlet is small and we rapidly reach the 80 kph sign marking its perimeter. But that is now irrelevant; a thud swells up in my chest that says 'accident'. For no reason, I slam my foot on the brake and slow down, despite the signs that tell me I can speed up. But then it becomes clear. The other car is juddering and shuddering but is still driving forward. I'm surprisingly close to it, which is odd considering how quickly I braked. It keeps going even though it's behaving so strangely. I'm now thinking and rationalising, that the driver mustn't know it's in trouble, or the driver can't control it. I'm well below the speed limit but slow down even more, even though there's a line of cars behind me, and the other drivers won't know

28 This account is best described as methodologically connected to ego-histoire and jurisography. See for instance John Docker, 'Of Pearls and Coral: Jurisography and Ego History' (2016) 20 *Law Text Culture* 18–32. Pierre Nora, '"Introduction" from Essais d'Ego-Histoire,' [trans. Stephen Muecke] in Vanessa Castejon, Anna Cole, Oliver Haag and Karen Hughes (eds), *Ngapartji Ngapartji, In Turn, In Turn: Ego-histoire, Europe and Indigenous Australia* (Canberra, Australia: ANU Press, 2014), 21–22. The originator of *ego-histoire*, Nora observes the practice of this form of writing, as history, in the face of complaints and criticisms of lack of objectivity and exhibitionism in this form of writing, in speaking of the contributions to the original collection published by Gallimard in 1887 that tested its practices: 'These are not phony literary autobiographies, pointless intimate confessions, abstract professions of faith, or attempts at basic psychoanalysis. The exercise was to clearly set down one's own story [histoire] as one would write someone else's; to try to apply to oneself, each with his or her own particular style and methods, the same cool, encompassing and explanatory gaze that one so often directs towards others.'

what's going on. I think the car is about to go into a spin. Instead it mounts a steep cutting, flips onto its head and turns, landing horizontally across the two single lanes of the highway, screeching metal on tarmac as it goes. I've pulled over and try to get out of the car to help but can't move. People, some bearing crowbars, materialise from the long lineup of cars now caught up in this accident. We weren't far from a speedway, and mechanics and a nurse serendipitously were on the scene. The driver and his passenger are extracted in pretty good condition, even before the police and ambulance arrive. It takes 20 minutes or more for me to get out of the car; my legs are like jelly and I guess I'm in shock. I speak to the police officer who turned up, and the road is freed up soon after.

A week later, a young police officer rang to obtain a statement. He said: 'You did really well'. I think I knew what he meant, but other than the record of calls on my phone, I had no ability to place where this happened. I would have been an evidential disaster. This event challenges the dramatic expectations and logical consequences of law: that our logical and reasoning minds are to be treated as operative and our bodies an unnecessary irrelevance. Yet if we rely on our minds only, we make mistakes and dangerous errors. As the theatrical reminds us, what is abjured in law is the training of our bodies to be aware and responsive, to be able to *notice*. Put another way, the Baconian presumption of logicality and rationality and the image of the mind as functioning step by step based on Lockean sense data is, whatever we might imagine, actually dangerous and irresponsible. I'd put my foot on the brake based on nothing other than a bodily reaction or intuition. If I'd waited for my rational mind to kick in, it would have been too late. But now, as I write the words noted earlier, *I am surprisingly close to it* nearly a decade later, something registers. I would have hit the car in that earlier, pre-logical, irrational phase, when I responded *before action as thought* could have been triggered. It would have been catastrophic to have acted rationality; the shock response now making some sense, because this was the body and not the mind in control.

There are a few ways to explain what happened here: that as an experienced driver I would have quickly realised that the other car was in trouble; that I saw something and ignored it, reacting only at the last minute; that I wasn't paying attention and again reacted at the last minute. The first is the most likely of these possibilities, but it can't be explained only through experience, but through Zen-like practices that heavily influenced Jerzy Grotowski's theatre practices. These train the self to neutralise the conscious, thinking mind, where 'right acting and right living … is already liberated from mind and hand, which already "exists" in the instant of execution when thought and muscle act together,'[29] as training to awaken and practice intuition '"by stilling the babbling brook" of conscious awareness'.[30] Or as Grotowski has it: '"He forgets about himself in the moment before and in the moment to follow" … in this acceptance of the present

29 Adrian Cairns, 'Zen and the Art of Acting' (2006) 2.5 *New Theatre Quarterly* 26–28, 27.

30 David Feldshuh, 'Zen and the Actor' (1976) 20.1 *The Drama Review: TDR* 79–89, 81.

moment … the participant "begins to live in relation to someone"'.[31] As practices I'd been introduced to as an adolescent in the early 1970s in theatre classes, these had become practised; having driven for over 30 years at the time of the accident, driving, too had become practised. The other car had held my focus through the driver's consistent, excellent driving, and my own driving practices that remain present, meaning that the disruption in the driving by the other car triggered a pre-logical response in one or other parts of my brain, prior to awareness, which was acted upon directly. It didn't enter my conscious mind because a new, second reaction grounded in my rational and conscious mind registered the erratic driving. *I am surprisingly close to it* didn't register because I'd responded by 'forgetting myself' in the 'moment before', habituated through practice and training that involved 'living in relation to someone' as a practice of response and responsibility.[32]

This story of driving tells of an event, but I don't recount it to be read as a legal problem or hypothetical to be solved, such as teasing out any tortious liability or problems of evidential deficit, or potentially criminal consequences. These forms of training in law become pre-logical and ingrained too, meaning that it is too easy to register this account as a story about individuals and thus an irrelevancy for 'real' law, and so losing the purpose of its recounting. So too the human and everyday registered in this story fails in jurisprudence's quest for the ideal and abstract, and tells the wrong story, in much the same way that Lehmann despairs of philosophical and theological antitheatricality. Jurisprudentially then, its theatrical purpose, which reveals the irrationality of rationality and the illogicality of logic, and the rationality of the seeming irrational and the logicality of the seeming illogical, will be missed. To notice before awareness occurs literally, like this situation, but it also responds to statute, case law, and client stories. The story confounds the expectation of legal doctrine that can accommodate notions of intentionality on the one hand, or unintentionality on the other, all the while holding onto the expectation of action as thought, bringing to life the challenge laid down by Rancière noted at the outset of this chapter that 'The rationality of action corresponds to a certain form of the whole: that constituted by a denumerable and coherent set of relations – relations of coordination between causes and effects, of subordination between centre and periphery'.[33] But what this account reveals, too, is that it is dangerous to ignore the ineffable and illogical, as theatre and its practices shows, though it might be better, at least momentarily, to turn to a physicist, in a call to the Baconian as proof, because who wouldn't believe a scientist, who found out the very same thing.

31 Lisa Wolford, *Grotowski's Objective Drama Research* (Jackson: University of Mississippi Press, 1996), 46 quotations of Grotowski, references omitted.

32 See Chapter 1, note 115.

33 Rancière, *Lost Thread*, 101.

The moment of thinking was fatal

The esteemed Danish physicist, Niels Bohr,[34] was fascinated by a seemingly odd phenomenon in Westerns: in a shoot-out, the person who went to shoot first (usually the villain) would inevitably be shot by his opponent (inevitably the hero). Presuming there was a psychological explanation, Bohr suggested that: 'Since the hero never shoots first, the villain has to *decide* when to draw, which impedes his action.'[35] In 1928 while visiting Bohr's Institute in Copenhagen, fellow scientist George Gamow challenged the hypothesis and using water pistols, Bohr, taking on the role of hero, killed off all the villains (his students including Gamow).[36] His instinct about the shootout was correct, that the *moment of thinking* was fatal.

Also familiar with the story was the theatre director and theorist, Eugenio Barba, the creator of a physical theatre practice called theatre anthropology, through the International School of Theatre Anthropology, which he founded in Denmark in 1979.[37] For Barba, Bohr's experiment only makes sense if it is understood through the differences between the bodily response of the hero and that of the villain, whose connection with the body is interrupted by thought.[38] The answer wasn't in psychology but in an understanding of a responding body. Barba was able to piece together the connection through his work, where he found a common strand of heightened physicality and work on the body across a wide range of theatre traditions; on the other hand, word, motivation, psychology, or mind, which had characterised most forms of Western theatre practice until the innovations that had begun in the late nineteenth century, which had no way of explaining how the shootout worked. Barba began his own theatre research after working with Grotowski in the early 1960s; Barba was one of the people who introduced Grotowski to the West.[39] Erika Fischer-Lichte observes of Grotowski that his techniques and practices created an entirely different actor or performer who 'no longer lends his body to an exclusively mental process but makes the mind appear through the body, *thus granting the body agency*'.[40] (my emphasis). In Bohr's story, the hero's body is *has been granted agency* through the deployment of an embodied mind, that is through the body, while the villain's body *is betrayed by thought*. In Barba's terms, the latter exemplifies what he terms a state

34 The material under this heading is adapted from and draws on portions of, but doesn't reproduce, Leiboff, 'Sara Lund' except where expressly cited.

35 George Gamow, *Thirty Years That Shook Physics: The Story of Quantum Theory* (New York: Doubleday, 1966), 56.

36 Gamow *Thirty Years*, 56.

37 Eugenio Barba, *The Paper Canoe: A Guide to Theatre Anthropology* (London and New York: Routledge, 1995), 34.

38 Barba, *Paper Canoe*, 34.

39 Grotowski, *Poor Theatre*, 127. Grotowski was fascinated with Bohr and his Institute, and his own brother, Kazimierz, a physicist, had apparently worked at the Bohr Institute. The idea of the institute apparently inspired the idea of establishing a Laboratory Theatre.

40 Erika Fischer-Lichte, *The Transformative Power of Performance* [trans. Saskya Iris Jain] (Abingdon: Routledge, 2008), 82–83.

he calls *to be decided*– and this is precisely what leads to the downfall of Bohr's villains. To be left in, or remain in a state of *to be decided* is deadly, literally,[41] through seeking to break down the conditions of experience through Aristotelian action as thought.

Law assumes that the correct mode of thought remains locked into the state of thinking, or 'to be decided'. Rather, *a body* that *is decided* makes no sense for law, because it lacks rationality and reason. The actor or performer is never and *could never be* a 'mindless' body, just as Bohr's hero is never just a mindless gunslinger. Instead, the actor's body functions through a heightened state of self-awareness and awareness *beyond the self*, as does the hero. This heightened sense of consciousness and awareness of self and others, functions at a level of responsibility and responsiveness to a community of interests.[42] Moreover, the actor or performer is trained to unite consciousness and instinct:

> It is the act of laying oneself bare, of tearing off the mask of daily life, of exteriorizing oneself. Not in order to 'show oneself off', for that would be exhibitionism. It is a serious and solemn act of revelation. The actor must be prepared to be absolutely sincere. It is like a step towards the summit of the actor's organism in which consciousness and instinct are united.[43]

And that is what makes it possible to enter the state that constitutes *is decided* – it involves a heightened presence, and deep understanding of self and of others,[44] that is, an awareness *of self* and an awareness *beyond the self*. Regardless, law is just as likely to assume that *is decided* is:

> merely an unthinking reflex at work. 'To be decided' is consonant with what we already know, so appears to be an exercise in thought*ful*ness. But if 'to be decided' is conceived of by law as a thinking mind divorced from the body, as a separate entity, it represents a response that is unconnected, unfeeling, and unresponsive to those around her or him.[45]

These two examples are variations on the same theme – one as an account of an actual situation, and other testing, and challenging, an expected and presumed form of conduct, and each has legal implications in and of themselves, but revealing something uncomfortable and counterintuitive for law and its dramatic expectations: that thinking and reason can be treacherous, while intuition and bodily responses are instead, and unexpectedly, responsible. This confounds, as Rancière neatly points to, the *presumption of action* as *rationality* that 'defines both a norm of legitimate social behaviours and a norm of composition of fictions.

41 Barba, *Paper Canoe*, 32, 34.
42 Leiboff, 'Sara Lund', 86.
43 Grotowski, *Poor Theatre*, 210.
44 Leiboff, 'Sara Lund', 86.
45 Ibid.

Such was the Aristotelian arranging of actions linked through bonds of causality according to necessity or verisimilitude'.[46] Law has taken up this presumption with gusto, in one denying and discarding anything other than rules and word, in combination with an expectation of causality that mistrusts the unexpected and denies the unknown, while the bodies of those interpreting law must recede in order to encode justice.

The stories also reveal something of the unexpected bodily responses of legal interpreters, and point to the remnant lives, lifeworlds and memories held within law's writing and recording and in doctrine, where swords and shields speak to more than mere allusion, and are held within doctrines like promissory estoppel.[47] Swords and shields aren't an accident in law, as the stuff of childhood games, or more particularly those most likely played by boys. Swords and shields, too, are reminders of the violence of law, and of law as sword in the hands of Perseus.[48] In chancing our arms like this, the presumptions that rational minds are in some way the sole means through which we process, reason and analyse law, are rendered nugatory. These bodily figures of speech and metaphors, such as the flick pass brief that can only ever be understood by someone who's played rugby union, with all that denotes, are just some of that ways that judgment and argument in law reveals and holds onto something of its remnant physicality. Despite what we imagine, bodies are operative in judgment, argument and practice, and law (as doctrine and principle, and through the narration of facts and accounting of precedent) holds a remnant bodily presence within the words on the page, that is, in judgment and law report. These are used to forgive, to exacerbate, to dismiss.

Take, for example, the case of Zane Alchin, dealt with in the Local Court in Sydney in 2016. Mr Alchin was found guilty of using a carriage service to menace, harass or offend. His remarks on social media slut-shamed and suggested women should be raped, prompting responses by others online who were disquieted by his remarks, including Paloma Brierley Newton, who took a screenshot of his comments and handed them to police. Though acknowledging that Alchin's conduct was 'quite disgusting' and that 'You overdid it', Magistrate Pierce took the view that Alchin hadn't actually threatened or incited anyone to rape.[49] He compared Alchin's conduct to conduct on a football field: 'If you're on the football field, you consent to a few bumps, so a few mildly explicit comments, in this analogy …

46 Rancière, *Lost Thread*, 101.

47 *Walton Stores (Interstate) Ltd v Maher* (1988) 164 CLR 387.

48 'And the sword of Perseus which is used to cut off the head of Medusa is the law': Joseph Smith, 'The Sword and Shield of Perseus: Some Mythological Dimensions of the Law' (1983) 6.3–4 *International Journal of Law and Psychiatry* 235–261, 261.

49 The remarks are taken from the following media reports: Melanie Kembrey, 'Sydney Labourer Zane Alchin Sentenced for Harassing Women on Facebook', *The Sydney Morning Herald*, 29 July 2016. https://www.smh.com.au/national/nsw/sydney-man-zane-alchin-sentenced-for-harassing-women-on-facebook-20160729-gqg8l8.html; Elle Hunt, 'Judge Compares Offensive Facebook Posts to Football in Sentencing Sydney Man', *The Guardian*, 29 July 2016. https://www.theguardian.com/australia-news/2016/jul/29/court-sentences-sydney-man-for-sexually-explicit-facebook-comments

your sexually explicit comments were the equivalent of socking someone in the jaw with a right hook'. Those who complained, including Paloma, overreacted, which caused Alchin 'to experience a great deal of pain which you didn't deserve'. The women were the problem; the magistrate tacitly created the conditions of the play and the rules of engagement by using football to deny the harm to the women involved,[50] all the while invoking the presumption of action as rationality by reframing the conduct as nothing other than a punch up on the football field. This shared physicality reorders and reframes abuse into nothing other than game designed to exclude. Law, even at the level of the Local Court, or Magistrate's Court, reorders conduct into a set of circumstances that are *to be decided*, reshaping conduct to meet or conform to expectation, that is as a dramatic text designed to reorder conduct. The women who challenged Zane Alchin *were (is) decided.*

Put another way, text and word overbear, registering causally as permitted within law's dramatic Aristotelianism, while anything else is denied as irrational, illogical and dangerously challenging to law, its doctrines, its certainties and presumptions. And broadly speaking, anything beyond text or word bears the mark of the theatrical, as the story of the highway and of the shoot-out point to, and as the circumstances surrounding the case involving Zane Alchin show, law is uncomfortable with the conditions of *is decided*, and reshapes events within the logics of *to be decided*, that is as drama. *Is decided* might seem hard to delineate from the long-established politics, practices and jurisprudences of feminism, race, and class, and more, as synonymous with the theatrical antonyms because of the deployment of instinct, disruption, liveliness and courage, transgression and/or imagination, and, what might not be immediately apparent: an unwelcome training in difference by being repudiated or abjured by law's benchmark physicality. A training in difference, from needing to negotiate the problems of flick pass briefs and swords and shields and of reshaping conduct within a benchmark legality of the kind that Magistrate Pierce comfortably negotiates, is largely brought about by being repudiated or abjured by law's benchmark physicality. Perversely, and perhaps surprisingly, learning how to function in law when marked by difference, learning how *to be decided*, can lead to the distress experienced by the participants in the Scottish Feminist Judgments Project. Through the theatre games they played, the body reveals something to the self: that she or he sublimated through learning *to be decided* wrought by dealing with practices, methods and logics that are counter-intuitive to that self at best, and antithetical at worst.[51]

These experiences reveal that physicality of practice and training is deployed all the time in law, and then reframed to meet the preformed expectations through

50 In late 2018, Mr Alchin was due to appear in Sutherland Local Court (in southern Sydney), in relation to an Apprehended Violence Order Application (2018/00066650) and a mention in the criminal case of *R v Zane Alchin* (2018/00067507) following a series of incidents relating to his girlfriend: Candace Sutton, 'Tinder Shamer in Prison Charged with Slicing Girl's Underwear'. https://www.news.com.au/national/nsw-act/courts-law/tinder-slut-shamer-in-prison-charged-with-slicing-girls-underwear/news-story/f06933aeaad51c90e265d636cf7e4eac

51 See Chapter 1.

the rewriting of events, forms of conduct and so on, by neutralising and negativing circumstances and experiences using the deferrals that are afforded in the condition of *to be decided.* But one form of physicality and training into the body means that it's also possible, through training, to become habituated into the practices imbued in the theatrical antonyms to shape new intuitions, to trigger different responses based in responsiveness.[52] To change what's expected in law seems to be impossible, but we need to remember that it's only relatively recent in law's history that formally realised judgments took shape as writing as an action drawn from the record, either first or second hand, of an oral delivery of judgment and of argument before the court. Law, as Bentham complained of the judges, was a work in progress, and created after the event, but more particularly, 'created' through the reporters who recorded the law. But even that wasn't vouchsafed, for the reports could be anything from the records and notebooks of judges and advocates, to an actual first hand report of the case. We forget that law was largely an oral activity, and words came after and recorded *ex post facto* in the law report, and its sources often far removed from the logical practices of judgment taken for granted in contemporary law.

Judgment and law reports

From orality to the book, from play to drama

The law report, or 'law on the books', is the oldest formal repository of the narratives and reasoning found in the common law world. The reports replaced the records and brief annotation of judgment contained in Year Books, from their Norman origins until their replacement by the reports in early modern England. The content of the Year Books was scant, and had to be supplemented by a helpmeet, the informally annotated texts and notebooks of lawyers, which functioned, along with the recollections of practising lawyers, as the only repository of the reasoning and logics of judgment. Law was as much a practice based in imagination and in memory, and as Winfield complains of the Year Books: 'Bench and Bar must rely on their own memories for earlier cases.'[53] Omitting precedent on the one hand and containing side remarks about the weather and the rudeness of certain judges,[54] the Year Books were later dismissed as offering intriguing insights as historical records, but nothing of law,[55] something barely comprehensible for lawyers trained to think of law reports holding only judgments of value and importance. We forget that judgment was (and still is up to a point in lower level cases) oral and evanescent, and would disappear unless recorded by a law reporter taking the words of the judge and turning them into the record of judgment held

52 See Chapter 1, notes 38–41.

53 Percy H Winfield, *The Chief Sources of English Legal History* (Cambridge, MA: Harvard University Press, 1925), 150.

54 Winfield, *Sources,* 155.

55 Ibid., 171. Also see Chapter 1, Manderson, note 44.

in the reports. Up until some point in the twentieth century, reports might also include the argument of counsel and the interventions of the court.

The law reports turned oral judgments and the *aides-mémoires* of the commonplace books and annotations, private and collective, on paper and dispersed through discussion, into a literary form, creating narrative expectations of judgment. Though these early law reports may have echoed the structure of judgments as delivered, scholarship suggests that it is more likely they were organised according to the structures of the commonplace book, personal notebook or treatise, supplemented by annotations and glosses on the law that would also be shared with other lawyers or the courts.[56] Though law likes to imagine itself uninfluenced by externalities,[57] the invention of the new technology of print in the early modern era triggered some of the changes[58] that would eventually lead to the normalisation of law in the form of judgment by the nineteenth century.

This isn't our normal story of law, which holds that ancient doctrine is held within judgment and has done so for time immemorial. Print, however, turned what had been a private practice of memorialisation and annotation of a personal or collective record of law into a stable record that could now validate the authority of judgment. These new reports, beginning with Plowden's, had to formulate what cases should look like. McGlynn treats Plowden's reports as transitional, acting as a transfer between the essentially personal, individual or collective shaping of law in the commonplaces towards a formalised law.[59] Plowden brought together material from a range of sources, including plea rolls and year books; but they weren't immediately taken up as the style to be adopted.[60] The reports, McGlynn argues, were part of new humanist concerns about learning, citation and argument,[61] and activities like taking, organising and retrieving notes, brought into law through the universities, which lawyers like Plowden and Bacon attended, before joining the Inns of Court.[62] Winfield, more archly, is probably closest to the mark in suggesting that the law reporters didn't quite know how to deal with their accounts, or topics, or where to place the emphasis in their writing.[63]

However, the genre best suited to the task of recording and then shaping orality or texts drawn from notes and then edited, was the play: the model for the early law report can be found in the medieval and early modern vernacular and community play. Though we imagine the play to be the work of a (single) literary

56 Margaret McGlynn, 'Idiosyncratic Books and Common Learning: Readings on Statutes at the Inns of Court', in Lorna Hutson (ed.), *The Oxford Handbook of Law and Literature, 1500–1700* (Oxford: Oxford University Press, 2017), 41–60.

57 See the criticism in James McBain, '"Attentive Mindes and Serious Wits"', in *Oxford Handbook, 1500–1700*, 80–96, 95.

58 David J Harvey, *The Law Emprynted and Englysshed: The Printing Press as an Agent of Change in Law and Legal Culture 1475–1642* (Oxford: Hart Publishing, 2015). Harvey is a New Zealand District Court Judge.

59 McGlynn, 'Idiosyncratic Books', 52.

60 J Harvey, *The Law Emprynted*, 161.

61 McGlynn, 'Idiosyncratic Books', 58.

62 Ibid., 53.

63 Winfield, *Sources,* 169.

genius who writes a set of words to be performed on a stage, the play is as much as anything a work of collaboration, with scenes and events improvised and the resulting interaction recorded as play text, and vice versa. The newly crafted law reports speak to the genre of medieval mystery, miracle and morality plays. After all, the recording of a field (law) *grounded* in orality (or in the notations and annotations of a script) would be able to find a cognate form in a medium, theatre, *grounded* and *practised* in much the same way. As Paul Raffield observes:

> The English legal system of the early modern period was derived from an oral tradition; its adversarial juridical procedures were predicated on an agonistic model in which competing narratores [senior counsel] presented contending stories and were judged on the basis of their persuasive skills. The parallels with drama are obvious and compelling, not the least being the recording of oral storytelling in textual form. It was in the sixteenth century, as the published Law Reports (especially those of Plowden) replaced the Year Books, and as an independent legal profession was recognized by statute, that standardization and systemization of the common law was established.[64]

The early modern report's rambunctious and richly embellished engagement in its life-worlds (that annoyed Bacon so much) was given short shrift in the emerging neoclassical formalisation of the shape and structure of judgments in the eighteenth century,[65] before settling the tightly formularised judgment as drama by the end of the nineteenth century.[66] Then, conditions of authorisation saw the reports displaced by judgment, which now bore so many of the elements of the well-made play (drama) patterned on Aristotle's instructions and prescriptions drawn from the *Poetics.* The report was rendered nugatory, as the expectations of causality in judgment through the logics of Austinian positivism imposed a rigidly unbending *stare decisis* and precedent as

64 Raffield, 'The Dramatic Imagination and the Dream of Law', 178.

65 Desmond Manderson and Cristina S. Martinez, 'Justice and Art, Face to Face' (2016) 28.2 *Yale Journal of Law and the Humanities* 241–263, 243–245 and 262–263.

66 This shift was paralleled in the new technics of control of theatre in the eighteenth and nineteenth centuries in England, replacing the more obviously bodily interventions in the early modern, where the *Vagabonds Act* 1572 restricted theatre and its practices physically. So common players of interludes (not belonging to any baron of the realm, or to any other honourable person of greater degree), had to have the licence of two justices at the least, or would be 'grievously whipped and burned through the gristle of the right ear with a hot iron of the compass of an inch about.': (14 Eliz.I, c. 5). Replaced by a licensing regime, the *Stage Licensing Act* 1737 (10 Geo 2 C28), all material to be performed was subject to censorship and licensing by the Lord Chamberlain, and performances of plays confined to the licensed Patent Theatres: Convent Garden and Drury Lane. However, it was possible to get around this system if texts were not used and if performances were not held in a theatre (also illegal, though impossible to police because texts weren't used). These other forms – burlettas, pantomimes and melodramas included – were eventually caught by the *Theatre Acts* 1843 (6 & 7 Vict c.88). All restrictions were removed in the UK in1968 with the passing of the *Theatres Act* 1968.

straightjacket, tightly confined by the conventions of dramatic Aristotelianism.[67] But now to go back, to a beginning of sorts.

The early modern report – orality as play

Paul Raffield is perplexed by a line in an anonymous play called *Thomas of Woodstock, or King Richard the Second, Part One*, written in the period 1591–1595. There, a character called Nimble (or a plodder, slang for an attorney-at-law) says: 'for I have plodded in Plowden and can find no law'.[68] Of course law was in Plowden but you had to go looking for it by reading into and through the stories and events, the individuals and personalities that are the stuff of his reports. Bacon's criticism of Plowden[69] is put into Nimble's mouth.[70] Plowden, however, thought that he shaped the law and judgment clearly and materially, and without superfluities. It's instructive to see how an eighteenth-century English translation of his introduction to the reports (from the original Law French), reframes Plowden as a denizen of the neoclassical (as an act of wishful thinking, it might be added), in which he accounts for his treatment of the arguments, interactions, and judgments reported:

> I have for the most Part reported Cases in a summary way, collecting together the *Substance* (as it appeared to me) of all that was said on the one Side, and on the other, and oftentimes of all that was said by the judges themselves, without reciting their Arguments Verbatim ... I thought that there were *few Arguments so pure as not to have some refuse in them*, and therefore I thought it best to extract the *pure only, and to leave the refuse* ... But this is a Task not easily accomplished, *for he who would reject a great Part of what was spoken as vain and superfluous, and relate only that which was pure and material*, ought to have not only great Understanding and Memory, but especially *an excellent and distinguishing Judgment*, for otherwise he may reject as ineffectual that which is very material, and approve as effectual that which is of no Weight.[71]
>
> (My emphases)

For all of their supposed removal of 'refuse', in the terms used by Fulbecke,[72] Plowden's reports contain vast amounts of material, not just pleadings, but detail and side matter. This incongruity between aim (which speaks of the *Poetics*, again at least through later neoclassical interventions) and style (which is detailed and generally very lively) is as much as anything a desire to appeal to generations of lawyers inured in the practices of

67 Rancière, *Lost Thread*, 101.
68 Raffield, *Art of Shakespeare*, 10.
69 Chapter 1, 19–20.
70 I have suggested elsewhere that Shakespeare pokes fun at Bacon in the play *As You Like It*: Leiboff, 'Theatrical Transmutability of Law's Texts', 249–253.
71 Plowden, *The Commentaries*, v.
72 Harvey, *The Law Emprynted*, 161.

the year book,[73] and of the law held within memory and commonplace book. 'Plowden's style was new', Harvey remarks (though he observes too that some of the last of the year book writers wrote in a stylistically similar fashion).[74] For all of his claims of summation, purity and materiality, Plowden's reports read as spectacle, as a survey of place, being and presence. And though credited with establishing the modern report, most of his stylistic devices were to be later discarded.[75] His reports contain highly detailed accounts of the positions of the parties and the detail of the law and reasoning and logic of the courts, and lots of personal and intriguing detail that would be considered irrelevant in the stripped back form of a contemporary judgment. There is law of course, but Plowden's accounts are too bounteous and too lavishly rich in their detail and particulars. We might just be there with the serjeants and justices, the litigants and their stories. These reports are of their time and place; they scold and they charm, sharing the warm breath of the lifeworlds out of which they were shaped.

There is a reason why they might read like this: for a late medieval/early modern lawyer, there would have been no better model to adopt to turn the oral and evanescent into a literary form than the recently banned popular theatre form, the lively and charming mystery play (along with something of the newer, much more ascetic morality play), accompanied by a *soupçon* of the rules of the *Poetics* guiding its structure (it's likely Plowden would have been familiar with something of Aristotle's *Poetics*;[76] he was certainly familiar with *The Ethics*.)[77] There were other forms of

73 Ibid.: Harvey notes that Fulbecke compared Plowden with another reporter, Dyer, remarking that their different styles would be preferred depending on the lawyer: Plowden had a fullness of argument, while Dyer had a strictness and brevity. Harvey suggests these reports were more like yearbooks. Dyer's reports were only published posthumously, but were of the same period as Plowden: 144. Compare Van Vechten Veeder, 'The English Reports, 1292–1865' (1901) 15 *Harvard Law Review* 1–25, 'his accurate, concise, and business-like notes have always been regarded as among the best of their class', 12.

74 Harvey, *The Law Emprynted*, 144, n. 3.

75 Ibid., 144; Richard O'Sullivan, 'Edmund Plowden, Master Treasurer of the Middle Temple,' (1957) 3 *The Catholic Lawyer* 44–58: 'we get a living picture of the scene in Court', 48.

76 The reports are organised into categories that hold something of the structure of the *Poetics*, but there's nothing in the writing that holds tragedy within it. The correct translation of the *Poetics* was available in England by the time Plowden began preparing his reports in around 1540, but translations of a version, in adapted and altered form, had been available from the fifteenth century. Micha Lazarus, 'Aristotelian Criticism in Sixteenth-Century England', *Oxford Handbooks Online* (Oxford University Press, 2016) DOI: 10.1093/oxfordhb/9780199935338.013.148. This work has overturned the belief that *Poetics* was unknown in England until the seventeenth century except in poorly translated forms. Lazarus traces its reception to 1540, and that suggests its influence might have extended into Shakespeare's later work. The first Latin translation published in England only appeared in 1623 (the same year Bacon published *De Augmentis*). It had been assumed, until Lazarus' work, that the only translations available before 1623 were inadequate.

77 O'Sullivan, 'Plowden', suggests that Plowden was deeply versed in Aristotle, as well as Aquinas, 50. See also Constance Jordan, 'Shakespeare's Law and Plowden's Authority',

entertainment, play and emerging drama during the latter medieval into the early modern, from masques and interludes to court based plays (of the kind Bacon created and advocated),[78] some secular plays, as well as street entertainment. McBain, among others, has noted the place that early drama had been included as part of training at the Inns of Court, where plays were written and performed from around the 1560s,[79] until they were replaced by entertainments and masques (by 1640).[80] Regardless, plays had been a staple of medieval English life for centuries, and would continue to influence training and thinking in law throughout the Jacobean period.[81]

The mysteries and moralities served a particular purpose: didactic and entertaining, sanctioned (up to a point), they were of and from their community.[82] The mysteries, presented annually or biennially as part of the Catholic feast of Corpus Christi, had been a staple of English life from the fourteenth century (if not earlier), until they were banned under the Reformation in 1534.[83] A cycle of the plays that could run for days, the mysteries presented all of the bible stories from beginning to end. Initially created by the clergy, they became the responsibility of the local guilds, who would each stage a single play that spoke to their trade or expertise – bakers would present the story of the loaves and fishes, goldsmiths the story of the Magi and so on. Their serious purpose of instructing in Christian doctrine aside, the mysteries are peppered with the local, and the very prosaic. Staged in the street, in churchyards and in marketplaces, Howes remarks that 'akin to the [contemporary] immersive theatre ... their historical stories in up-to-date settings, making references to local landmarks, disputes and characters in order to root the action not only in the [then] contemporary moment, but in their particular location'.[84] Each play in a cycle varied in its tone and seriousness, from

in Kevin Curran (ed.), *Shakespeare and Judgment* (Edinburgh: Edinburgh University Press, 2017), 71–87, 85; Suzanne Corcoran, 'Theories of Statutory Interpretation', in Suzanne Corcoran and Stephen Bottomley (eds), *Interpreting Statutes* (Leichhardt: Federation Press, 2005), 8–30, 11–12.

78 Chapter 1.

79 McBain, 'Attentive Mindes', 95.

80 Alan H Nelson, 'The Universities and the Inns of Court', in Richard Dutton (ed.), *The Oxford Handbook of Early Modern Theatre* (Oxford: Oxford University Press, 2011), 280–291.

81 See generally Raffield, *Art of Law in Shakespeare.*

82 Some plays and entire cycles of the plays are extant: Wakefield, Coventry, York, and Chester (the latter in their original form). Records reveal that they were performed in other locations across the country, including Clerkenwell in London, though nothing remains of their texts. The play created by the mechanicals in *A Midsummer Night's Dream* hearkens to the mysteries, albeit in classical guise, now as a mark of learning.

83 They continued until 1576 in some locations, albeit under threat of punishment (the *Vagabonds Act* 1572 restricting actors: see note 60 above). The repression of the mysteries that speaks to the apparatus of power and the repression of difference. See also Peter Stallybrass and Allon White, *The Politics and Poetics of Transgression* (Ithaca, NY: Cornell University Press, 1986).

84 Hetta Elizabeth Howes, 'Medieval Drama and the Mystery Plays', *British Library*, 31 January 2018, https://www.bl.uk/medieval-literature/articles/medieval-drama-and-the-mystery-plays

dealing with the serious and mystical and then moving straight to comedy with barely a breath between them. In the Chester plays, Noah is a drunk and Mrs Noah is too much of a gossip to realise that she needs to get onto the boat, eventually being carried off by her sons. In the York cycle, incompetent soldiers argue whilst nailing Jesus to the cross, as slapstick and as piety in one. It isn't hard to imagine that some of the characters are based on locals and their foibles, speaking to the life and lifeworlds of the community out of which they were created and in which they were presented.[85] The mystery plays were bound up in their community in time and in place, and as Howes remarks, were 'civic undertakings, expressive of civic attitudes and values as well as the religious ideas that are their main concern. *It is not therefore surprising that the mystery plays often offer, as a kind of aside, social comment*' (my emphasis).[86]

The politico-religious dimensions of their demise was patent, not only because of their Catholicism, but because of their traits of carnivalesque.[87] They, with other forms of popular theatre, were the subject of Elizabeth's *Vagabonds Act* 1572.[88] Less so the morality play, but it too had run its course by around 1550. Instructing in how to achieve Christian salvation, the genre began around 1400, in a play called *The Castle of Perseverance. Everyman*, the best known of the moralities, appeared around 1500. In these generally serious plays, an individual, human character is usually set on a journey or a challenge, encountering named and personified virtues and vices (temptation, perseverance, hope and so on), 'before ultimately turning to righteousness and salvation'.[89] But again, like the mysteries, the morality plays were also unable to resist the comic. As Howes notes, 'the serious themes are counterpointed by moments of farcical comedy, primarily provided by the vice characters'.[90]

Plowden would have been no stranger to the culture of the play, and it's not hard to find elements and features of the mystery and the morality in his reports, from individuals as personified figures of vice or virtue in *Saunders*,[91] and the detailed recounting of people, places and events, peppered with remarks and asides along with commentary. His reports take for granted the importance of recording more than the bare material facts, and we see and are asked to pay attention to the detail of lives and motives and circumstances in the narration of both the law and the facts, and of the interactions between advocate and judge. But we, too, are to

85 Howes, 'Medieval Drama and the Mystery Plays'.

86 Anonymous, 'Popular English Drama – The Mystery Plays', *Harvard's Geoffrey Chaucer Website,* undated, https://chaucer.fas.harvard.edu/pages/popular-english-drama-mystery-plays

87 Mikhail Bakhtin, *Rabelais and His World* [trans. Hélène Iswolsky] (Bloomington: Indiana University Press, 1984), 15.

88 See note 60 above.

89 Howes, 'Medieval Drama and the Mystery Plays '.

90 Ibid.

91 *R v Saunders and Archer* (1573) 2 *Plowden* 473; 75 ER 706. See especially Crofts, *Wickedness*, 63, 67–69, 89–100 and for a discussion of the place of the moralities and the movement to the individual in law see Gaakeer, '"*Sua Cuique Persona?*"', 293–294.

learn from the moral or a caution reported along with the law and its rationale. The Catholic Plowden's reports are morality and mystery in one, but with an eye to Aristotle's *Poetics*. And though the reports spilled out of law and into the wider world (Shakespeare drew on them)[92] their liveliness, the richly embellished image of law wouldn't last.

Though Raffield suggests that law and drama were to learn from and imitate each other during the first decade of Jacobean rule,[93] neither Plowden nor Shakespeare were to retain their influence into the era through the influence of the neoclassical drawn from the *Poetics*. Bacon aside, Coke was also critical of Plowden's rambling, interrupted style of report.[94] Shakespeare was pushed aside,[95] in favour of one of Bacon's friends,[96] the classically trained Ben Jonson. In the hilarious five-act *Bartholomew Fair* of 1614, a strictly imposed unity of time, place and action (everything occurs strictly as it happens) of the neo-classical is combined with a biting wit poking fun at law. As playwright Steve Walter archly puts it: '"Aristotalitarianism" is ubiquitous, from the neo-classicism of Ben Jonson or Dryden or Corneille, with their distaste for the unruly pleasures of Shakespeare'.[97] To which we might add, the unruly pleasures of law rendered through Plowden. If law turned to theatre to try to find a lexicon and orthography in the early reports, it would find its next model in the drama of the neoclassical, as an expression of Baconian rationality after the Restoration, as another instance of exchange between law and drama. Theatre, in all of this, was nowhere to be seen. If in the early seventeenth century Plowden is in decline, by the eighteenth century translations of his reports into English are now 'corrected', their rambunctiousness contained,[98] and their liveliness now gives way to the expectations of a rational legal neoclassicism, as vehicle of legal antitheatricality, in report and judgment.[99]

92 Raffield, *Art of Shakespeare*, 9.
93 Ibid.
94 Winfield, *Sources*, 188–189.
95 Shakespeare, c.1564–1616, predeceased both Bacon and Jonson.
96 Ben Jonson (1572–1637) was a friend of Francis Bacon, whom Jonson celebrated and eulogised: Ben Jonson, '(On) Lord Francis Bacon' 1625. https://sourcebooks.fordham.edu/mod/1625jonson-bacon.asp; Ben Jonson, 'On Lord Bacon's Birth-Day', *The Works of Ben Jonson* (Boston: Phillips, Sampson, and Co., 1853), 834. Jonson's plays, though mostly comedies, would conform to Bacon's approved kinds of dramatic poesie. Jonson in turn had praised *De Augmentis* for its literary and moral guidance: Stanley Stewart, 'Jonson's Criticism', in Richard Harp and Stanley Stewart (eds), *The Cambridge Companion to Ben Jonson* (Cambridge: Cambridge University Press, 2000), 175–187, 186.
97 Steve Walter, 'Aristotle Didn't Know Anything about Theatre: Why Do Playwrights Still Adhere to the Philosopher's Over-Simplistic View of Drama? It's a Greek Tragedy', *The Guardian*, 4 October 2010. https://www.theguardian.com/stage/theatreblog/2010/oct/04/aristotle-poetics-theatre-sophocles-euripides 4. He attributes the term 'Aristotalitarianism' to playwright Timberlake Wertenbaker.
98 Crofts, *Wickedness*, 103–104.
99 See text at note 70 above.

Neoclassical drama: the report moves to judgment

It's not completely surprising that reports, as a genre, stuttered and declined during the seventeenth and early eighteenth centuries,[100] in part because of the political and social turmoil along with the regularisation of empiricist and rationalist logics,[101] and the forging of the norms of nascent modernist legalities hostile to the embellished lifeworlds of the original reports, and because of the technology of print. Veeder observes of the late seventeenth-century attempts to control the reports:

> The license of the press prompted the enactment soon after the Restoration of a licensing act, requiring, among other things, that all books concerning the common law of the realm should be printed only upon the special allowance of the lord chancellor or the judges, or by their appointment … At all events this licensing act, which expired in 1692, did not materially improve the standard of reporting.[102]

The tussles over the veracity of the reports is echoed in the near contemporaneous scraps that attended the emerging boundaries of literary property, or copyright law: should law only recognise a property in determinable and literal marks on a page, or the sentiment (that is, what makes the work what it is) of a literary work? Two cases heard between 1760 and 1769 illustrate how the move was made from the latter to the former, roughly at the same time that the new model of report took hold. Burrow's reports (1757–1771), were, Veeder observes 'of the utmost value in themselves as a record of the services of Mansfield, Foster, Wilmot, and Yates, exercised, moreover, a most beneficial influence upon subsequent reporting'.[103] I'll return to Burrow soon, but there is something in the shift in law during the eighteenth century that takes us into the difficulties facing this boundary setting in copyright law, through the reporting of the following two cases, and the shape that the reports were to take.

The development of copyright concepts and the rise of the methods of empiricism ran hand in hand during the eighteenth century and privileged 'book' and 'composition' – the 1760 Equity decision in *Tonson v Collins*,[104] and the reasoning of the majority in 1769 common law decision in *Millar v Taylor*,[105]

100 Michael Bryan, 'Early English Law Reporting' (2009) 4 *University of Melbourne Collections* 45–50, 48.
101 Veeder 'The English Reports', 19 is glowing of the developments: 'From the Revolution the reports increase in value and importance; they deal more with modern conditions. The development of commerce, and the consequent variety and importance of personal property and of contracts, the growth of maritime jurisprudence, the development of equity, and the general introduction of more liberal and enlightened views of justice and public policy, all combined to give a new tone and impulse to the common law.'
102 Ibid., 4.
103 Ibid., 22.
104 96 ER 180.
105 (1769) 98 ER 201.

incidentally reported by Burrow. These earlier methods, now lost from copyright law, include framing a work as *book* (both physical and conceptual), and the looser conception of the *composition*, and later replaced by a division between idea and expression, drawn from Locke's *An Essay Concerning Human Understanding*. Locke claims that knowledge is made by the mind processing ideas that are experienced through the senses or the process of reflection based on observations of the external or material world. Ideas are, in their simple or complex form, the building blocks of knowledge; it is the application of human reason to those ideas that provide for certainty and stability of the knowledge. It is Locke's conception of ideas – or that which is *ideal* in the terminology of the eighteenth century – and their apparent adoption into the distinct ontological categories of *idea* and *expression*.

In his speech in *Tonson v Collins*,[106] Yates, who was to become the sole dissenting judge in *Millar v Taylor*,[107] argued that there is no way of knowing an author's work other than through their style, or the marks on paper, neither of which was a known species of property.[108] We are left with impression that anything other than the literal and verifiable is to be discarded for law, in Yates' position that must have been personal. In reply, Blackstone responded that: 'Style and sentiment are the essentials of a literary composition. These alone constitute its identity.'[109] Nine years later in *Millar v Taylor*, Aston J was concerned that: 'The plaintiff's supposed property has been treated as quite ideal and imaginary; not reducible to the comprehension of man's understanding; not an object or law, nor capable of protection',[110] but 'has *indicia certa*; for, though the sentiments and doctrine may be called ideal, yet when the same are communicated to the sight and understanding of every man, by the medium of printing, the work becomes a distinguishable subject of property'[111] Willes J held that the 'literary composition is as of the material; which always is property. The book conveys knowledge, instruction, or entertainment: but multiplying copies in print is a quite distinct thing from all the book communicates'.[112]

The influence of the neoclassical on law, in combination with the formalisation of empiricism and rationality, strips anything other than the literal from the protection of property rights in copyright law. It's inevitable that Plowden's form of report writing would be replaced with a more austere form of reporting, as was happening across law.[113] Reporting, in a sense, had been responsible for taking a

106 *Tonson v Collins* (1760) 96 ER 180, 190.
107 *Millar v Taylor* (1769) 98 ER 201, 229–250.
108 *Tonson*, 185–186.
109 *Tonson*, 189.
110 *Millar*, 219.
111 *Millar*, 221–222.
112 *Millar*, 216.
113 Frederick G Kempin, Jr, 'Precedent and Stare Decisis: The Critical Years, 1800 to 1850' (1959) 3 *American Journal of Legal History* 28–54, remarks that 'modern lawyers are quite prone to assume, without conscious thought, that the approach of eighteenth century lawyers and modern lawyers to legal problems is identical': 28.

more or less unstable set of documents and turning them into authorised texts. But for this same reason, the reports were suspect, in the same way that copyright would turn away from style and sentiment as that which should be valued as property, in favour of marks on a page.

The standard history of law tells us of a triumphant moment when, with the establishment in 1865 of the Incorporated Council of Law Reporting (and their offshoots), law is rescued from the vagaries of the nominate reporters, Plowden included. This narrative includes the heroic moment when, at the end of the eighteenth or beginning of the nineteenth century,[114] proto-authorised reporting of judgment begins when the superior courts authorise the reporting of cases by barristers authorised to undertake the task, at the same time that the doctrine of *stare decisis* was approved in judgment,[115] establishing and formalising in law the elements and function of the binding nature of precedent. The nominate reports, unlike the authorised reports, were potentially suspect. After all, the reports had been, and would continue to be, a creative and improvised form of writing; some were a verbatim oral report then structured as judgment, others were personal notes of participants in court or the records of individual judges, while others still were nothing other than the published notebooks of individual advocates or of

114 Kempin, Jr, 'Precedent and Stare Decisis' 30; TFT Plucknett, 'it is to the nineteenth century that we must look for the final stages of the present system' (Plucknett, *A Concise History of the Common Law*, 5th edn, 350, 1956); Holdsworth 'the modern theory was substantially reached in the late eighteenth century' (WS Holdsworth, 'Case Law' (1934) 50 *Law Quarterly Review* 180–195); Allen, of the 'finishing touches' that 'it had reached a high state of development by the end of the eighteenth century, but needed the continually improving mechanism of the succeeding age to give it final and definitive form', Allen, *Law in the Making*, 5th edn (1951), 225.

115 The authority for the principle of *stare decisis*, the binding nature of precedent, derives from the remarks of Parke J in *Mirehouse v Rennell* (1833) 1 Cl. & F. 527, 546, 6 ER 1015, 1022–1023, incidentally reported the year after Bentham's death in 1832. Bentham's hostility to judge-made law and the erratic nature of the common law seems to hang as a ghostly presence in these remarks, as does the reference to 'law as a science', adopting the new 'scientific' sense of the word beyond that of science as knowledge, the same year that the word 'scientist' was coined:

'The precise facts stated by your Lordships have never, as far as we can learn, been adjudicated upon in any court; nor is there to, be found any opinion upon them of any of our Judges, or of those ancient text-writers to whom we look up as authorities. The case, therefore, is in some sense new, as many others are which continually occur; but we have no right to consider it, because it is new, as one for which the law has not provided at all; and because it has not yet been decided, to decide it for ourselves, according to our own judgment of what is just and expedient. Our common-law system consists in the applying to new combinations of circumstances those rules of law which we derive from legal principles and judicial precedents; and for the sake of attaining uniformity, consistency and certainty, we must apply those rules, where they are not plainly unreasonable and inconvenient, to all cases which arise; and we are not at liberty to reject them, and to abandon all analogy to them, in those to which they have not yet been judicially applied, because we think that the rules are not as convenient and reasonable as we ourselves could have devised. It appears to me to be of great importance to keep this principle of decision steadily in view, not merely for the determination of the particular case, but for the interests of law as a science.'

judges. Nothing much had changed since Plowden, or the earlier private sharing of the commonplaces during the era of the Year Books.

But now the new authorised reporters had access to judge's notes, and judges could then correct the version of the report to be published. They were to be modelled on the intermediate reporting practices of Sir James Burrow (1701–1782),[116] who was credited with creating the *modern* report, including 'a headnote to each case that contained few facts and stated the relevant proposition of law as concisely as possible'.[117] Winfield remarks that in Burrow, case, judgment, outlines of ground or reason are 'right', even if not taken down verbatim.[118] It's not surprising that twentieth-century commentators would so conclude, for Burrow was a man in the image of Francis Bacon; like Bacon, he was a polymath and elected as a Fellow of the Royal Society (set up in Bacon's honour) on 7 April 1737, as 'A Gentleman well versed in Natural and Mathematical knowledge'. Scientific and rationalist, Burrow constructs reports that are stripped of superfluity and are solely concerned with that which is material (and that which isn't is given no explanation). They read as if deploying the highly formularised rules of neoclassical drama, now well-established as the norm deep into the eighteenth century. Setting up a clear linear structure grounded in the classical unities of time, place and action, the neoclassical had moved well beyond its nascent form in Ben Jonson's plays. Its instructions, derived from the *Poetics*, are given shape by England's first Poet Laureate, John Dryden (1631–1700):

> all the Rules by which we practise the *Drama* at this day, either such as relate to the justness and symmetry of the Plot; or the Episodical Ornaments, such as Descriptions, Narrations, and other Beauties, which are not essential to the Play; were delivered to us from the Observations that *Aristotle* made, of those Poets, which either liv'd before him, or were his Contemporaries ... Out of these two has been extracted the Famous Rules which the French call, *Des Trois Vnitez*, or, The Three Unities, which ought, to be observ'd in every Regular Play; namely, of Time, Place, and Action.[119]
>
> As for the third Unity which is that of Action, the Ancients meant no other by it then what the Logicians do by their *Finis, the end or scope of any action: that which is the first in Intention, and last in Execution: now the Poet is to aim at one great and compleat action, to the carrying on of which all things in his Play, even the very obstacles, are to be subservient*; and the reason of this is as evident as any of the former.[120]
>
> (My emphasis)

116 Winfield, *Sources*, 190.
117 Bryan 'Early English Law Reporting', 49.
118 Winfield, *Sources*, 190.
119 John Dryden, *An Essay of Dramatick Poesie* (London: Herringman, 1668), 10–11.
120 Dryden, *Dramatick Poesie*, 12–13.

Burrow follows this instruction to the letter – keeping only the essentials and discarding what's unnecessary, but more significantly, embedding *causality* as that 'one great and compleat action' in his reports, and in judgment, causality and the boundaries of the denumerable become the norm, whether in the form of precedent, of circumstance or of doctrine. Causality establishes boundaries and limits, and strips away those embellishments that intrude upon the 'justness and symmetry of the Plot'. In judgment, *pre*formed text becomes the norm, enabling judgment to be carefully crafted to meet these neoclassical expectations.[121] Judgment becomes a form of writing to be performed, grounded in a preordained plot that follows an expected order of action, and generating the conditions through which law's dramatic pretence becomes the standard form of law: positivist, empiricist and unreceptive to lives and lifeworlds beyond inherited conceptions of law. Reports have become compilations of judgment, and with some exceptions written judgments have become the product of its judicial creators.

Victorian law: judgment as well-made play

By the time the Incorporated Council of Law Reporting is established in 1865, judgment has overtaken reports as the site of authorisation. Judgments now cohere and law is normalised, affording the conditions for *stare decisis.* Formalised judgment appeals to the temperament of the Victorian legalities (not least as determined within the logics of John Austin's positivism), which sees law turned back into self as a perfected technic of interpretation. Embedding supposedly ancient legal norms, this new Victorian legality is replete with Bacon's logics and Locke's politics and philosophy, having turned its back on its more lively antecedents, denying the theatrical that had been a part of the law in the medieval and early modern. But the reports, or should I now say, judgments, have started to change their shape, too, taking on the characteristics of Victorian melodrama, in a form that belies the move to the neoclassical, in the first part of the nineteenth century,[122] but foreshadowing the shift to judgment as well-made play. The asceticism of a Burrow *report* is retained, up to a point, by the end of the nineteenth century, but *judgment* now bears all the hallmarks of the well-made play, all the while holding a tension between holding onto precedent, narrating the facts and conforming with the expectations of positivism. The writing of the judgments, their politics and sentiment, moves towards the conventions of the well-made play, and where reported, the texts corrected by the judge, whose original oral utterances are accepted as written law.

121 Michael Meehan, 'Blackstone's Commentaries: England's Legal Georgic?' in Wilfrid Prest (ed.), *Re-Interpreting Blackstone's Commentaries: A Seminal Text in National and International Contexts* (Oxford: Hart Publishing, 2014), 59–71; for the neoclassical in Australian judgments: Michael Meehan, 'The Good, the Bad and the Ugly: Judicial Literacy and Australian Cultural Cringe' (1990) 12 *Adelaide Law Review* 431–448.

122 Chapter 3.

The well-made play is the sentimental cousin of the neoclassical Aristotelian drama, via melodrama. A tightly confined formula imposes a set of rules: action begins *in media res*, or at least part of the way through events that will become clear as the play progresses. Generally the plays take a hero through a series of stops and starts, but we know that nothing will stand in the way of what is intended, as inevitable, and will be resolved by the end of the play. From comedy to tragedy, and the new naturalism of Ibsen and Chekhov, the model of the well-made play (and its adaptations) takes us from expected paths, until a conclusion is reached after a series of problematisations. This, too, is the structure of judgment that became the standard by the end of the nineteenth century and was inherited into the twenty-first century. Verbosity becomes the hallmark of judgments that bear the weight of *stare decisis*, along with the demands of causality, and the expectations of positivism.

Law is now normalised but is also unbearable. Law, as report and judgment, tells both what happened, and what could have happened, and in its writing reveals so much of the circumstances in which law is conceived and understood. This is the presumptive form of the judgment inherited into contemporary common law thinking: an introductory overview of the circumstances surrounding the case begins the judgment, followed by the material (not all) facts on which the case turns being set out, along with the law, and then the relationship between those facts and law and applicable legal principles. A problem that has to be solved, usually involving a difficulty with the law in terms of its scope or application or interpretation, or where the court finds itself dealing with potential changes to or new approaches to existing law, will involve a detailed explication and consideration of conflict or transformation, within the limits that law will permit (generally based on the position of the court in the hierarchy), and finally there is the reasoning involved and a decision reached – as dénouement.

Just as theatre had begun to challenge the same norms by the end of the nineteenth and the beginning of the twentieth century, as the demands of Aristotelianism, the neoclassical and the well-made play suffocate the life out of theatre. Theatre in England is unable to avoid the strictures of the Lord Chamberlain, and in its struggles to deal with an unyielding text, something of the move back to the body of actor and the space of theatre starts to unfold by that millennium. Law, through judgment, on the other hand, is now unable to move, the burden of the demands of words paralysing any possibility of law turning to the lifeworlds out of which it had been created,[123] buttressed by A.W.B Simpson's observations that law and judgment:

123 David Sugarman, 'Promoting Dialogue Between History and Socio-legal Studies: The Contribution of Christopher W. Brooks and the "Legal Turn" in Early Modern English History' (2017) 44.S1 *Journal of Law and Society* S37–S60 accounts for the work of historian of law, Christopher Brooks who hypothesised that there was a decline in law and institutions after 1670, including a decline in the role of the Inns, and that law was now divorced from the interests of ordinary people, S47–S48.

> moved over time from the collective consciousness of a tightly knit group of lawyers based on oral tradition, to a more formal system of approved reports of the deliberations of courts, and then shifted again in the nineteenth century to the idea that there were key principles of the law enshrined in the ratios or decisional reasoning of the 'leading cases', nuggets of canonical law that could be used to convey principles to students in training colleges like Harvard and Oxford and so reproduce the cadres of lawyers able to identify and apply precedents in the professional discourse of the law.[124]

The dramatic qualities of judgment now provide the perfect device behind which the legal interpreter can hide from the lifeworlds of the law, and more particularly offer a device that permits them to avoid engaging in the lives and lifeworlds of those affected by law. While so much a part of late medieval and early modern law and even into the eighteenth century, in the face of challenge, is pushed to one side, and replaced by law that retreats into the abstract as ideal, with all of its consequences for law's lost presence – that is what we assume through the presumptions of a positivist jurisprudence, though the reality of law, at least in the early nineteenth century, might surprise.

124 Joshua Getzler, 'Brian Simpson's Empiricism' (2012) 3.2 *Transnational Legal Theory* 127–139, 133.

3 Law's lost presence

The TSST

> It is necessary to tear the seamless web. To break the strands that trap and hold the imagination in the dead zone of a sticky and immobile *lex*, the iron cage of a putatively comprehensive rule, decision, or other major mode of code. The minor rends ... the peripheral passions, enthusiasms, tones and relationships, movements and moods, potentially intervene as critique in law ... in the past that was discarded, the practices that were denied, the strangers who were kept out.[1]

The Trier Social Stress Test ('TSST'), used to assess physiological markers of stress in humans, is intentionally confronting and unnerving for participants, who appear before a 'mock' expert committee whose members are 'trained to withhold any type of social engagement or positive feedback; they do not smile or nod, and stick closely to scripted instructions and responses'.[2] Participants find themselves facing a simulated job interview and an impossible numeracy test, all designed to create failure, and compounded by the demands of the trained 'committee members' who *actively* work to *physically* withhold any kind of normal human interaction to assess how participants respond to stress, which registers through hormonal markers and heart rate – the micro measures of the body which overbear any rationalising and logical accounts of their interaction with the committee. Whatever a participant might think of their performance, their body will reveal just how they're actually responding.[3] Though it's the participants who are being tested, it's the panel members who are denied of their humanity in order to make the test work, that is, they have to be *trained to physically suppress* any functioning human physical responses, and are bound by the script that demands conformity. Its purpose to induce stress responses in the participant, but the TSST, with its suppression of human response and interaction, along with the demand for

1 Peter Goodrich, 'How Strange the Change from Major to Minor' (2017) 21 *Law Text Culture* 30–53, 30–31.

2 Andrew P Allen, Paul J Kennedy, Samantha Dockray, John F Cryan, Timothy G Dinan and Gerard Clarke, 'The Trier Social Stress Test: Principles and practice' (2017) 6 *Neurobiology of Stress* 113–126, 114.

3 Melissa A Birkett, 'The Trier Social Stress Test Protocol for Inducing Psychological Stress' (2011) 56 *Journal of Visualized Experiments: JoVE* 3238.

conformity through an unyielding script, operates as an exemplary display of antitheatrical legality and its deferral to thinking, order, morality, ethics and propriety/belief.[4]

It's not a long step to find the TSST in law, from techniques used in cross-examination, where counsel turns against and stonewalls the cross-examinee who is forced to answer 'yes' or 'no',[5] to its tests and techniques of problem solving,[6] and passed onto its students through the use of cyphers such as A and B or Whiteacre and Blackacre, to strip legal analysis of human foibles, and to train in objectivity and strip back any subjectivity might creep into legal decision-making. These logics are passed into and are presumed to be the basics of law, but are instead a Victorian invention, involving a rewriting of law as a set of abstract principles.[7] These principles and abstractions denude law, as shaped through the cases, of their lifeworlds and liveliness, none more so than in the omnipresent reasonable man, person, or woman whose presence pervades law.[8] The reasonable *man* is everywhere in law, and is exemplary of the technics that imbue law's *lost* presence, which will wend through this chapter as a dramaturgical troubling of the foundational circumstances that supposedly gave birth to the him, at a pivotal moment in time in the shaping of law.

Wherefore art thou, reasonable man?[9]

It's not surprising that John Gardner has to ask: 'Who is the "reasonable person", that "excellent but odious character" who seems to inhabit every nook and cranny of the common law?'[10] My question is instead: 'Why are you the reasonable man in the first place?' He's traced, somewhat mystifyingly, to someone entirely different,[11] the 'man of ordinary prudence' who first makes an appearance in the 1837 case of

4 Chapter 1.
5 Alison Young, 'The Waste Land of the Law, the Wordless Song of the Rape Victim' (1998) 22.2 *Melbourne University Law Review* 442–465.
6 For example the two tests for causation teased out by Justice James Edelman, then on the Federal Court of Australia, before his elevation to Australia's ultimate court, the High Court: Justice Edelman, 'Understanding Causation and Attribution of Responsibility', presented at the Commercial Conference of the Supreme Court of Victoria/University of Melbourne, Banco Court, 7 September 2015. www.fedcourt.gov.au/digital-law-library/judges-speeches/speeches-former-judges/justice-edelman/edelman-j-20150907
7 See Chapter 2, note 120.
8 John Gardner, 'The Many Faces of the Reasonable Person' (2015) 131 *Law Quarterly Review* 563–584; Caroline Forell, 'Reasonable Woman Standard of Care' (1992) 11 *University of Tasmania Law Review* 1–16.
9 *For what cause or reason? on what account? why?* are you the reasonable man: 'wherefore | wherefor, adv. (and n.).' *OED Online*. Oxford University Press, December 2017, Web. Accessed 20 January 2018.
10 John Gardner, 'Equality, Responsibility and the Law by Arthur Ripstein' (2001) 51.3 *University of Toronto Law Journal* 273–308. Gardner quotes the non-lawyer and playwright AP Herbert, *Uncommon Law* (London: Methuen, 1935), 4.
11 Gardner, 'The Many Faces', 564.

Vaughan (or Vaughn) v Menlove.[12] This case is treated as authority for the foundational principle that objective determinations of conduct are to be used in law over a position of subjective good faith.[13] I will return to *Vaughan* presently, but for most of us in law, this is the beginning and end of it. Reasonableness, shaped through the prism of objectivity as rationality, which rules over its bothersome antonym, that most treacherous of alterities, subjectivity.[14] Equipped with the physiognomy of a featureless avatar, it's supposed (because he holds the mirror up to the men who created him), the reasonable man is put to work in much the same way as the committee members who facilitate the TSST, a blank cypher whose job it is to reframe the circumstance of those who come to law. Rather than law responding to an actual person with their real hurts and concerns (subjectivity), their experience is filtered through, and hence replaced, with the life of someone else entirely, the reasonable man (as objectivity). And though largely an analytical paper exercise in law, where the denial of response is already inbuilt into the advice offered and the guidance given, the effect is no different from that of the TSST, turning away from lived experience in the face of a structured script,[15] as an exemplary instance of legal antitheatricality, and with concomitant consequences for justice, fairness and the lifeworlds of law, and for health and well-being of those caught in its wake.

Yet this couldn't be further from the circumstances surrounding *Vaughan v Menlove* and its agent, the prudent man. Instead, the case – its afterlife and reception in law – has been reordered to manifest the conditions of antitheatrical legality in order to conform within law's Baconian inheritance. To theatricalise *Vaughan*, is to reveal what Maria Aristodemou observes of theatre (as Lacanian woman), which: 'can dissimulate, form, deform and reform and in the process express a different system and a different law',[16] literally, as a Goodrichian minor practice as dramaturgy, that affords techniques that allow us:

> To cut a hole in the fabric of law [...] to insist upon more than law within the institution of legality ... to let the phantasm through the breach and in doing so breaks down the abstraction of the legal norm ... The minor, the child, threatens to make law real and all too human ... a visceral mode of occupying an institutional space, a lifestyle in contestation with a form of life. As ontology, as minor gesture, singular life, there is a sense of resistance, of interruption and of puncturing that veers away from the abstraction and ... closed, epistemology of law.[17]

12 (1837) 3 Bing (NC) 467,132 *Eng Rep* 490.
13 Forell, 'Reasonable Woman', 2–3.
14 'reasonable, adj., n., and adv.' *OED Online*, Oxford University Press, December 2017, Web. Accessed 20 January 2018.
15 See Chapter 2 in connection with the circumstances of the accident I account there.
16 Maria Aristodemou, 'The Seduction of Mimesis: Theatre as Woman and the Play of Difference and Excess in Aeschylus's Oresteia' (1999) 11 *Cardozo Studies in Law and Literature* 1–33, 4.
17 Goodrich, 'How Strange', 50, reference omitted.

Once ruptured, law never looks the same again, and though it would prefer us to turn away rather than face this disruption of an origin in story rendered through theatre practices.[18] It's much easier to work with the law as the TSST, but that doesn't mean it's the right thing to do for law and its validity. What's more troubling is that disrupting expectations in law does precisely the same thing that the TSST does to its participations, bring back to ourselves as corporeal and present, reminding us that we've imbricated a particular expectation of normality that's now built into our bodies, and return the abstract back to the human, as a practice of theatre, that is by reading Vaughan back to its life and lifeworlds, as law's lost presence, tearing that fabric, even just a little and unravelling the seamless web.

Vaughan I

You will have begun this as a bodily response if you have noticed the small nick in the fabric of law's assumptions: *Vaughan* talks of the 'man of ordinary prudence', not the reasonable man.[19] You might have reoriented these words and turned them back to the language of reason, but I'd ask you not to do this but hold onto the language of prudence even if it grates and irritates. John Gardner, for one, is chary of making too many claims of *Vaughan*, for good reason, observing that 'he made his inaugural contribution (*it is widely claimed*) in 1837' (my emphasis).[20] We can find the reasonable man in *Vaughan* if we want, but that involves cherry-picking select phrases to transform the prudent man into the reasonable man, and then to take the further step of asking the reasonable man to speak for an objectivity grounded in abstraction, as expectation.

Reading law's lost presence through *Vaughan* moves theatricalisation into the dramaturgical, as a studied means through which a text is revived, and which then manifests the challenge to an existing set of assumptions, such as a key doctrine or principle in law.[21] A somewhat ineffable term, there is a range of practice that falls under the rubric of dramaturgy, but I use one mode in connection with theatrical jurisprudence: to delve into the circumstances surrounding a text, such as a play, and manifest the time, place and social conditions of which it's a part, and its modes of connection with the present. This aspect of dramaturgy has a twofold purpose: to unfold what sits behind the scant and bare words on the page and to find those points of connection with the new circumstances in which the text will be read, seen, heard and so on, to prevent what theatre director Peter Brook observed that: 'once gone, the moment is gone and it cannot be recaptured slavishly by imitation';[22] of faithful

18 Compare Kathryn Temple, 'Blackstone's 'Stutter': The (Anti)Performance of the Commentaries', in Wilfred Prest (ed.), *Re-Interpreting Blackstone's Commentaries: A Seminal Text in National and International Contexts* (Oxford and Portland, OR: Hart Publishing, 2014), 3–20, 8–11.
19 'prudent, adj. and n.' *OED Online*, Oxford University Press, December 2017, Web. Accessed 20 January 2018.
20 Gardner, 'The Many Faces', 564.
21 Leiboff, 'Theatricalizing Law'.
22 Brook, *Empty Space*, 151.

productions that had been kept alive for 40 or more years (at the time in 1968), but 'none of these had more than antiquarian interest'.[23]

What concerns Brook is the twin points of connection with the present, and the problem of an understanding of the text beyond repetition. A footnote or sentence holding what resides in a case is even more concerning, so as a dramaturgical starting point, it seems as good a place as any to find out what the case was about. What's patent from the start is that *abstract* reason and objectivity was nowhere to be found, meaning the case is exemplary of law as invented tradition,[24] as a Hobsbawmian 'set of practices, normally governed by overtly or tacitly accepted rules and of a ritual or symbolic nature, which seek to inculcate certain values and norms of behaviour by repetition, which automatically implies continuity with the past'.[25] Law, in this mode, is subject to repetition,[26] as imitation as imagined, both ancient and modern,[27] using the invented or imagined pasts to justify law, doctrine and principle. What dramaturgy does is delve into the text, challenging a closed and perfected exegesis, to rethink those productions of 'antiquarian interest', and challenge slavish repetitions of what we think the text is *meant* to mean, not just as analysis or history but to render the text dramaturgically as a means by which it will be theatricalised and brought back into ourselves as a practice of response and responsibility to law.

Rending the seamless web

Common law depends on a presumptive antiquity of the kind presumed by Ronald Dworkin's seamless web, to which Peter Goodrich's remarks are directed. Law is imagined as a complete system, holding within it all the principles needed to deal with any new situation that comes its way, as updated and reordered through each new iteration. The seamless web has to presume that law is perfection rendered as principle, in the mode of Bacon's Year Book, and in the neoclassically formed textbook summations of Blackstone's *Commentaries*,[28] and again in the nineteenth-century textbooks and treatises which went about the task

23 Ibid., 18.
24 Of a vast and significant literature, Peter Fitzpatrick, *The Mythology of Modem Law* (London: Routledge, 1992); Desmond Manderson, 'Apocryphal Jurisprudence' (2001) 26 *Australian Journal of Legal Philosophy* 27–59.
25 Eric Hobsbawm, 'Introduction: Inventing Traditions', in Eric Hobsbawm and Terence Ranger (eds), *The Invention of Tradition* (Cambridge: Cambridge Universoty Press, 1983), 1–14, 1.
26 For an extended reading of the historicisation of Blackstone in this review essay, Christopher Tomlins, 'Re-Interpreting Blackstone's Commentaries: A Seminal Text In National And International Contexts' (2015) 36 *Adelaide Law Review* 599–621.
27 A hymnal of this name was introduced into the Church of England in the 1850s, following agitation in the 1830s: *Hymns Ancient and Modern*. https://en.wikipedia.org/wiki/Hymns_Ancient_and_Modern as a response to the non-conformist practices of hymn singing and its popularity.
28 For Blackstone as neoclassical, see Manderson and Martinez, 'Justice and Art' 241–263 and 258–259

of turning Bentham's shapeless heaps of odds and ends into a coherent and rational ordering of the law.[29] Law as principle is supposed to be the work of the courts, but as the fashioning of the reasonable man will reveal, the textbook and treatise writers are *or can be the generators of principle.* David Sugarman famously accounts for their interventions,[30] 'correcting' infelicities and recording what the law really ought to have been. Having no formal role in its institutional practices the law textbook/treatise functions as a nineteenth-century version of the commonplace, regularising and ordering the mess of law into coherent principle, that mode of principle on which the seamless web is premised. It's the treatise/textbook that's instrumental in creating principle, as liberal, abstract and rights based,[31] and in the process transforming medieval concepts into a necessary ancient narrative to support this new politics.

But let me clarify, for 'nineteenth century' is too broad in its periodisation – for this is a *mid-late nineteenth-century* practice. Despite the early century interventions of Jeremy Bentham and some continued desire amongst its practitioners to maintain its trajectory, the early mid-nineteenth century becomes hostile to rationality and neoclassicism, politically and socially, and in law. What grounds this challenge is a desire to return to a perfected past, medieval, Gothic, and romantic. *Vaughan*'s afterlife reveals something of the reordering that has left us with a legacy of the inevitable and consistent march of rationality, in the manner in which the prudent man, almost medieval in his common decency and virtue as a practice, which is later 'corrected' and transformed into the reasonable man.

Recorded almost as an afterthought in a footnote, A.W.B. Simpson remarks that *Vaughan's* significance was recognised by Percy Winfield, who acknowledged 'that [*Vaughan*] did not feature prominently in later nineteenth-century cases. It was, however, treated as a leading case in Sir Frederick Pollock's [1887] treatise … *as decisive in adopting an objective concept of negligence*' (my emphasis).[32] It's not the courts but a textbook and treatise writer who elevates and shapes the case.[33] Simpson, too, reminds that the courts were creating new law, rather than the maintenance of what had already been, for 'what happened in the nineteenth century was not the substitution of new law for old law, but the creation of law where there had been none before'.[34]

29 Leslie J Moran, 'Law and the Gothic Imagination', in Fred Botting (ed.), *The Gothic* (Cambridge: DS Brewer, 2001), 87–109, 89.

30 David Sugarman, 'Legal Theory, the Common Law Mind and the Making of the Textbook Tradition', in William Twining (ed.), *Legal Theory and Common Law* (Oxford: Blackwell, 1986), 26–62.

31 David Sugarman and Ronnie Warrington, 'Land Law, Citizenship and the Invention of Englishness: The Strange World of the Equity of Redemption', in John Brewer and Susan Staves (eds) *Early Modern Conceptions of Property* (Abingdon and New York: Routledge, 1995), 112–143, 132.

32 AWB Simpson, 'Legal Liability for Bursting Reservoirs: The Historical Context of 'Rylands v. Fletcher'' (1984) 13.2 *The Journal of Legal Studies* 209–264, 211, n. 6.

33 Sugarman, 36, indicates that Pollock's work was based on lectures at the Inns of Court.

34 Simpson, 'Legal Liability', 215.

So, too, the determination of cases by civil juries, with the judge confined to issuing directions that were rarely appealed. *Vaughan* was rare: both the initial direction of the judge to jury in the original assize trial was reported, along with the Court of Common Pleas determination of the correct law to be applied in the case.[35] Multiple reports of the Common Pleas decision exist, all of which differ in matters of substance, fact and evidence, and the text of the judgments,[36] some of which might be the source of Pollock's assertion. In William Hodges' Reports, for instance, we find that the defendant Menlove's land was a close, with a barn nearby, a detail that doesn't appear in the authorised *English Reports*, and in a slightly snippy footnote gloss, refers to an argument of Serjeant Talfourd, who appeared for Vaughan in this and an earlier case he cites in argument.[37] Gale and Whatley, in their 1839 treatise on easements,[38] becomes a treatise that repeats a sentence in the report contained in the version of the case contained in the *English Reports*, that of the Common Pleas report in *Bingham's New Cases*, attributed to the assize judge:[39] that the defendant would be 'bound to proceed with such *reasonable caution* as a prudent man would have exercised under such circumstances' (my emphasis).[40] But in *Carrington & Payne's Reports* of the assize trial of 1836, also included in the *English Reports*, this phrase doesn't appear. Rather, the assize judge, Patteson J, directs the jury to consider:

> whether the defendant has acted as a man of ordinary skill and prudence would have acted, or whether through his negligence and carelessness the plaintiff's property has been consumed. It is not enough that the defendant should have acted *bona fide*, for if you think that by his injudicious want of care the injury has been occasioned, he is liable in this action.[41]

'Reasonable caution' appears nowhere in this passage; *prudence* functions as its animating sensibility, but it's not hard to see how the compound '*reasonable* caution' combined with 'prudent *man*', might create the reasonable man, especially

35 Ibid.

36 The *English Reports* lists the other reports of the case, including S.C. 4 Scott, 244; 3 Hodges, 51; G L. J. Q P. 92; 1. Jur, 215: at Nisi Prius, 7 Car. & P. 525.1: *Vaughan v Menlove* (1837) 3 Bing NC 468 (1837) 132 *English Reports* 490, 490.

37 William Hodges, 'Vaughan v Menlove' Court of Common Pleas Vol. III: From Hilary Term, Seventh Will. IV to Michaelmas Term, First Vict. 1837 (London: Henry Butterworth, 1839), 51–55.

38 CJ Gale and TD Whatley, *Treatise on the Law of Easements* (London: S. Sweet, 1839), 241. In the hearing before the Court of Common Pleas, a Whately, Whatley or Whateley appears, and different spellings are adopted between the different reports. Whatley is a member of Middle Temple, while another barrister, a member of the Inner Temple, William Whateley joined the Oxford Circuit. Serjeant Talfourd was a member of Middle Temple.

39 The report adopted by the *English Reports.*

40 Gale and Whatley, *Easements*, 241; *Vaughan v Menlove* (1837) 132 *English Reports* 490, 492.

41 *Vaughan v Menlove* (1837) 7 Car & P 525, 132 *English Reports* 232.

since this instance is sometimes confused with the Common Pleas judgments. Later writers' decision to strip the case of prudence and transform it into reason, deals with an inconvenient distraction for law as it formalised in the mid-late nineteenth century, and that had signalled its obeisance to reason and rationality of the century before, and having to fix the principles in a case like this that had seemingly turned away from the ideals of a neoclassical and abstract law.[42]

Jurisography as dramaturgy, *via* prudence, as theatrical jurisprudence

> Oh, what a tangled web we weave
> When first we practise to deceive!
> (Sir Walter Scott, *Marmion*, 1808)

The blank slate

Hans-Thies Lehmann reminds us, through theatre, that:

> no law (and certainly no law that is 'good' or 'democratic') stands on a *blank slate*; it always includes earlier and coming generations ... [and] enlists the extralegal power to which it owes its origin and continued existence. And so, the standing order, whatever form it may assume, no longer proves recognizable as violence – *only revolt against it appears violent.* On the other hand, the dimension of time undermines the principle of legality insofar as it depends on proceedings such as majority decisions. *Time introduces the problem of missing, false, borrowed or feigned voices and their relation to judgment.*[43]
>
> (My emphases)

Contesting the origin story of the reasonable man and what will be a call to the prudent man as theatrical invokes that 'revolt that appears violent', and the Derridian original violence that turned the prudent man into the reasonable man. No hue or cry seems to have been raised about the strategic manoeuvre that turns prudence into reasonableness and then into rationality to maintain the trajectory of the story of law that had begun with Bacon. This slippage of language seems to have been widespread, in any case. A quick perusal of the *OED* around the period of *Vaughan* and into mid-century shows that there 'prudent' means what it says: a prudent person who acts with or shows foresight, who has or exercises sound judgment in practical affairs, who is circumspect, discreet, cautious and far-sighted.[44] To be prudent involves conduct and action, characterised by, exhibiting or proceeding from prudence; it's judiciousness, sensible.[45] And another definition in the *OED*, now for the word 'reasonable'. Among a slew of

42 For the multivalenced features of prudence, see generally Robert Hariman, 'Theory without Modernity', in Robert Hariman (ed.), *Prudence: Classical Virtue, Postmodern Practice* (University Park, PA: Penn State University Press, 2003) 1–32.

43 Lehmann, *Tragedy*, 107.

44 'prudent', *OED Online*. In an obsolete sense also wise, discerning, knowledgeable (2.).

45 'prudent', *OED Online*.

definitions, a related term, if not a cognate word: a person who is sensible, sane, having sound judgement, wise, or *prudent*.[46] The electronic *OED* then adopts an =, with prudent now equated to 'reasonable', and with yet another step, with 'rational'. It's in the reverse but nonetheless reasonable is being equated to prudent. Rational, then, is defined as the faculty of reasoning; having sound judgement, being sensible, sane, and lucid, and that which involves reasoning, as opposed to emotion, intuition.[47] These conjunctions and equivalents bring that which is prudent to that which is rational and reasonable, a perfect form of violence. To be prudent doesn't involve reason or rationality, for they are very different things indeed.

Reframing prudence

As Des Manderson and Cristina Martinez remind: 'The prudent artist, like the prudent lawyer, proceeds according to his past experience in order to profess good judgment in the present'.[48] James Parker reminds, too, of the material and bodily as it imbues juris*prudence*; rather than being confined by the limitations of legal philosophy, prudence is material, it's practice, it's conduct and craft, it's performed, it's embodied action.[49] In jurisprudence, though, prudence is turned back on itself, as a practice of judgment and reasoning through *phronesis*,[50] though with the potential for enrichment through the imaginative, as reframed by Dutch jurisprudent and judge Jeanne Gaakeer, drawing on the work of Paul Ricoeur.[51] But there's more to prudence than practical reasoning,[52] or the practice of office within the Ciceronian tradition.[53] Rather, as Hariman reminds, prudence offers the 'activation as a field of possible articulations',[54] including a feature of the classical where 'prudence represents the ideal of the individual and the society advancing together rather than at the expense of each other'.[55] It's the latter than we find in *Vaughan*, and in one of the advocates on Vaughan's behalf, Serjeant Talfourd, more of whom later in this book, and who will turn up, from time to time, in this chapter, in surprising ways.

Prudence, however, has been more or less lost from the contemporary legal imaginary. Hariman laments its place as 'the set of minor techniques for accommodating system to lifeworld, though never a basis for reflecting on or changing the system'.[56] Prudence requires *presence*, not in the metaphysical,[57] but in its theatrical sense, that

46 'reasonable', *OED Online*.
47 'rational 1b', *OED Online*, Oxford University Press, December 2017, www.oed.com/view/Entry/153586. Accessed 20 January 2017.
48 Manderson and Martinez, 'Justice and Art', 259, reference omitted.
49 Parker, *Acoustic Jurisprudence*, 36, references omitted.
50 Ibid.
51 Jeanne Gaakeer, 'Configuring Justice' (2012) 9 *No Foundations: An Interdisciplinary Journal of Law and Justice* 20–44.
52 Hariman, 'Theory without Modernity', 4.
53 Parker, *Acoustic Jurisprudence*, 37; Parsley, 'Mask and Agamben'.
54 Hariman, 'Theory without Modernity', 2.
55 Ibid., 14.
56 Ibid., 17.
57 Parker, *Acoustic Jurisprudence*, 136.

moves from 'product to process, from mediated expression to direct contact, from representation to presentation, from discourse to body, from absence to presence',[58] of the kind bound up in the impatient re-narrations of leading cases and their principles by A.W.B. Simpson,[59] but more particularly in Genovese, McVeigh and Rush's jurisography, which works 'to consider the form and formation of jurisprudence as a conduct of relationships with law, as much as to tell stories of law ... as a conduct of life,'[60] that offers the most potent practice of prudence.

Jurisography holds within it the practices of dramaturgy;[61] or more particularly 'in making a case for the *dissent* of dramaturgy',[62] as a further practice of the kind I've already traced, of which dramaturg Hana Worthen asks more, that 'impels a *searching inquiry* into the material conditions and cultural work of theatre ... to formulate its *contestable nodal knots* in relation to the material ... at the *politico-aesthetic nexus* of performance' (my emphases).[63] So too law read jurisographically returns the texts of law to the lifeworlds out of which they were created, not as history or as a return to an ideal state, but to press on our expectations and assumptions in law, and to think law differently.[64] *Law's lost presence* isn't a hankering for some ersatz nostalgia of an idealised or imagined legal Arcadia, but through the theatrical and the techniques of dramaturgy, materially challenges and troubles presumptions of law, both then and now. The contestable nodal knots of law involve a complex of physical and spatial conditions through which the past presses onto the present, as presence, and the present, through presence, onto the past. This kind of dramaturgy takes us into word, text, time, place, space, the emplacement and demeanour of bodies to be read then and now, and now and then, as multiple dimensions and layers that troubles the linearity and unambiguity of law, disrupted by triangulating or quadrangulating through myriad possibilities of encounter, engagement and interaction, unravelling the seamless web thread by thread.

What becomes apparent is that once a case like *Vaughan* is stripped of all of these features and enters the realm of principle, it's so much more easily verballed, echoing Lehmann's observation that time introduces the problem of missing, false, borrowed or feigned voices and their relation to judgment.[65] It also runs contrary

58 Jon McKenzie, *Perform or else: From discipline to performance* (London: Routledge, 2001), 38.

59 Chapter 2.

60 Ann Genovese, Shaun McVeigh and Peter D Rush, 'Lives Lived with Law: An Introduction' (2017) 20 *Law Text Culture* 1–13, 10–11.

61 Marett Leiboff, 'Theatricalizing Law'.

62 Hana Worthen, 'For a Skeptical Dramaturgy' (2014) 24.3 *Theatre Topics* 175–186, 175.

63 Ibid., 175–176.

64 Tomlins, 'Re-Interpreting Blackstone's', 621: 'The "history" in which for 200 years Blackstone was a foe to be hated has in the last 20 years been enlivened by the recreation of him as an ally to be welcomed. Historicists may stand amazed but history in the hands of law is simply not stable.'

65 Lehmann, *Tragedy*, 107.

to the doctrine of precedent, that's either tightly bound as being 'on all fours' with the earlier case or thinly connected because of textual and factual difference, including its transfiguration through time, place and circumstance. Peter Brook, reminding us that time and space read very differently when one is familiar with events and close to them, as he recounts in 1968 in *The Empty Space*:

> A man came forward, and I gave him a sheet of paper on which was typed a speech from Peter Weiss's play about Auschwitz, *The Investigation* … The volunteer was too struck and too appalled by what he was reading [and] … something of his seriousness and concentration reached the audience and it fell silent. Then at my request he began to read out loud … immediately the audience understood.[66]

Can I now ask you to turn back to Patteson's J words, and the words from the *OED*, and read them out loud, with awareness, just as this man read the words from Peter Weiss's play? Notice what you bring to the words and what you don't, what you understand and what you don't. In reading, be aware that there's something not quite right with the transmission of the case, and with some awareness that more is going to come, about which you don't know the details yet. Be present, literally, as you read, not looking for answers or trying to analyse as you go, just as the student actor who was asked to read the list of dead at Agincourt, not as names but as lived individuals, 'as if the butchery had occurred in living memory'.[67] As I turn now to 1837, the year of the Court of Common Pleas decision, can I ask that this be read as if in living memory, perhaps at a moment of transition or of disruption as a clue to help? If you could be present and aware in your reading, not as an abstract exercise in the metaphysics of presence or of imitation, but of law of the past as if it was present, in the here and now.

'By particular desire', a one off reprise of the neoclassical tragedy *Ion* 'written by Mr Sergeant Talfourd',[68] was publicised in a weekly bill for the Theatre Royal, Covent Garden for Friday 28 April 1837, with the lead one of Talfourd's friends, the new actor-manager of the theatre, one William Charles Macready.[69] Talfourd was exceptionally busy that year. *Vaughan* had already been heard and decided in January, and as the representative for Reading in the House of Commons, gave notice of his new copyright Bill in May.[70] A celebrity in his own right, and with

66 Brook, *Empty Space*, 27–28.

67 Ibid., 27–29.

68 *Theatre Royal*. https://ubir.buffalo.edu/xmlui/handle/10477/2734. Talfourd's son, Francis, was a writer of burlesques, and also a member of the Middle Temple.

69 Richard Foulkes, 'Macready, William Charles (1793–1873)', *Oxford Dictionary of National Biography*. https://doi.org/10.1093/ref:odnb/17741: www.oxforddnb.com/view/10.1093/ref:odnb/9780198614128.001.0001/odnb-9780198614128-e-17741. Talfourd appeared for Macready the year before in an assault case.

70 Isabella Alexander, *Copyright Law and the Public Interest in the Nineteenth Century* (Oxford and Portland, OR: Hart Publishing, 2010), 92–99.

famous literary and theatre friends, a profile of him was published that year in *The New Monthly Magazine and Humourist*,[71] one of many circulating in popular periodicals of the time.

The conjunction between *Vaughan*, the reprise of Talfourd's tragedy, and his fame remind us that old cases aren't just antiquarian footnotes, but that like all law, emerge from their own time and place. Abstraction winnows away circumstances that matter, then and now, and to dramaturgically revive it, as it were, is a step towards understanding how the case was ordered. 1837 is serendipitous, a year of coincidence that reveals something of a dialectical reordering of the institutions and practices of the previous century and longer. *Vaughan* is argued and decided during the Hilary term of the Court of Common Pleas, on 23 January 1837, against the backdrop of an emerging neomedieval Gothic revival, a romantic reaction against neoclassicism and its rationality, given some impetus through the romantics, including the work of the Scottish lawyer, novelist and poet, Sir Walter Scott, who died in 1832.[72] And John Constable dies in 1837, the painter of picturesque, proto-impressionist romantic landscapes, typified by the monumental *The Hay Wain* of 1821,[73] with its depiction of the actual Suffolk countryside where he grew up, a rural idyll of a tenanted cottage in the foreground, the hay carriers on the haywain or haycart also in the foreground and haymakers far off into middle distance (and his father's mill tucked away to one side), valorising rural life and work.

The year marks the end of the reign of William IV; his death in June means that Victoria, at the age of 18, is now monarch, ringing in an era of profound change, though some of it had already begun under her uncle, whom she succeeded. Significant changes to law and its organisations and institutions were in train, and will unfold over the next 20–30 years. Those already afoot lead to the demise of the ancient rank of Serjeant (dating back to just after the Norman Conquest), of which Talfourd was a member, having lost in rank to Kings or Queen's Counsel (and seen as a consolation prize for unsuccessful applicants for silk), a process that began when Bacon insisted on being granted this new title. The end began once they lost their exclusive right to practice in the Court of Common Pleas, a tussle fought out between 1834 and 1846.[74]

71 LB, 'Memoir of Mr. Serjeant Talfourd, M.P.' (1837) *The New Monthly Magazine and Humourist*, 213–220.

72 For Scott's *Ivanhoe* and the Victorian (or nineteenth-century) literary as jurisprudence see William P. MacNeil, *Novel Judgements: Legal Theory as Fiction* (London: Routledge, 2012).

73 John Constable, 1776–1837: https://www.tate.org.uk/art/artists/john-constable-108 accessed 12 December 2016; John Constable, *The Hay Wain* 1821, *The National Gallery*, https://www.nationalgallery.org.uk/paintings/john-constable-the-hay-wain, accessed 12 December 2016.

74 In 1834, the Lord Chancellor, Lord Brougham, opened Common Pleas to all barristers. This continued for six years, when the Queen overturned the edict, until legislation was passed in 1846, ending this monopoly, and consolidated with the passing of the Judicature Act.

Formalised legal training would be revived later in the century, having been non-existent since the latter part of the seventeenth century,[75] and along with the establishment of the Incorporated Council of Law Reporting in 1865, begins a process of regularisation of legal institutions. This ushered in 'a noticeable change in the self-conception of the bar and bench … between the eighteenth century and nineteenth century … [where] professional values eclipsed the values of gentility'.[76] Again coincident with 1837, the University of London was formally established, twice, once by William IV, and accidently dissolved on his death, only to be reinstituted by Victoria at year's end.[77] A secular institution, its inauguration was bitterly opposed by Oxford and Cambridge, institutions only open to members of the Church of England. It housed the first university law school in England, at what's now University College London, instituted 10 years earlier, and founded or inspired by Jeremy Bentham; his auto-icon sits in the neoclassical building that houses UCL. Common law would only begin to be taught at the original universities much later in the century.[78]

Two years earlier, in 1835, the same year as the fire that engulfed Menlove's land and two cottages on Vaughan's property, John Austin, who'd been appointed Professor of Law at the new law school's inception, called it quits, after a singularly unsuccessful tenure in his attempt to garner acceptance for his new jurisprudence.[79] A more famous fire the year before, in 1834, saw most of the Palace of Westminster, the site of Parliament and the law courts, burnt down. The design of its replacement, designed by Barry and Pugin selected through competition in 1836, was the new Gothic revival, of which Pugin was an advocate, a highly political decision to return to a medieval style against the neoclassical of the earlier century.[80] Work on its design was well underway in 1837, with building itself beginning in 1840.

Pugin's adherence to medievalism was set out in his 1836 self-published polemic, *Contrasts: or a Parallel between the Noble Edifices of the Fourteenth and Fifteenth, and Similar Buildings of the Present Day; Shewing the Present Decay of*

75 Holdsworth traces the decline and fall of the educational system of the Inns of across three periods: (i) the late sixteenth and early seventeenth centuries; (ii) the Commonwealth period; and (iii) the latter part of the seventeenth century: WS Holdsworth, 'The Disappearance of the Educational System of the Inns of Court' (1921) 69.3 *University of Pennsylvania Law Review* 201–222.

76 Conor Hanly, 'The Decline of Civil Jury Trial in Nineteenth-Century England' (2005) 26.3 *The Journal of Legal History* 253–278, 262.

77 The university was established using William's 'Royal will and pleasure', and had to be reincorporated by Victoria.

78 Leiboff, 'Ghosts'.

79 Brian Bix, 'John Austin', in Edward N. Zalta (ed.), *The Stanford Encyclopedia of Philosophy* (winter 2016 edition). https://plato.stanford.edu/archives/win2016/entries/austin-john/

80 The Royal Courts of Justice on the Strand, designed to house the new High Court and its divisions, replacing four existing and competing courts, Common Pleas, Exchequer, Chancery and King's Bench or Queen's Bench following the investigations and inquires that resulted in the *Supreme Court of Judicature Act 1873*. The new court building opened by Queen Victoria in 1882 used a Gothic-inspired architectural style.

Taste, which advocated a return to the sensibility of the medieval in architecture and beyond. The same sensibility was taken up by his near contemporary, the influential art critic John Ruskin, as a desire to return to a communal sensibility of the Middle Ages, both socially and artistically. By 1848 a group of seven artists and writers inaugurated the Pre-Raphaelite Brotherhood, who turned too to the artistic practices of the late medieval, and for some, as a genre as well as art practice. Three years before, in 1845, Friedrich Engels, published *The Condition of the Working Class in England*, and the same year that the Pre-Raphaelites formed, in 1848, he and Marx published *The Communist Manifesto*. By mid-century, the Arts and Crafts movement had been founded by William Morris, as a political and artistic movement against the institutionalisation of *laissez-faire* and industrialisation.

There was a far from subtle interplay between the social, political and cultural, and at the same time that Pugin was advocating a return to a medieval past, in 1837, Chartism, the movement seeking the vote for working men, was initiated, with the formal movement beginning in 1838. That year sees the first instalment of Charles Dickens' *Oliver Twist*, and the last of his serialisation, *The Pickwick Papers*; its later publication in novel form would be dedicated to Talfourd. Most social change, however, was a long way off, and would become worse as the century progressed, particularly for those living in poverty and those struggling financially. At least two competing pressures were at play. On the one hand, the rise of the middle class and the growth of *laissez faire* saw law smooth the way for capital. On the other, and also squeezing the life out of the former as well as placing an impossible burden on the others, was the continuing legal benefit attached to the aristocracy and landed gentry.

We see exactly these concerns played a few years before Pugin publishes his polemic, in Thomas Love Peacock's 1831 satirical play-novel *Crotchet Castle*, where the aptly named characters play out the positions of neoclassicism, medievalism and progressive rationality, along with science and economics, including Mr Chainmail who hankers for the return of the Middle Ages, the Reverend Dr Folliott, a Tory classicist, and Mr Mac Quedy (QED) a Scottish rationalist. The nouveau-riche Mr Crotchet, of said castle, sums up their competing positions in the following term, as

> The sentimental against the rational, the intuitive against the inductive, the ornamental against the useful, the intense against the tranquil, the romantic against the classical; these are great and interesting controversies, which I should like, before I die, to see satisfactorily settled.[81]

The novel's humour is riven with serious concerns, with digs at law, education and significant personages of the time, including a savage description of the local lord of the manor, local justice and Member of Parliament, as an embodiment of the evils that were live and horrendous in early nineteenth-century England:

81 https://ebooks.adelaide.edu.au/p/peacock/thomas_love/p35c/index.html

> Sir Simon Steeltrap, of Steeltrap Lodge, Member for Crouching–Curtown, Justice of Peace for the county … By administering the laws which he assists in making, he disposes, at his pleasure, of the land and its live stock … in a circumference of several miles round Steeltrap Lodge. He has enclosed commons and woodlands; abolished cottage gardens; taken the village cricket-ground into his own park … committed many poachers; shot a few; convicted one-third of the peasantry; suspected the rest.[82]

Sugarman and Warrington remind that at least up until the 1870s, England was a 'patrician polity', and though the first industrial nation, the superior position of the landed only began to erode in the last quarter of the nineteenth century.[83] Land and law provided 'the construction of memory, consciousness and identity, a process binding together and privileging particular conceptions of "justice" and "Englishness"'.[84] The landed and aristocratic held a political, cultural and economic hegemony: in government, parliament, law, civil service, armed forces, and church.[85] They would be excused obligations in contract through the device of equity;[86] it was their 'natural privilege to take loans and then be excused of the bargain',[87] a practice would extend well into the nineteenth century.[88] Inevitably this would place pressure on anyone entering into contracts with them – the middle class and lower classes all bearing the burden of aristocratic and landed privilege. The closeness of this relationship was able to continue because 'a significant proportion of the aristocracy took up the law in some form, as late as the 1880s'.[89] These links with the judiciary only began to break down gradually from the 1820s onwards, which accelerated late in the century. By the mid-nineteenth century a now more middle-class judiciary had misgivings about privileging the landed.[90]

In 1849, Talfourd became one of those non-landed, middle-class judges in the Court of Common Pleas. The bench at the time of *Vaughan* appears to be non-landed, as the sons of professionals.[91] Nicholas Tindal, the Cambridge educated Chief Justice, though, was a Tory Solicitor-General and descendent of John Fortescue, among other legal luminaries, his own family of lawyers and clergymen, and the most patrician of all four justices who heard the review. He was the only one of the four who lived into the next decade, and the youngest. John Vaughan, one of the last of the King's Serjeants, died in 1839; his father was a doctor. Both

82 Ibid.
83 Sugarman and Warrington, 'Invention of Englishness', 121.
84 Ibid., 126.
85 Ibid., 121.
86 Ibid., 123–124.
87 Ibid., 125.
88 Ibid.
89 Ibid., 123.
90 Ibid.,132–133.
91 Justice of the Common Pleas, https://en.wikipedia.org/wiki/Justice_of_the_Common_Pleas

Stephen Gaselee, who retired at the end of Hilary term 1837, and died in 1839 and James Park, who died in 1838, were the sons of surgeons. Tindal, the youngest of the four judges, died in 1848. All four were born at the height of Georgian England (Gaselee in 1762, Park in 1763, Vaughan in 1769, and Tindal in 1776), and part of a generation inured in the neoclassical, but would have been unable to ignore the competing philosophical positions of the time, and the influence of the Romantic movement of Wordsworth, Coleridge and the Gothic, with its companion in theatre, the melodrama that Peacock had satirised, too, in *Crotchet Castle.*

Theatricalising *Vaughan*

Melodrama

Serjeant Talfourd so excited those in attendance in1834 at Westminster Hall in his summation in defence of Tait's Magazine against Richmond,[92] they broke into applause, Talfourd having 'held his audience in breathless attention ... his hearers, forgetting that they were in a court of justice, where such demonstrations are never permitted'.[93] In the 1830s, law is visible and on display, as theatrics,[94] or more particularly, at least in the public's mind, as melodrama, that popular theatre form made up of a heady mix of emotion, romanticism, and sentimentality that first developed in eighteenth-century France as a reaction against the formal demands of neoclassical drama. One of the progenitors of the well-made play, English melodrama of the early nineteenth century managed to avoid the Lord Chamberlain's licensing regime until the passage of the 1843 *Theatres Act*, its segmented scenes, the use of *tableau vivants* and musical interludes failing to meet the expectations of Aristotelean drama. Drawing on the improvisational practice of Italian *commedia dell'arte*, with standard story lines and stock figures, including Harlequin and Columbine (later adapted into pantomime and Punch and Judy), eighteenth-century German romantic *Sturm und Drang*, such as Schiller's *Luisa Miller* and Goethe's *Faustus*, melodrama's sensational plots press on the emotions, as comedy or comedia or the ordinary, generating fear and pity, hatred and hope, evoking the sublime and sometimes the ridiculous.

Melodrama was far from universally approved, and seen as the genre of the lower classes. Talfourd's friend Macready who, in the first decades of the nineteenth century, transformed the practice of theatre by introducing rigorous rehearsals, attended to *mise-en-scène*, and insisted on a high standard of ensemble acting, along with his intellectual ability to penetrate and to express the psychological nature of his characters,[95]

92 Anonymous, 'Serjeant Talfourd' *The London Journal: and Weekly Record of Literature, Science and Art* (1847) 6.146, 11 December 1847, 233–234.

93 Anonymous, 'Mr. Sergeant Talfourd, M.P.' (1838) 31 *The Mirror of Literature, Amusement, and Instruction* v–viii, vii.

94 Simon Stern, 'William Blackstone: Courtroom Dramatist?' in Prest, *Re-Interpreting Blackstone's Commentaries*, 21–30, 24–25.

95 Foulkes, 'Macready'.

would refuse the popular forms of melodrama and pantomime, the forms of theatre for which the nineteenth century was famed, and despite its immense possibility for income, to retain the mark of legitimacy against melodrama's illegitimate origins outside of the patent theatres. And Talfourd, though famed for his neoclassical *Ion*, was to deploy something of a kinship with and the 'atmosphere' of melodrama in his *Glencoe* of 1840,[96] absent its stock characters, and written for Macready, like his play of 1838, *The Athenian Captive*.[97]

Melodrama's stock characters of hero, villain and heroine, and stock plot devices of villainy and deceit and, if lucky, the redemption from a fate worse than death or, if not, punishment both fair and unfair meant that as a genre it was formulaic and created to produce the kind of emotion-laden reactions of fear, pity, sympathy, terror, excitement and the like. This was popular theatre that entertained and spoke to the concerns of its mostly non high-brow audiences. Aside from its stock features, melodrama was heterogeneous in style and subject, ranging from the exotic to the local, creating terror through gothic horror, and the familiar, such as it was, in the form of the nautical, urban, domestic, rural and prison melodrama. Crime, both true and fictional, was its mainstay, epitomized by the true crime melodrama, *Maria Martin or Murder in the Red Barn*, which drew on the circumstances of a murder committed in 1827 in Suffolk, and the trial of the accused in Bury St Edmonds the following year. The public flocked to the trial, much to the consternation of the Chief Justice of Exchequer who was responsible for its administration, generating nascent *sub judice* contempt rules designed to neutralise prejudice, for plays depicting the events running before and during the trial, its mix of revenge and villainy, innocence and tragedy providing a mainstay of the genre throughout the nineteenth century.[98]

And there was the legal melodrama at its most distressing and abject in *The Factory Lad* of 1832. Dealing with law and the denial of justice, and its complicity in the upheaval of rural life and the harmful effects of industrialisation, and the intervention of a corrupt justice called Bias, this melodrama inverts the normal course of events where the hero triumphs over evil.[99] While melodrama as imagination, within rhetorician Peter Brooks' characterisation of melodrama as that 'fictional system for making sense of experience',[100] this is melodrama as genre in the raw. In many respects it operates in precisely the opposite register to the sentimentalisation of law as exculpation and avoidance which Honni van Rijswijk,

96 Allardyce Nicoll, A *History of English Drama 1660–1900, Volume 4; Early Nineteenth Century Drama 1800–1850* (2nd edn, Cambridge: Cambridge University Press, 1955), 79.

97 Ibid., 48.

98 *Red Barn Murder*, https://en.wikipedia.org/wiki/Red_Barn_Murder, accessed 17 July 2018.

99 Sarah Grochala, *The Contemporary Political Play: Rethinking Dramaturgical Structure* (London: Bloomsbury Methuen, 2017), 52–55.

100 Peter Brooks, *The Melodramatic Imagination: Balzac, Henry James, Melodrama and the Mode of Excess* (New Haven, CT and London: Yale University Press, 1976 and 1995), vii.

drawing on Robert Meister, who reads melodrama as code for sentimentality and as a device for the bystander to avoid the consequences of law and its effects, correctly identifies for melodrama.[101] *The Factory Lad* is something different, that confounds Brooks' Romantic Socialism,[102] its rawness and denial of redemption denies melodrama's usual stock responses and forces its audiences to acknowledge the realities of law at its most brutal.

Salop

In 1851, Thomas Menlove died of gas poisoning in Salop Gaol, at the age of either 68 or 70. Seven years earlier, his name appeared in *The Jurist* as insolvent debtor No. 64–872.[103] and *The London Gazette* of Saturday 6 April 1844 contains notice of a Creditor's Petition for Thomas Menlove, Late of Petton, Salop, Farmer, whose location is the Gaol of Shrewsbery.[104] Salop, as it's referred to here and in the judgment, was the original name of the border county of Shropshire. Abutting Wales, the county is and was rural, but in the late eighteenth and early nineteenth century was at the heart of the Industrial Revolution, and Shrewsbery or Shrewsbury as it's now styled, its county town and the site of the assize trial in *Vaughan v Menlove.*

Menlove and his fate was the subject of brief exchange on a message board sometime in the last few years, going something like this:

> Found him in prison on the 1851 census I've been going over some notes and the death cert of my ancestor Thomas MENLOVE shows that he died in Salop Gaol in 1851 after gas leaked into his cell! Are there any records from Salop Gaol which might shed light on what he was doing there. PRISONERS born in Shropshire who were present in the Institution on the night of 30th March 1851 Thomas MENLOVE, Debtor, M, 70, Farmer, b. SAL, Petton.
>
> I wonder if this imprisonment is related to his 1837 conviction for one of his hay bails catching fire and burning his neighbours house? Maybe he couldn't pay the fine and they locked him up for 15 years until he died?
>
> A Thomas Menlove, farmer, of Petton was involved in a lawsuit over a hay bail that caught fire and burnt a neighbouring property in 1835. He was ruled

101 Honni van Rijswijk, 'Interventions into the Feeling of Popular Justice: Australia's Stolen Generations, the Problem of Sentimentality, and Re-Encountering the Testimonial Form', in Cassandra Sharp and Marett Leiboff (eds), *Cultural Legal Studies, Law's Popular Cultures and the Metamorphosis of Law* (Abingdon: Routledge, 2016), 71–94, 82–83.

102 Brooks, *Melodramatic Imagination*, 87–88. Compare Elaine Hadley who takes, instead, a genre approach to melodrama, as a response to new forms of regulation in the eighteenth and nineteenth centuries: Elaine Hadley, *Melodramatic Tactics: Theatricalized Dissent in the English Marketplace, 1800–1885* (Stanford, CA: Stanford University Press, 1995).

103 *The Jurist* (1844), 123.

104 At 392.

liable in 1837. I hardly think that warrants still being in prison 24 years later though?[105]

Menlove, it seems, lost everything, though whether his decline into bankruptcy and debtors prison had something to do with the dispute with Vaughan, or if he was sliding into debt anyway before or after the case, is a moot point. Though Menlove lived at Petton, the land where the hayrick caught fire was at another site, Burlton, a mile away, or some 20 minutes away by foot. Menlove possessed the land at Burlton freehold, on which there were some farm buildings,[106] but there's a box located in the Shropshire archives containing two draft agreements from January 1835 for the sale and purchase of a farm and land at Burlton and for the sale of land at Burlton, with Thomas Menlove named in each.[107] Whether Menlove is buying or selling, or was successful in the sale or *vice versa* is for someone else to pursue, but it's hard to avoid wondering if there was some coincidence between these draft agreements and the fire on land at Burlton later that year.

Burlton, or to be more precise, Burlton Hall, isn't just any location,[108] and nor its owner, Robert Chambre Vaughan, the plaintiff in the case. He can be located at 'Vaughan, of Burlton Hall' in Burke's 1837 listing of the *Landed Gentry*, at pages 238–242, and as updated and adapted over the years.[109] He's a relatively young man at the time of the fire and the case, having been born on 3 June 1796, and an Oxford graduate, who was married, and incidentally a descendant of Edward III, for whom the middle-class, Nonconformist by birth, pupillage trained, and politically left wing and reform-oriented Talfourd appears.

Simpson fills out some detail of the events surrounding the case drawn from the local press (one Tory and the other progressive), given the paucity of the records of the case (either lost or misplaced,[110] which is the case for many of the records from Shropshire). Vaughan, patently, was a wealthy man of property; Menlove, a respectable freehold farmer. The two cottages were occupied by Vaughan's servants, Thomas Ruscoe and Thomas Bickley, the former a domestic servant and the

105 https://www.rootschat.com/forum/index.php?topic=435224.0, accessed 20 September 2018.

106 Simpson, 'Legal Liability', 211–212.

107 XD3651/D/5/773: 'Draft agreement: George Wycherly with Thomas Menlove (Jan 1835) Shropshire Archives box 481 Jan 1835 Description: re sale and purchase of farm and lands at Burlton (Two copies)' XD3651/D/5/774: 'Draft agreement: Thomas Menlove with John Cheshire (Jan 1835) Shropshire Archives, box 481, Jan 1835 Description: Agreement for sale and purchase of land at Burlton. Related People: Menlove, Thomas, Cheshire, John,'

108 Burlton Hall, a Grade II listed building in Loppington, Shropshire. https://britishlistedbuildings.co.uk/101212510-burlton-hall-loppington#.XDbillwzaUk, accessed 12 September 2018.

109 *Burke's Genealogical and Heraldic History of the Commoners of Great Britain and Ireland*, Volume 2.

110 Simpson, 'Legal Liability', draws on further accounts from local newspapers to tell more of what happened: 210–212.

latter a labourer.[111] In July Menlove stacked some hay on his property; it spontaneously combusted on 1 August 1835, and on the morning of Friday September 4, at about 4 o'clock, the hayrick burst into flames, and the resulting conflagration spread across the carriageway between the two properties by a strong westerly wind and burnt down the two cottages.[112] What's left out of the law reports, but was reported in the newspapers at the time, was that a strong westerly wind fanned the conflagration.[113] The cottages weren't insured, the policy having lapsed. An estimate for the cost of rebuilding them was £147. The defendant's own loss in the fire was variously estimated at between £100 and £600, though in the assizes this sum was stated to be £500. At trial, Vaughan was awarded £5.

The case can't help but conjure images of fire rupturing and disrupting the idyll of a bucolic countryside like that in *The Hay Wain*, and the seemingly joyful work of harvesting and transporting hay, albeit on the opposite side of England and of an imagined past. The case displays something of the stock concerns and characters of melodrama – the demanding gentry, the farmer, either good hearted or careless, the homeless servants, all feed into potential theories of the case that would also form the thematic of any melodrama. So in one possible scenario, Menlove might have acted as expected, drawing on his wealth of farming experience to rectify the problem using accepted practice and but for the change in the wind, the rick would have survived. Now in another, Menlove becomes arch villain, that he wanted the land to burn to obtain an insurance payout or that he was pigheaded, stubbornly ignoring advice to demolish the rick and move it away from the edge of his own property. Or it was Vaughan who lacked care, failing to renew his insurance policy, leaving his workers without homes and seeking to avoid responsibility by turning the case onto Menlove, in much the same way that Sugarman and Warrington observed, that the landed gentry and aristocracy would always win. Another was that jurors might not want to upset the local gentry,[114] or that this was an instance of a feud between the neighbouring landowners. There's one more possibility, but I'll come to it later.

Menlove used an iron rod to make an aperture or chimney, and removed some of the hay but some words would be used to damn him in Common Pleas in the

111 Ibid.

112 Ibid., and from the account of the facts in both of the *English Reports*. There are discrepancies in the chronology between each.

113 Ibid.

114 By 1848, the editors of the *Law Times* were agitating for civil juries to be dispensed with 'shaken, and partly dissipated by that sternest of monitors, and most sweeping of reformers, Common Sense', comparing them to quack doctors. Legal resentment of jury amateurism is exemplified in the comments of *The Times* that at the assizes held at Monmouth, 'the composition of common jury lists seems to be conducted on the principle of selecting the most uneducated and incompetent persons to be found in the respective counties with the requisite qualifications', with *The Jurist* regretting that juries were usually composed of 'persons with scarcely sufficient education to understand the ordinary conversational language of educated men, and quite incapable of any close or acute reasoning'. Hanly, 'The Decline of Civil Jury Trial', 261, 262, 265, references omitted.

mode of melodrama: that he said his stock was insured and he'd chance it. But at the assizes, he was said to have not been insured for his losses, and claims that the *rick was poorly constructed*, which caused the problem in the first place, came later, seemingly much to the frustration of his counsel. There was something that didn't make sense at all about the case, and that was why Menlove took the step of asking Common Pleas to review the rule that Patteson J applied in the case. The assize judge seemed to be sympathetic to Menlove, and there was only a relatively small award of damages against him. There seemed to be only one purpose, and that was that Menlove wanted to have his name and actions cleared.

Vaughan II

Talfourd, it was jested in the contemporary periodicals, never appeared for anyone who lost, in part because he would, as Serjeant, appear first. But the periodicals all agree that he would never cross-examine an honest witness with hostility. Though nothing's said so in this case, what's apparent is that at Common Pleas,[115] his arguments are modest and confined, though devastating. It suggests a number of things – that he's either unsympathetic to Vaughan, or at best, neutral, or that he's unsure about Menlove's liability. Vaughan's two servants are given more attention in the account of the case and the plaintiff next to none, to perhaps neutralise the optics of the landed gentry pursing a farmer, with all that would mean at the time, including conjuring images of *The Factory Lad*, and the rural melodramas of the era. Talfourd's submissions are confined to an existing principle in law, involving prudence as associated with *knowledge or scientier*: Menlove knew of the dangerous state of the rick, and yet negligently and improperly allowed it to stand. Talfourd relied on the circumstances of an earlier case,[116] when weeds were burnt close to a neighbouring property which then caught fire, where liability was determined by adopting the ordinary prudence test in the absence of any precise awareness of what had occurred. In the earlier case:

> there were no means of estimating the defendant's negligence, except by taking as a standard, the conduct of a man of ordinary prudence: that has been the rule always laid down, and there is no other that would not be open to much greater uncertainties.[117]

What Talfourd's doing here is making nothing of Menlove's actions, but is bringing into play an earlier case and *its* fact circumstances and law as *proxy* for this case. Richards, for Menlove, instead argues that the prudent man standard was impossible to measure, and rather that the case:

115 Despite the inconsistencies in the different reports, I'll now keep to the version of the case in the Court of Common Pleas as reported in *Bingham's New Cases*, the version included in the *English Reports*, with a comment at n. 113.

116 *Thomas v Morgan* (2 Cr. M. & R. 496), the authority glossed in *Hodges Reports* at n. 35. Talfourd appeared in *Thomas*, a point unremarked in *Bingham*.

117 *Vaughan*, 492.

> ought to be estimated by the faculties of the individual, *and not by those of other men*. The measure of prudence varies so with the varying faculties of men, that it is impossible to say what is gross negligence with reference to the standard of what is called ordinary prudence.[118]
>
> (My emphasis)

Richards holds onto judicial remarks in an attempt to provide a clear authority for the problem of the using the *standard* of the prudent man, for it becomes a test 'of other men', otherwise, but unwisely adds the reference to 'the varying faculties of men'. As authority, he cited Patteson J (the assize judge who heard the case) in *Crook*, who'd said: 'I never could understand what is meant by parties taking a bill under circumstances which ought to have excited the suspicion of a prudent man', and Taunton J: 'I cannot estimate the degree of care which a prudent man should take.'[119]

This argument didn't work. While abstract tests of objectivity weren't considered in the case, despite the later claims, *standards* were considered. Standards, meaning something like standards of decency, or standards of behaviour, isn't cognate or synonymous with objectivity (unless calculable as a weight or measure). But it's barely touched on, because what's concerning Tindal CJ more is the lack of direct causality or causation, even considering the evidence about the incorrect building of a rick and a subsequent failure to demolish. The test created turns to the *care or caution* to be taken by the prudent man, which turns on evidence of Menlove's actual conduct or the absence of conduct. And in this, he holds, there was nothing new for:

> *care taken by a prudent man* has always been the rule laid down; and as to the supposed difficulty of applying it, a jury has always been able to say, whether, taking that rule as their guide, there has been negligence on the occasion in question. Instead, therefore, of saying that the liability for negligence should be co-extensive with the judgment of each individual, which would be as variable as the length of the foot of each individual, we ought rather to adhere to the rule which requires in all cases a regard to *caution such as a man of ordinary prudence would observe*.[120]
>
> (My emphases)

Care or caution, a subset of prudence, becomes the determining factor in the case. Yet our eyes turn to the latter sentence, with its reference to 'the length of the foot of each individual' and its echo of the Chancellor's foot and its relationship with equity, mean that we decode the word of the Chief Justice into objectivity, and *overlook* the remarks about caution and care. But it's not objectivity, it's the problem of determining standards of behaviour. We see this played out in the

118 *Vaughan*, 492.
119 *Vaughan*, 492.
120 *Vaughan*, 493.

thought experiment of the Chief Justice, who proposes that the same rule would apply: 'just as if a chemist making experiments with ingredients, singly innocent, but when combined, liable to ignite; if he leaves them together, and injury is thereby occasioned to the property of his neighbour, can anyone doubt that an action on the case would lie?'[121]

If designed to offer neoclassical balance and symmetry, it's an odd cognate scenario. If it's to comfort Menlove, letting him know that he wasn't really to blame but it was just because a different attitude to care and caution was applied, it's an odd comparator. On the other hand, two of the elderly justices are having none of it. Gaselee J is reported as having delivered no judgment, while Park J and Vaughan J are seemingly untroubled by any law, though Park J holds onto existing maxims in Law French, and then concludes that: 'After he had been warned repeatedly during five weeks as to the consequences likely to happen, there is no colour for altering the verdict, *unless it were to increase the damages*' (my emphasis).[122] And though not expressed in so many words, Vaughan J was unimpressed with Patteson J, and appears to suggest that he would have found Menlove criminally liable if he could:

> It was, if anything, too favourable to the Defendant to leave it to the jury whether he had been guilty of gross negligence; for when the Defendant upon being warned as to the consequences likely to ensue from the condition of the rick, said, 'he would chance it,' *it was manifest he adverted to his interest in the insurance office.* The conduct of a prudent man has always been the criterion for the jury in such cases: but it is by no means confined to them … *Here, there was not a single witness whose testimony did not go to establish gross negligence in the Defendant. He had repeated warnings of what was likely to occur, and the whole calamity was occasioned by his procrastination.*[123]
>
> (My emphases)

It's not unusual that appellate level courts, who don't see or hear the witnesses, might miss what's apparent to a trial judge. Menlove, in the minds of Park and Vaughan JJ, is attempting to fraudulently obtain insurance monies or, if we follow the logic of Sugarman and Warrington, law is to run with the interests of the landed over everyone else. Yet Patteson J seems to have been chary of awarding anything more than nominal damages, and this might have been because of Captain Swing.

Swing

Menlove's hayrick went up in flames not long after the Swing Riots of 1830–1831.[124] The riots and what they represented would seem to be the only reason

121 *Vaughan*, 493.
122 *Vaughan*, 494.
123 *Vaughan*, 494.
124 Eric Hobsbawn and George Rudé, *Captain Swing* (London: Phoenix Press, 2001) (first published 1969 by Lawrence and Wishart).

why Menlove might have wanted the trial reconsidered, despite the small quantum of damages awarded against him. It seemed to be an excessive response but it seems that Menlove wanted to do anything that would dissociate him from any association with fire, either as a form of arson or as form of protest against his neighbour.

The circumstances of the riots appear in *Crotchet Castle* at least twice, with Swing protestors terrifying the Revered Dr Folliott, but it's the actions of the odious Sir Simon Steeltrap that triggers the riots. Dispossessed, poverty stricken tenant farmers and farm workers, whose livelihoods were lost or seriously compromised with the introduction of farm mechanisation, and enclosure laws that turned common lands over to individual property owners, ousting those who'd had access to the land for centuries, turned to violence to express their anger at their treatment. Swing rioters burnt or threatened to burn hayricks, and damaged farm machinery that took their work away from them. Owners would be threatened with letters in the name of the fictitious Captain Swing, with the assistance of literate and concerned middle-class supporters. Ricks would be set alight, catching barns and other farm property.[125]

The newly invented lucifer match made this an easy task,[126] and incendiarism remained the mechanism of choice for arson, either as protest of for insurance, in 1830s–1840s rural England.[127] Fires would be lit at night or over weekends; Menlove's fire took hold at 4 a.m. Silence was the watchword; 'threshers on the spot where fires began saw nothing, and suspicious "strangers" vanished into thin air',[128] the reverse situation of witnesses who suddenly appeared to speak against freeholder Menlove. Swing was notorious, and was the subject of significant commentary, and in the hands of the middle class, treated with sympathy given the plight of impoverished rural workers. Melodramas about Swing appeared in 1831,[129] including *Swing; or the Rick Burner* of 1831,[130] which was performed in the counties. The commentary was deeply concerned with the reasons why Swing happened in the first place, and because of the heavy handed response of the Whig government of Lord Melbourne, which prosecuted protestors and supporters with zeal,[131] with 2,000 tried in 34 counties, with some hanged, and over 400 transported to Australia for periods of 7 to 14 years, though capital punishment was repealed in 1837.[132] Among those transported were Thomas Cook, an 18-

125 Robert Hughes, *The Fatal Shore: A History of the Transportation of Convicts to Australia 1787–1868* (London: Vintage Books, 2003) 197–200.

126 Robert Kuhlken, 'Settin' The Woods on Fire: Rural Incendiarism as Protest' (1999) 89.3 *The Geographical Review* 343–363, 345–346, references omitted.

127 Eric Richards "Captain Swing' in the West Midlands' (1974) 19.1 *International Review of Social History* 86–99; Steve Poole, "A Lasting and Salutary Warning': Incendiarism, Rural Order and England's Last Scene of Crime Execution' (2008) 19.2 *Rural History* 163–177.

128 Ibid., 48.

129 Frederick Burwick, *British Drama of the Industrial Revolution* (Cambridge: Cambridge University Press, 2015), 2015, 166–175.

130 Ibid., 168–169.

131 Ibid., 199.

132 David Jones, *Crime, Protest, Community, and Police in Nineteenth-Century Britain* (London: Routledge and Kegan Paul, 1982) notes the paucity of records from Shropshire.

year-old solicitor's clerk from Whitchurch in Shropshire (some distance from Petton and Burlton), who anonymously penned a threatening letter to one William Churton, a cabinet maker and auctioneer, who'd helped put out rick fires,[133] and who was transported to Australia.

What's not posed at the trial or at Common Pleas is the possibility, or even probability, that Menlove was framed, and that his rick went up in flames not because of his negligence but because of payback or threats made to him; this might explain why the damages award against him was so small. Whatever really happened, Menlove's bankruptcy was a swingeing punishment, though there is a final, albeit deferred, triumphant ending to this story. His son, Edward is born on his father's farm at Petton, at the height of Swing, his birth recorded on 24 February 1831. He learnt his agricultural and pastoral skills from his father, and left England at the age of 22, moving to the Antipodes in 1853,[134] around two years after his father died, coming first to Melbourne in Australia, and then after a brief return to England, on to New Zealand in 1863, where he prospered, becoming one of the largest landholders and civic leaders in the North Otago region of New Zealand's South Island, marrying and having three daughters and two sons. Given his success in New Zealand, it seems hard to fathom that he learnt poor farming practices from Thomas Menlove. From what's written about him, we know Edward was a wonderful employee, and after his death, this was published in the local newspaper at Oamaru in the district that he'd been involved in building:[135]

> Sir, me and my mates have just read from your paper the news that our old friend Mr Menlove has died. When this news gets among my 'brother swaggers' it will be met with sorrow from all of them, I'm sure... Many's the Swagger, when meeting another on the rocks has passed along the standing word, 'make for Teddy's; you'll get a feed there'. Yes sir, and we got it every time. That's the kind of man he was – a big-hearted, straight forward, fine fellow, and one of nature's gentlemen. To this we all rise and sing in chorus. 'Yes, yes; he was.'
>
> I am, etc., Bill the Swagger.[136]

Edward, or Eddie, Menlove succeeded, it seems, because of what he learnt from his father, and seemingly because of what happened to his father, as evidenced by his kindness to the itinerant swaggers.

133 Ibid., 198–199.

134 'Death of Mr Edward Menlove', *Oamaru Mail* (1903) XXVIII.8243, 27 July. https://paperspast.natlib.govt.nz/newspapers/OAM19030727.2.5; 'Old Colonists: Mr Edward Menlove': *The Cyclopedia of New Zealand [Otago and Southland Provincial Districts]*. http://nzetc.victoria.ac.nz/tm/scholarly/tei-Cyc04Cycl-t1-body1-d4-d28.html

135 His success comes however from the dispossession of Māori.

136 Shanann Carr, *Remembering Edward Menlove*. https://culturewaitaki.org.nz/epitaph/remembering-edward-menlove, 2009-2010.

The (real) origin of the reasonable man

There are so many unanswered questions about *Vaughan v Menlove*, but what's not in dispute is the principle that comes from it: that a prudent man test was approved in the case, and that care and conduct was the measure applied. Reasonableness, such as it was, had no place in the case, and nor did objectivity or subjectivity. But if abstract concepts of reasonableness had applied, as opposed to prudence, it's just as likely that Menlove wouldn't have been found liable if *Blyth* had been the law, but perhaps not, because the case overtly favours the inaction of a large corporate entity.

Over 20 years later, in the 1856 Exchequer case of *Blyth v The Company of Proprietors of The Birmingham Waterworks*,[137] the reasonable man makes his actual appearance, with some nod to the prudent man and conduct that holds onto something of prudence. The adoption of both adjectives tells us that these aren't synonyms and confirms that the prudent man and the reasonable man aren't one and the same. Baron Alderson now holds that the corporation wasn't liable, now in an exceptional situation of an extreme polar blast:

> Negligence is the omission to do something which a reasonable man, *guided upon those considerations which ordinarily regulate the conduct of human affairs*, would do, or doing something which *a prudent and reasonable man* would not do. ... The defendants had provided against such frosts as experience would have led men, *acting prudently*, to provide against; and they are not guilty of negligence, because their *precautions proved insufficient against the effects of the extreme severity of the frost* of 1855, which penetrated to a greater depth than any which ordinarily occurs south of the polar regions. Such a state of circumstances constitutes a contingency against which no reasonable man can provide.

At the tipping point of regularising law, the logics of law inherited into the twentieth and twenty-first century are given form. The scant references to prudence in *Blyth* nod to *Vaughan*. Now conduct is registered within the interests of commercial enterprise. Bacon's promise, as it were, is complete. Prudence, as embodied responsibility, is about to be forgotten about, and verballed, along with the revival of the ideals and community of the medieval and middle ages. This story has been swept out of view in order to hold onto the pretence of the continuity of law since at least the seventeenth century, as rational, logical and reasonable.

The third

Beyond the fringe, beyond the pale[138]

The dramaturgical reconsideration of *Vaughan* has a twofold purpose. The first is to theatricalise what is assumed to be a principle in law and correct its history, and

137 (1856) 11 Exch 781, 156 ER 1047.

138 These terms aren't just randomly adopted. They are references to actual things and places, but read carefully to make sure you know what's at stake.

the second is to use it to return to the TSST, and what it would entail in the circumstances of any widespread adoption of artificial intelligence ('AI') in law. AI replaces lawyers in reading, interpreting and applying law, and, it's claimed, the elimination of the need to judge.[139] It's law, but not quite as we know it, as Richard Mohr shows in exquisitely drawn detail.[140] A document appears as if it's nothing other than a phone or electricity bill, but it's actually a demand for the payment of a fine for driving over the speed limit. The document and its payment methods presume the existence of an offence. In its one sidedness, this is a diabolically efficient deployment of law without any alternative possibility, and if adapted to the TSST, is much more efficient and rational, dispensing entirely with human interaction.

Not only is there no one to talk to in order to challenge the payment of the bill – sorry, notice of a speeding offence (for that's what it is) – but the very possibility of a challenge in law is rendered nearly impossible, a presumptive guilt embedded in the payment system. Payment produces a legal consequence – the loss of demerit points that might lead to the loss of a driver's licence. This is law administered by machine (a speed camera and the computer that generates the document) *qua* machine (the payment mechanism), bypassing human intervention that might inconveniently query things like camera error, of angle error and intervening events.[141] If the TSST tests stress through the denial of human interaction and the deployment of a set script, law decided by machines is the ultimate in faceless law, where script and facelessness demands acquiescence, it's an impossible, diabolical instance of 'computer says no'.

Of course, the machines aren't intervening on their own. As Dominique Hogan-Doran SC explains for judges who mightn't appreciate its consequences: 'Because human beings program predictive algorithms, their biases and values are embedded into the software's instructions … Algorithms are also what make intelligent robots intelligent.'[142] For law, it's not just biases and values, but the quality of law used, and

139 Mireille Hildebrand and Jeanne Gaakeer (eds), *Human Law and Computer Law: Comparative Perspectives* (Dordrecht: Springer Netherlands, 2013); Mireille Hildebrandt, *Smart Technologies and the End(s) of Law: Novel Entanglements of Law and Technology* (Cheltenham: Edward Elgar, 2015); 'Applications of Artificial Intelligence to Legal Informatics', Wikipedia. https://en.wikipedia.org/wiki/Applications_of_artificial_intelligence_to_legal_informatics, accessed 9 July 2017; Lucy Marks, 'Artificial Intelligence Law Firm Aims to Roll Out in Remote, Low Socio-Economic Communities', *Australian Broadcasting Corporation*, 14 November 2017; Erin Winick, 'Lawyer-Bots Are Shaking Up Jobs', *MIT Technology Review*, 12 December 2017. https://www.technologyreview.com/s/609556/lawyer-bots-are-shaking-up-jobs/

140 Richard Mohr and Francesco Contini, 'Reassembling the Legal: The Wonders of Modern Science in Court-Related Proceedings' (2011) 20 *Griffith Law Review* 994–1019.

141 Ashley Pearson and Kieran Tranter, 'Code, Nintendo's Super Mario and Digital Legality' (2015) 28.4 *International Journal for the Semiotics of Law* 825–842; Kieran Tranter, 'Disrupting Technology Disrupting Law' (2107) *Law, Culture and the Humanities*. https://doi.org/10.1177/1743872117704925, 10–11.

142 Dominique Hogan-Doran SC, 'Computer Says 'No': Automation, Algorithms and Artificial Intelligence in Government Decision-Making' (2017) 13 *The Judicial Review* 1–39.

without realising it, the non-legal presumptions of the programmer. AI law must inevitably strip subtlety and complexity from law, its histories, its possibilities for variation, in favour of the two lines of principle as shaped not through the courts but through the repetition, correct or not, found in textbook, treatise, or social media, regardless of its veracity, an ontological redrawing of law as scraps of social media that imbricates the law of the Year Books but denying justice in its wake.

AI law is dystopian promise of law as drama, dispensing with complexity and promising certainty, where *judgment is always present, and where it precedes law* in the algorithm. Algorithms, after all, are just a script, and that script is held in the hands of the programmer, whose knowledge and understanding of the complexities of law, or lack of it, will be determinative, as the ultimate ghost in the machine. Law isn't perfectible but programming has to be, so *whoever writes the program holds judgment in their hands.* This is law as brutalist and diabolical, brooking no possibility of variability or circumstance, the TSST as automaton and as promise in the denial of human interaction and the perfectibility of the strictures of the script.

AI law discards text in favour of 'txt' and #, for whom the niceties of judicial interpretation are annoyance rather than explication, and law and its lifeworlds subdued, in much the same way that the nineteenth-century textbook and treatise writers subdued and verballed *Vaughan*. The algorithm and its creator will rebuff the unknown, the unique, and deny challenges to unfair and hostile precedent. Algorithms can't notice what's behind the loose thread, or find the way in to strip a little at it to open the seamless web, unlike the theatrical that gives us the ability to *notice*, to find the nodal knot or point at which precedent can be broken into.[143] And nor is there any way of noticing the non-legal presumptions and assumptions that have no authorised basis, as problematised through all the variations I teased out of the circumstances in *Vaughan v Menlove*, and all of the lost, hidden situations that exist now and in the future that can't be taken for granted.

Even haphazard, everyday misconceptions and trivialities can actively shape reasoning and interpretation. In 2010, I carried out a quasi-empirical study that asked different generations of lawyers to respond to questions that dealt with cultural, historical, pop cultural and literary references used in judgment,[144] not to test knowledge but to find out what these variabilities, predilections and presumptions meant for the reading of the same legal text across these groupings. The three examples I'm including here represent three different kinds of questions. The first is grammatical but includes a contemporary concern based on an historical past. The second involves an old legal concept and an old word that might have a range of meanings. And the third involves the use of words by a member of the House of Lords as part of a judgment. The nature of the responses ranged from troubling to amusing to deeply disturbing, and are included in Table 3.1 below.

143 Mark Antaki, 'The Turn to Imagination in Legal Theory: The Re-Enchantment of the World?' (2012) 23 *Law and Critique* 1–20; Peter Goodrich, 'The New Casuistry' (2007) 33 *Critical Inquiry* 673 at 682 and 707; David Gurnham, *Memory, Imagination, Justice: Intersections of Law and Literature* (Aldershot: Ashgate, 2009).

144 Chapter 1: Talkin' 'bout law's generations.

Table 3.1 From the Law's Gens Project

		1925–1953	*1954–1965*	*1966–1975*	*1976–1985*	*1986–2000*
Q12						
Correctly answered 'False'		66.7%	76%	72%	70%	54%
Correctly answered 'False', excluding overseas born participants		100%	90%	87.5%	75%%	56.5%
Q30						
Assumpsit	Legal term	50%	23.1%	9.1%	10%	1.8%
	Wrong, 'Assume', no answer	50%	76.9%	90.9%	90%	98.2%
	'Assume' as a sub-answer	16.7%	7.7%	18.2%	20%	12.7%
2. Hogshead	Who got the answer right?	66.7%	30.8%	18.2%	0%	7.3%
Q 35						
What are 'the sixties'? And how many got the answer right?		16.7%	30.8%	18.2%	20%	14.5%

Question 12 asked: 'Is the following statement true or false?' 'All people born in Australia between 1950 and 1960 received free university education in Australia, whenever they undertook their university education.' The politics or history behind the question wasn't its purpose, though it's inevitable that this where reader would go. There was a period of free tertiary education from the early 1970s and into the mid-1980s, principally available to people born in the period from about 1955 through to the late 1960s. People born before then might have received free tertiary education through Commonwealth Scholarships or bonded education. Deeply unequal circumstances now mean that most university students would now leave university with large debts, and for obvious reasons, there is resentment about a benefit unavailable to them. Grammar was the point of the question, but it's more than obvious that reading is bound up in what texts can mean, not just what they actually mean.

The parts of the sentence mattered: 'All people … whenever'. The sentence was constructed to be read with these modifiers in place, regardless of whether it could be known that only a very small part of the population gained access to university when it was free. Lifeworlds matter. My research assistant, a recent law graduate, Daniel Byers, worked with the data carefully, revealing a difference based on local familiarity, confirming that the grammar wasn't attended to with care. Rather, knowledge of events or assumptions about the circumstances was what mattered to the lawyers and law students who participated in the study.

Another question, this time with a connection to *Vaughan*, and really a question of legal knowledge: Question 30 turned to the headnote of *Coggs v Bernard* (1703) 91 Eng. Rep. 26: 'Assumpsit to take up a hogshead of brandy in one cellar, and lay it down in another. Breach, that tam negligenter he put it down in the latter, that it was staved, gist.' Two of the questions that follow will be included here. The question was two-fold, with assumpsit, a legal term likely to have been lost, and its closeness to the word 'assume'. Knowledge of the legal term dropped markedly across the age groupings, but there wasn't much variation when it came to using the word 'assume' in its place, with the marked difference existing at the point of not attempting a response (a possibility offered to participants), or just getting it wrong. Knowledge of hogsheads declined with age, or with drinking patterns.

And a final example, Question 35, one of a double header that continued to Question 36. It asked: 'In her decision in *Fisher v Brooker* [2009] UKHL 41, concerning the authorship of the opening organ solo of *A Whiter Shade of Pale*, Baroness Hale says at 20: "I agree that … this appeal should be allowed and the declarations made by the trial judge restored. As one of those people who do remember the sixties, I am glad that the author of that memorable organ part has at last achieved the recognition he deserves."'

Again a number of questions followed but one response is enough, and it's truly surprising, because even those who lived through the sixties were unable to find a meaning. The sixties on their own, even with the supporting components in the phrase, were indecipherable, but then again her Ladyship missed the joke, because if you really had been there, you wouldn't have remembered …

The point of all of these instances is that they show how much law is in the hands of the non-legal knowledge we hold within us, and the likelihood or not of our turning back to ourselves or whether we'll consider our assumptions. But what this reveals and confirms is that law is bound up with so many other aspects of our lives, whether we want to believe this or not

To know how it stands now resolved

> 'Aha!' said the old man, 'Aha! who was talking about the Inns?' 'I was, Sir,' replied Mr. Pickwick—'I was observing what singular old places they are.'
>
> 'You,' said the old man contemptuously 'What do you know of the time when young men shut themselves up in those lonely rooms, and read and read, hour after hour, and night after night, till their reason wandered beneath their midnight studies; till their mental powers were exhausted; till morning's light brought no freshness or health to them; and they sank beneath the unnatural devotion of their youthful energies to their dry old books? They are no ordinary houses, those. There is not a panel in the old wainscotting but what, if it were endowed with the powers of speech and memory, could start from the wall, and tell its tale of horror – the romance of life, Sir, the romance of life.'[145]
>
> (Charles Dickens, *The Posthumous Papers or The Pickwick Club*, 1837)

145 H Spenden Steel, 'Origin and History of English Inns of Chancery' (1907) 13.8 *The Virginia Law Register* 585–593, 593, includes this extract from Dickens, *The*

When the Council of Legal Education in 1852 revived training for barristers after a 150-year hiatus, it omitted a key component of the original legal education. Until the seventeenth century, a broadly humanist education was the norm for those attending the Inns of Court,[146] and the preliminary training undertaken at the defunct Inns of Chancery.[147] Plowden, at the Inns of Chancery in the sixteenth century, O'Sullivan tells us, would have been schooled in 'ethics and politics, and learnt the outlines of the classical and Christian jurisprudence that gave life and energy to the Common Law'.[148] Once at the Inns of Court, he would undertake exercises in the law, in mooting and in disputations in term time and in vacation.[149] Dinners at the residential Inns, except at moots, were devoted to argumentation around a case, where 'they learned, in Shakespeare's phrase, to practise rhetoric in their common talk'.[150] The liberal arts, or humanities, were as much a part of their education as the Inns' 'intense intellectual and social life. Dancing was part of the ancient ritual of the place, and they were also given to music and to drama; with regular times for Revels, and Grand Christmas and the Reader's Feast'.[151] Blackstone, as mentioned earlier in this book, lamented the loss of this broadly humanistic training,[152] though he was writing when there was no legal training for lawyers at all, unless through a private pupillage, of the kind Talfourd undertook with Chitty.

Training at the Inns ceased during Cromwell's Commonwealth, and its brief revival at the Restoration didn't last.[153] Holdsworth's diagnosis was simple: 'The age was corrupt. The standard of public morality was low … [with] the injury inflicted upon English law by the Benchers of this period … all public teaching of English law was stopped for nearly a century and a half'.[154] Of course, there was always Oxford or Cambridge, where there was a modicum of a broadly humanist or scientific education before qualifying. What this involved in the eighteenth and into the early nineteenth century, was to be in commons at an Inn, initially for 4 years, or 16 terms. That meant attending dinners and other events as required, but nothing in the shape of actual training. These requirements were trimmed during the eighteenth century; 'eating

Posthumous Papers or The Pickwick Club (London: Chapman and Hall, 1837), 211 without citing, seemingly because of expected familiarity with the passage.

146 In particular, Wilfred Prest, *The Inns of Court under Elizabeth I and the Early Stuarts, 1590–1640* (London: Longman, 1972); Wilfred Prest, *The Rise of the Barristers: A Social History of the English Bar 1590–1640* (Oxford: Clarendon Press, 1986); see generally the contributions in Jayne Archer, Elizabeth Goldring and Sarah Knight (eds), *The Intellectual and Cultural World of the Early Modern Inns of Court* (Manchester: Manchester University Press, 2011).

147 Steel, 'Inns of Chancery', 586.

148 O'Sullivan, 46.

149 Ibid.

150 Ibid.

151 Ibid., 46–47.

152 Chapter 1.

153 David Maxwell-Fyfe, 'The Inns of Court and the Impact on the Legal Profession in England' (1950) 4 *Southwestern Law Journal* 391–397, 394–395.

154 Holdsworth, 'Disappearance', 216.

your way to the bar' was all that was required, other than a brief formulaic exam with a Bencher. Unsurprisingly, these new barristers had next to no knowledge of the law.

Some help would come from crib books, or brief texts, such as the small book by Roger North KC, jurist and polymath, very belatedly published in 1824, nearly 100 years after his death in 1734. North, a biographer and musician, and amateur architect, Bencher of Middle Temple, and Cambridge graduate, makes a number of observations of what makes a really good lawyer. He needs to know something of English history and be a general scholar, and 'read, commonplace, report, and converse about law',[155] and 'although it is not necessary for counsel to know what the history of a point is … it is a wonderful accomplishment, and, without it, a lawyer cannot be accounted learned in the law'.[156]

Whatever part this little book played in the development of later nineteenth-century legal training, it wasn't based on this latter passage, though, but rather the lesser sentiment in a phrase from this quote I intentionally omitted: 'to know how it stands now resolved'. 'To know how it stands now resolved', a *perpetual present without presence*, is the archest of Baconianism, and a deceit held within rationalism that intentionally omits from law's antecedents those aspects of law's presence, from history to prudence, from letters to rhetoric, all of which embed presence and an account of the ineffable in law that's otherwise the plaything of an absent law. If in 1831, Peacock's Mr Crotchet wanted to see philosophical controversies settled before he died,[157] by mid-century, of those he listed, it was rhetoric (as ornamentation), the sentimental, the romantic, and intuition that were gone.

Rhetoric's longstanding 'philosophical and political meaning … *was that of the historical and practical-human character of reason and of knowledge*'.[158] As Peter Goodrich has shown, rationalist and empiricist philosophy stripped rhetoric of what it actually did, 'from the study of argument to the appreciation of ornament, from dialectics to aesthetics, from semantics to a species of grammar',[159] instead turned it into that 'shadowy and twilight sphere of the cave, to the realm of appearance and of the probable as yet unilluminated by the real or truth'.[160] Rationalist 'abstraction, formality and neglect of history would inevitably lead to the perception of rhetoric as an oppositional category, as a non-science, as illogical and eventually as foul play … erroneous, deceitful and dangerous',[161] against

155 Ibid., 217.

156 Roger North, *A Discourse on the Study of the Laws, with notes and illustrations* (London: Published by a Member of the Inner Temple, 1824), 40.

157 Above, notes 81–82.

158 Goodrich, *Legal Discourse*, 98. See also, Peter Goodrich, 'Rhetoric and Law', in Michael J MacDonald (ed.), *The Oxford Handbook of Rhetorical Studies* (Oxford: Oxford University Press, 2017), 613–624.

159 Peter Goodrich, *Legal Discourse: Studies in Linguistics, Rhetoric and Legal Analysis* (London: Macmillan, 1987), 104. Peter Goodrich, 'Rhetoric as Jurisprudence: An Introduction to the Politics of Legal Language' (1984) 4.1 *Oxford Journal of Legal Studies* 88–122; Peter Goodrich, 'Law and Language: An Historical and Critical Introduction' (1984) 11 *Journal of Law and Society* 173–206.

160 Goodrich, *Legal Discourse*, 99.

161 Ibid., 108.

rationalism's much more stable practice, as based in Locke, of 'informing and instructing'.[162]

The theatricalisation of *Vaughan v Menlove* is an act of transgression. Transgression is one of the theatrical antonyms set up against ethics. Transgression involves breaking rules, and the idea that it might be able to reveal something missing in ethics seems dangerous, transgressive even. But its ethics as rules that is bound up in the theatrical antonyms, including that which is moral and morality. If transgression breaks rules it is also an action of moving, for transgression is simply an activity of stepping over, of movement and atmosphere: 'Bodies construct atmosphere on the arch of their movement. Atmosphere constructs bodies between its folds … bodies of flesh as well as discourse, materialities that keep on fluctuating between the abstract and the concrete'.[163]

Rhetoric, jurisography, prudence, and the theatrical antonyms remind us of that fluctuation, the materialities rendered through movement betwixt and between. Through it we find what's been lost in and of law through legal antitheatricality and its twin agents of rationality and reason. The depth of stories that fan out of *Vaughan v Menlove*, theatricalised through jurisography and dramaturgy, reveals that law's lost presence is able to be restored, to find a new presence for law, but also showing what's at stake if law is ossified through AI. The lines traced to discover that prudence was locked away behind reason, can't happen in isolation or by reading the two lines of principle. Stitching prudence back into place, as a lost principle of law, at the same time undoes law's seamless web. Granted, reason and the reasonable man did find their way into law through another case, but this means restoring the place of prudence, care and caution back into law, and the deep responsibility that it places on all of us, to act with care and caution.[164] That means learning, bodily, to understand what prudence demands.

162 Ibid.

163 Andreas Philippopoulos-Mihalopoulos, 'The Funambulist Atmosphere' *The Funambulist Papers* 29. https://thefunambulist.net/philosophy/guest-writers-essays-29-the-funambulist-atmosphere-by-andreas-philippopoulos-mihalopoulos; Andreas Philippopoulos-Mihalopoulos, 'Withdrawing from Atmosphere: An Ontology of Air Partitioning and Affective Engineering' (2016) 34.1 *Environment and Planning D: Society and Space* 150–167.

164 Gaakeer, '*Sua Cuique Persona*?'

4 The moral theatre

Dumb show

> Perhaps the law of the theatre is to be a theatre of the law: to stage the law in order to see what it 'really' means.[1]
>
> Body, rhythm, breathing, the here and now of the unthinkable presence of the body, its eroticism, these undermind the Logos.[2]
>
> By coming to know the mystery of another, one comes to know his own. And *vice versa*: by coming to know one's own, one comes to know the mystery of another... One might think that meeting is a creative feature exclusive to theatre, but after all if we analyze certain phenomena, for example in literature, we can find many analogies. In theatre, no doubt, meeting is essential.[3]

It's nearing the end of the nineteenth century. Law has regularised its practices, with judgment now held tightly in the hands of its authorising source, and perfected as Aristotelean drama, at the very least holding to the pattern of the well-made play and sometimes creating the perfection of the tragic. There's no need to read any extraneous material in the newly authorised law reports, though the arguments of counsel are retained, though like the earlier commonplaces and commentary, unnecessary, truth be told. The textbook and treatise, however, is elevated, its learned authors, who are sometimes cited in court, perhaps in recognition of their role in regularising law into a unified and coherent whole, sweeping aside the unruliness of what's gone before, tidying up and correcting judgments to say what they really should, keeping unruly and rambunctious antecedents at bay.

Now John Austin's jurisprudence is belatedly recognised, reiterating what's now a process of legal reasoning and interpretation, establishing law as inward looking and reiterative, cementing in place the logic of 'knowing how it stands now

1 Lehmann, *Tragedy*, 113.

2 Hans-Thies Lehmann, 'From Logos to Landscape: Text in Contemporary Dramaturgy' (1997) *Performance Research* 55–60, 57; See also Lehmann *Postdramatic Theatre*.

3 Jerzy Grotowski, 'On the Genesis of Apocalypsis', trans. Kris Salata (2008) 52.2 *TDR: The Drama Review* 40–51, 41. Salata notes that the Polish version of *Towards a Poor Theatre* was edited by Leszek Kolankiewicz, using shorthand notes of meetings held after the 1969 opening of the masterpiece *Apocalypsis cum figuris*, the tenth anniversary of the founding of the Laboratory Theatre. That text was corrected by Grotowski, 51.

resolved'.[4] So be it if black means white, person means man (in the extraordinary and infamous string of 'persons' cases); it's simply the law dictating the outcome, and not, heaven forbid, the outcome of a political choice or personal preference. Even better, because the amateur has been removed from any decision-making, law is now held close within its circle, something made easier now that the teaching of law through a regularised syllabus does its job of 'informing and instructing',[5] without anything more. There's no need for conversation or commonplacing,[6] though the occasional moot is welcomed as an opportunity to demonstrate advocacy skills.

This is the law that had crystallised by the end of the nineteenth century, as immemorial and ancient as the new set of court buildings that confirmed its antiquity. But just like these buildings, this law was neoteric, albeit with a set of stories in place that read of antiquity. Like the buildings on the Strand, there was so much that was invented tradition, along with the creation of narratives that would damn entire earlier periods of law if they failed to conform with the new traditions invented, like the neutering of inconvenient interventions, such as prudence, or the return to the medievalism of the first half of that century, and Holdsworth's dismissal of the 'corrupt age' before the mid-nineteenth century.[7]

At the same time, theatre was moving in an entirely different direction, away from the presentation of words as display or as entertainment. Though Macready's work in the early to mid-nineteenth century brought together play text and ensemble, by the end of the century upstaging through the star system had become the norm, or, in a more genteel form, the elegant display of a literary production. Now:

> At the turn of the twentieth century, the theater, along with the other representational arts, gradually became aware of its inner emptiness and began to project this void outwards … theater was no longer concerned with staging the real, but with exposing presence … the *hic et nunc* of performance, and to reinstate it within its specifically scenic dimension, after several centuries of feudal subservience to literature (to 'Your Highness The Word,' as Baty so pleasantly put it; as for Artaud, he denounced the attitude of 'grammarians and introverts, that is to say, of Westerners').[8]

What's generated instead is theatre that demands presence,[9] pushing 'on the borderline of logic and reason, on the threshold between what is thinkable and beyond reasoning'.[10] This is theatre of response, responsiveness, and ultimately,

4 Chapter 3.
5 Chapter 3.
6 Chapter 3.
7 Chapter 3.
8 Jean-Pierre Sarrazac, 'The Invention of 'Theatricality': Rereading Bernard Dort and Roland Barthes', trans. Virginie Magnat (2002) 31.2/3, 98/99 *SubStance* 57–72, 57–58, 61, 65–66.
9 Leiboff, 'Muteness', Leiboff, 'Forbrydelsen'.
10 Lehmann, 'From Logos to Landscape,' 56.

responsibility pressed onto the bodies of those who are brought into its ambit, like this gormless spectator whose impatience and irritation was rewarded with mortification.

In September 2002, the Brisbane-based *Grin & Tonic Theatre Troupe* presented a new version of cult classic Japanese television series *Monkey*.[11] A thin hessian wall divided the circus performance space from the public park it was using. Just before the play was about to begin, and to the audience's dismay, the walls were breached, intruders scrambling through at ground level, yelling at each other and audience members, swilling beer and pushing audience members from their seats. No one in authority appeared, exacerbating the consternation of audience members who were the direct recipients of their attentions, some of whom remonstrated, their agitation and anger on display and curiously, creating further attention from the intruders. Then the intruders breached the imaginary fourth wall, with the angriest audience member hot on their heels. The last laugh was on the audience, and this hapless spectator in particular. The intruders moved to the performance space revealing who they were, with the angry audience member now caught in a no man's land, as the audience shuffled with embarrassed laughter, applause, and mutterings, realising what had happened. The angry audience member had become aggressive, but defused when (as would have been planned) the intruder/actors stepped into the performance space, now shifting into 'character', saving the spectator from himself as he moved to throw a punch.

A physical response to danger created by the threat of the intruders overwhelmed commonsense while rationality and reason was unable to counter the raw viscerality created, and designed to destabilise and discomfit physically, provoking a dangerous and transgressive response, initiating and provoking potential lawlessness. This dumbshow, like all physical interventions in theatre, does two things. First, they force spectators, bodily, to abandon the complacency of expectation, bringing us into the place of theatre. Second, they deny the expectation of entertainment, instead generating encounter, writing something new into the bodies of those who are brought into its orbit. This *Monkey* was brilliant, but most of it's evaporated from my memory, except for the dumbshow, now deeply etched and inscribed, and now forming my clearest memories, as encounter that generated response, responsiveness through the physicality of encounter. Of course, this is what was intended. Encounter, Grotowski says, is 'an extreme confrontation, sincere, disciplined, precise and total – not merely a confrontation with his thoughts but one involving his whole being from his instincts and his unconscious right up to his most lucid state'.[12]

The mode of theatrical used in *Monkey* couldn't be further away from the politeness of literary display of drama, or theatre as amusement that was the norm at more or less the same time that law normalised and regularised its practices. The changes to theatre generated at the end of the nineteenth and into the early

11 This small portion is drawn and adapted from Leiboff 'Muteness', 384–391.

12 Grotowski, *Poor Theatre*, 57. Also see Kris Salata, *The Unwritten Grotowski: Theory and Practice of the Encounter* (New York: Routledge, 2013).

twentieth century (let alone those that came after) came too late to be encoded into law, which retained the dramatic expectations laid down in the mid-late Victorian, as already traced. Its practices of reading, interpreting and applying are those of drama as display: here is dénouement, there is the stock character, now let's hear from the chorus.[13] And to reiterate the point I've already made, I'm not talking about law as display or law within the trial, but the use of concepts from drama to normalise law and its interpretation. This is drama ossified, a literary presence unable to find ways to move from expectation. It couldn't be more different from the demands of the moral theatre. It's somewhat ironic, given that morals are included in the list of those forms of conduct that ground legal antitheatricality, to see this reference now to something called the moral theatre. But as already been touched on at the end of Chapter 3, it's *rule bound* morality that's been brought into in its sights. The moral theatre describes the demands of response and responsibility bound up in Grotowski's theatre, and which grounds theatrical jurisprudence, and it's sitting in plain sight in the dumbshow in *Monkey*.

Towards a poor theatre, towards a theatrical jurisprudence

Towards a Theatrical Jurisprudence draws on Jerzy Grotowski's legacy, its words a play on the title of a collection of Grotowski's writing, interviews and workshops, *Towards a Poor Theatre*,[14] published in 1968 in English. Grotowski's experiments developed a new morality, ethics and responsibility of theatre,[15] in large part through the revolutionary work that took shape in the first phase of experimentation in Poland at his Theatre Laboratory,[16] working with his co-founder Ludwik Flaszen,[17] the latter as dramaturg, theatrologist and translator, and who incidentally coined the phrase 'poor theatre', and his other collaborators.[18] This earliest phase, from 1959 to 1969, became known as *Theatre of Productions*, and the phase out of which theatrical jurisprudence is drawn.[19] This early work nearly all occurred in then Communist Poland; in 1969, Grotowski brought his actors to the US, and abruptly ended this first phase of work.[20]

13 Chapter 2.

14 Grotowski, *Poor Theatre*.

15 James Slowiak and Jairo Custo, *Jerzy Grotowski* (London and New York: Routledge, 2007), 10.

16 First at the Theatre of 13 Rows in Opole, in one or two more manifestations, before moving to Wroclaw.

17 Jarosław Fret and Leszek Kolankiewicz, *Rhizome* (Film), Theatre Olympics 2016. www.theatreolympics2016.pl/en/calendar/rhizome, accessed 20 May 2017.

18 For more see, Paul Allain and Grzegorz Ziółkowski (eds), *Voices from Within: Grotowski's Polish Collaborators* (London: Polish Theatre Perspectives/TAPAC: Theatre and Performance Across Cultures, 2015).

19 Followed by Theatre of Participation/Paratheatre (1969–1978), Theatre of Sources (1976–1982), Objective Drama (1983–1986), and his final phase, Ritual Arts or Art as Vehicle (1986–1999), which passed to Thomas Richards on Grotowski's death.

20 Grotowski would eventually leave Poland for good, in part because of the political pressures brought about during the last years of the Communist regime, moving to the US, to UC Irvine, and finally, from 1986 until his death in 1999, he was based in Pontedera in Tuscany, where he established a centre of performance research,

Grotowski created techniques and methods that hadn't been imagined in theatre before, as a radical theatre practice, changing theatre and its modes of training, its grammatical forms and its character, forever.[21] His influences were broad and eclectic, from the writings of mystic and gnostic Meister Eckhart, Carl Jung's work on myth and archetype, through to Stanislavski (whose work he said he was continuing), the guidance of Indian mystics, the theatre forms of East Asia, the work of Jewish mystic philosopher Martin Buber, and existentialism, among a host of other sources, to help establish a theatre that creates a live communion between actor and spectator.[22]

In the chapter of *Towards a Poor Theatre* that goes by the same name, Grotowski records that it was physical work, from Meyerhold's biomechanics and back to Stanislavki's physical work, along with the physical practices of Dullin and Delsarte,[23] which he would draw on to break down obfuscating techniques of theatre (tricks that overlay, that are fake). This physical work would be an essential component that would help ground the 'poor theatre'. Working with a closely held group of actors and collaborators, he developed physical exercises and breathing techniques, as a means through which to work on the self, which would manifest awareness and knowledge in the actor. Out of this work, the actor would emerge as *embodied* mind, who 'no longer lends his body to an exclusively mental process but makes the mind appear through the body, thus granting the body agency'.[24]

> We abandoned make-up, fake noses, pillow-stuffed bellies … We found that it was consummately theatrical for the actor to transform from type to type, character to character, silhouette to silhouette – while the audience watched – in a poor manner, using only his own body and craft. The composition of a fixed facial expression by using the actor's own muscles and inner Impulses achieves the effect of a strikingly theatrical transubstantiation, while the mask prepared by a makeup artist is only a trick.[25]

transmitting his legacy to his American disciple and collaborator, Thomas Richards. There are many Grotowski's, and many legacies of his, work, from the Pontedera *Workcenter of Jerzy Grotowski and Thomas Richards*, www.theworkcenter.org/, accessed 12 November 2017, and *Instytut Grotowskiego, The Grotowski Institute*, located in one of Grotowski's original theatre spaces, the Laboratory Theatre, in Wrocław in Poland, as archive and library and a research centre, maintaining an encyclopaedia of Grotowski's work, and also holding events and theatre workshops: www.grotowski.net/en, accessed 12 January 2017. The images reproduced in this chapter are licensed through *The Grotowski Institute*.

21 For some discussion of this influence, see Interview with Paul Allain, 'Grotowski's Influence: Barba, Brook And Beyond', *Essential Drama*, 19 November 2017, http://essentialdrama.com/tag/paul-allain/, accessed 12 July 2018.

22 Grotowski, *Poor Theatre*, 19; Slowiak and Custo, *Grotowski*, 13.

23 Grotowski, *Poor Theatre*, 16.

24 Fischer-Lichte, *Transformative Power of Performance,* 82–83.

25 Grotowski, *Poor Theatre*, 20–21.

We see this extraordinary responsiveness manifested in the photographs of some of Grotowski's key actor collaborators, especially the astonishing Ryszard Cieślak, in work carried out in the middle of that first phase of Grotowski's project. They are 'holy actors', who are sacrificing their bodies, as *via negativa*, in whom all blocks are removed and body and mind are integrated.[26] This is what Grotowski calls trance, where a different form of consciousness transforms the actor, generating a heighted state of alertness, but who is, at the same time, able to remain in the present. Trance is that nearly impossible state of being where thought and action are one and the same. We see this in the extraordinary and consummate Cieślak, in the images of him in *The Constant Prince*. This is what constitutes presence, the here and now (*hic et nunc*). He's not acting because this is what he's become, but is what Grotowski terms the *total act*.[27] There's no need for words to know what's going on; even in these black and white photographs, we must respond, and we must notice, not just for the sake of it but in the depths that connect us to the confrontation bound up in myth and archetype, that fractures our life-masks. This isn't display or entertainment; what we see is that embodied mind impelled through impulses, created deep in the body which precede movement and action, now moving into view.[28]

> It is the act of laying oneself bare, of tearing off the mask of daily life, of exteriorizing oneself. Not in order to 'show oneself off', for that would be exhibitionism. It is a serious and solemn act of revelation. The actor must be prepared to be absolutely sincere. It is like a step towards the summit of the actor's organism in which consciousness and instinct are united.[29]

Grotowski reminds us not to mistake the 'holy' actor with holiness in the religious sense: 'It is rather a metaphor defining *a person who, through his art, climbs upon the stake and performs an act of self-sacrifice*' (my emphasis).[30] As already mentioned, holy actors aren't acting, but live that which has become part of their being. In noticing what these actors tell us through their bodies, it's not just the inestimable Cieślak who we should be paying attention to, but the women, especially Maja Komorowska in Figure 4.2, lachrymose, her despair and distress manifesting even in the fall of her hair. Flip your head over to achieve the same result if you're sceptical. What someone watching you will see is someone flipping their head over, just as people who attempt to mimic Grotowski's exercises look like people mimicking Grotowski's exercises. It won't resemble the despair and distress that extends even to the ends of her hair, just as mimicry can't produce the responsiveness in the body that Grotowski's exercises were created to produce. Now hold an intense despair in your body, holding whatever triggers your distress.

26 Ibid., 16–17.
27 Slowiak and Custo, *Grotowski*, 20, citing Grotowski in Osiński, references omitted.
28 Ibid., 64–68, citing Grotowski's interview with Richards, references omitted.
29 Grotowski, *Poor Theatre*, 210.
30 Ibid., 43.

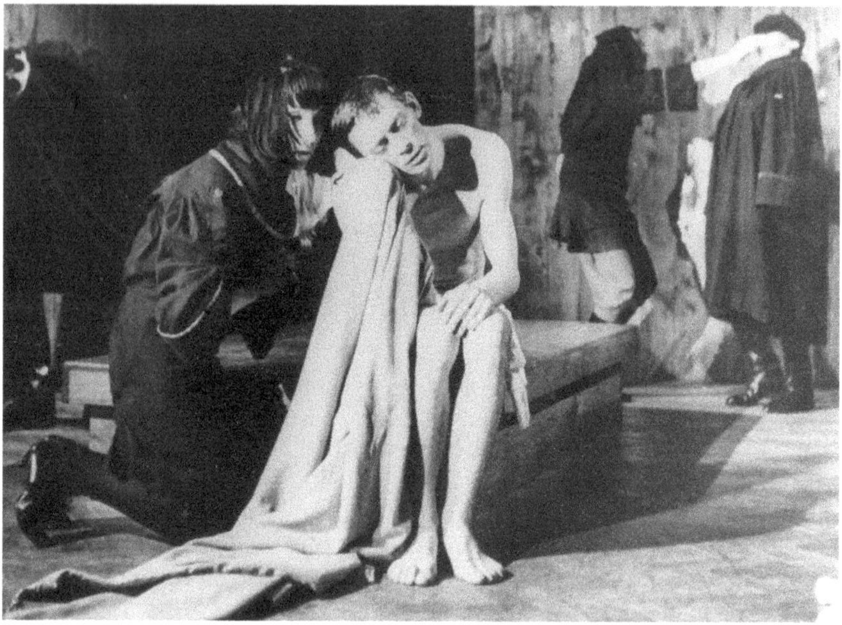

Figure 4.1 The Constant Prince, Wrocław 1965, Rena Mirecka and Ryszard Cieślak
Source: Photograph: Wincenty Kowalski. www.grotowski.net/en/media/galleries/constant-prince-wroclaw-1965-01. Reproduced with permission, under licence.

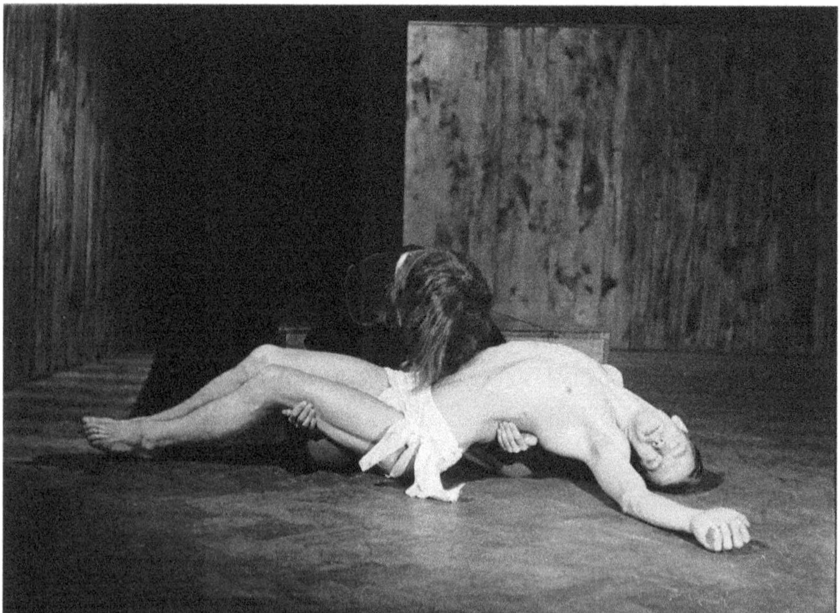

Figure 4.2 The Constant Prince, Wrocław 1965, Maja Komorowska and Ryszard Cieślak
Source: Photograph: Wincenty Kowalski. www.grotowski.net/en/media/galleries/constant-prince-wroclaw-1965-02. Reproduced with permission, under licence.

That'll look something like the fall of her hair, or absent hair, the fall of her head, which triggers her move.

When we look at these images, we see something, raw and despairing held in the body,[31] out of which we have to respond, unless there is something that we want to avoid, or where we have no inclination to accept our own humanity and those of others. These impulses aren't a form of everydayness, and not a form of impulsiveness (though there is something of impulsiveness that holds this bodily). Grotowski names this sign a human reaction that is a clear and pure impulse, registered in the extraordinary. He doesn't intend or want his actors to be natural or naturalistic, but in a move not far from Artaud's flames, that in moments, of terror, joy, danger, a person doesn't behave naturally.[32] Slowiak and Custo suggest that Grotowski was trying to differentiate between what's natural, organic, and primal, as opposed to what's quotidian, the latter what he wants to avoid and the former exactly what he wants in his actors.[33]

Poor theatre 'is capable of challenge itself and its audience *by violating accepted stereotypes of vision, feeling and judgement – more jarring because it is imagined in the human organism's breath, body and inner impulses*' (emphasis mine).[34] It requires what Grotowski calls 'warm openness',[35] based on 'human interest … on a feeling of sympathy, a feeling of acceptance',[36] in relation to both actor and spectator. That breath, body and inner impulses goes to the core of our being, and in registering the challenge through the actors and the confrontation of myth and archetype generated through the challenge of expectation (of text and of the expectation of its appearance), Grotowski wants us to question those stereotypes of vision, feeling and judgement. The 'poor theatre' is a theatre of bravery that is demands that we, as spectator, turn expectation back onto ourselves. Grotowski demands that we move beyond the surface into a receptivity *through* another, *to be aware of self and beyond self.* Grotowski's spectator 'undergoes an endless process of self-development, whose unrest is not general but directed towards a search for the truth about himself and his mission in life'.[37] And this is what's at the core of poor theatre, and through it, theatrical jurisprudence.

Work on the body is one part of Grotowski's theatre practice. His work with text is another, adopting techniques that fragment, disrupt and reimagine classical theatre texts, such as in the extraordinary and despairing *Akropolis*, where this classic of Polish theatre was retold through the dead of Auschwitz. Ludwik Flaszen accounts for the development of the play in 'Akropolis: Treatment of the Text', a chapter in *Towards a Poor Theatre*,[38] but it was Józef Szajna (1922–

31 Eugenio Barba and Ludwik Flaszen, 'A Theatre of Magic and Sacrilege', trans. Simone Sanzenbach (1965) 9.3 *The Tulane Drama Review* 166–189.

32 Slowiak and Custo, *Grotowski*, 17–18.

33 Ibid., 20.

34 Grotowski, *Poor Theatre*, 22.

35 Ibid., 47.

36 Ibid.

37 Ibid., 40.

38 Ludwik Flaszen as a Jewish child avoided murder after being sent from Poland to Uzbekistan. Flaszen is included in the group portrait of children, many of whom are Polish Jewish refugees, in a classroom in Andyzan, Uzbekistan, held in the United

2008), who designed, codirected, and functioned as a de facto dramaturg for *Akropolis* (1962),[39] and was a Polish survivor of Auschwitz (as well as of Birkenau and Buchenwald).[40] In 2016, Leszek Kolankiewicz writes of *Akropolis*' history, and its repeated performances, transformed in each version, in discussing a new film created about it, and featuring filmed excerpts from some of the original production:

> The production by Jerzy Grotowski and Józef Szajna, a survivor of KL Auschwitz, was inspired by Tadeusz Borowski's vision showing the world of concentration camps as a system where death is a mass phenomenon, but it is not demonic, rather a consequence of the operation of *a totally ordinary mechanism, governed by the laws of management and economics.* It depicted a community of inmates building their own camp and going obediently to the gas chamber at the end. The human wrecks re-enacted Biblical and Ancient Greek myths in collective hallucinations, and eventually also the myth of resurrection of the dead, i.e. the myths Wyspiański recalled in Acropolis, but mocked and desecrated in the camp's reality …[41]
>
> (My emphasis)

Just as the Laboratory Theatre's performance contained Wyspiański's self-commentary on his own play, the remix will include a self-commentary by Ludwik Flaszen, literary director at the Laboratory Theatre. On top of that, Flaszen will appear in it himself, remixing his own confessions of a Jewish survivor.

Grotowski's work with text, as accounted for in *Towards a Poor Theatre*, is that of excavation rather than interpretation, a practice that involves moving beyond the limits of text and reordering it through a practice of montage, bringing in a range of sources, along with the lived experience of the actor, to modify and recreate the text, a technique that would also be essential to his work on bringing actor and spectator together, through the practice of confrontation with myth and archetype. An absence of shared myth or archetype might become legible if brought to the surface through the bodies of actor and spectator, becoming perceptible by speaking *to* the now. Grotowski called this an act of transgression,[42] a mode of provocation that would lead to the fulfilment of the

States Holocaust Museum: https://www.ushmm.org/search/results/?q=ludwik+flaszen, accessed 7 December 2017.

39 Allen J Kuharski, *Voices from Within: Grotowski's Polish Collaborators* edited by Paul Allain and Grzegorz Ziółkowski, and 'Acting with Grotowski: Theatre as a Field for Experiencing Life' by Zbigniew Cynkutis' (2017) 61.4 (T236) *TDR: The Drama Review* 180–183. Kurashki notes that though not a full-time company member, Szajna was an early and influential supporter of the Laboratory Theatre in Opole, and was fully credited as cocreator with Grotowski on all five versions of *Akropolis* mounted between 1962 and 1967.

40 Ibid. 'The visual dramaturgy of the production was of a piece with his other work more than with the subsequent productions of the Polish Lab … a crucial reminder that the performance practice casually ascribed to 'Grotowski' included such shared visual/spatial thinking around significant dramaturgical content'. 181–182.

41 Kolankiewicz, *Rhizome.*

42 Grotowski, *Poor Theatre*, 19.

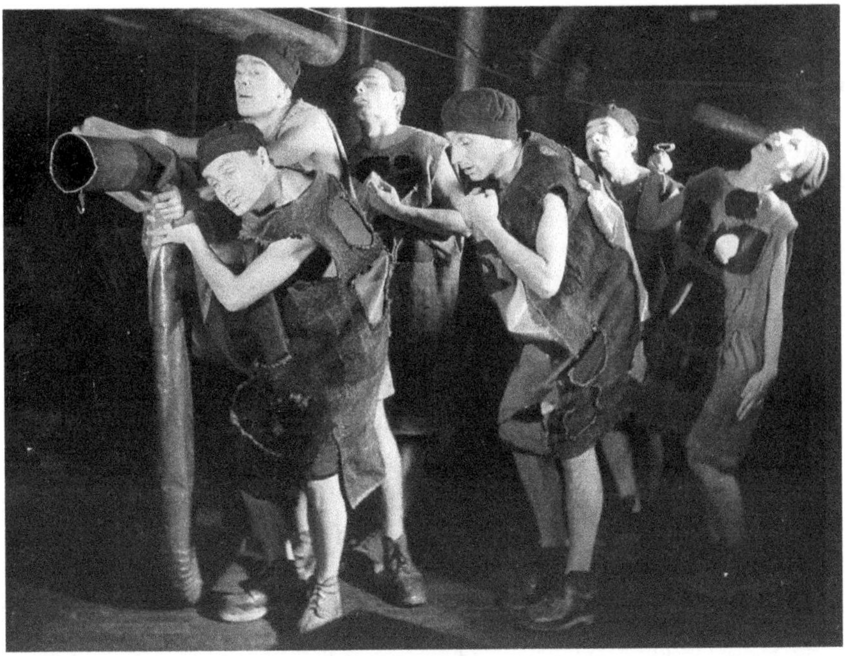

Figure 4.3 *Akropolis Version III*, Opole 1964, Zygmunt Molik, Ryszard Cieślak, Mieczysław Janowski, Andrzej Bielski, Gaston Kulig and Rena Mirecka

Source: Photograph: Laboratory Theatre/The Grotowski Institute Archive. www.grotowski.net/en/media/galleries/akropolis-opole-1964-nr-inw352. Reproduced with permission, under licence.

self. A mere display or identification with the story would be unable to register any effective response in the spectator, or indeed in the actor. Instead, Grotowski got his actors to confront their response to the myth, and embody that confrontation, which would then, in the absence of a common belief system, allow the actor and spectator to share and experience 'some universal truth' in the myth, or indeed to challenge the myth, as accounted for in the chapter called 'The Theatre's New Testament':[43]

> Every classical performance is like looking at oneself in a mirror, at our ideas and traditions, and not merely a description of what men of past ages thought and felt. Every performance built on a contemporary theatre is an encounter between the superficial traits of the present day and its deep roots and hidden motives … it is a sincere and absolute search into our historical ego; it is realistic because it is an excess of truth; it is social because it is a challenge to the social being, the spectator.[44]

43 Ibid., 59.
44 Ibid., 52–53.

Associated with this practice is his adoption of the term blasphemy, through which he sought to challenge ingrained traditions against one's own experiences, which are in turn determined by the collective experience of the time. This would expose 'secrets' deeply held, even if that runs counter to the stories retold. Slowiak and Custo use the example of the dissonance between the myth of the American soldier as hero and liberator, against the reality that not all are, meaning the truth is more complex than the myth, even though it's based in reality too. Through blasphemy, the actor provokes a response in the spectator that allows us to reconsider our roots and stories or myths and accept sharing the shame or blame.[45]

Grotowski didn't just train the body, or work on the self for its own sake. In 'The Theatre's New Testament', he insists that a broad training of actors is needed, beginning in childhood, to continue and develop throughout their lives, as part of their practice and not for the sake of embellishment, and:

> ought to receive an adequate humanistic education, aimed not at imparting an ample knowledge of literature, the history of theatre and so on, but *at awakening his sensibility* and introducing him to the most simulating phenomena of world culture … [and] would continue his studies in the fields of literature, painting, philosophy etc, to a degree necessary in his profession and not in order to be able to shine in snobbish society.[46]
>
> (My emphasis)

Towards a theatrical jurisprudence?

This very brief traverse through the first phase of Grotowski's work in Theatre of Productions can't and doesn't attempt to cover every facet of his work. Rather, what's been extracted are those elements that offer something of a jurisprudence. In briefly tracing the features of Grotowski's work during Theatre of Productions, accounted for in *Towards a Poor Theatre*, some words and concepts immediately jump out as reading jurisprudentially, that is, as a practice of prudence. Along with the response and responsibility bound up in the holy actor and presence, revealed through *via negativa*, it's the means by which text, in law, can be read, transformed and brought back into time and place, and re-read through now and then, that is the mark of Grotowskian blasphemy, that brings this to bear, as a moral theatre, out of which Grotowski's influence on theatrical jurisprudence can be traced to these five points:

- Classical play text and the possibility of montage – as excavation of law, its principles, doctrines and cases, in particular drawing on the technique of montage that can be drawn upon through externalities to both break into and elucidate law as dramaturgical.

45 Slowiak and Custo, *Grotowski*, 66.
46 Grotowski, *Poor Theatre*, 51.

- Confrontation and transgression – to bring myth and archetype into the present, as a restoration of long-standing and deep concepts lost through the technocratic, as a restoration of injustice as 'mirror' rather than as times past, exemplified by Szajna's dramaturgy of Auschwitz and as the 'operation of a totally ordinary mechanism, governed by the laws of management and economics'.[47]
- Encounter and impulse – a depth of awareness of legal text and in the humanity (and its artefacts) that produces a legal self who works to understand the factors that trigger herself or himself to notice, largely shaped in and beyond himself or herself, in order to notice injustice in the law. What Szajna or Flaszen would know and notice because of the injustices directed to them couldn't be known by others, but what they can do is find the means by which we, now, can notice, as impulse.
- The holy actor – her self-sacrifice reordered within the holy lawyer, who becomes an amalgam of spectator and actor, uniting consciousness and instinct, and mind and body, challenging stereotype by bringing the warm breath of connection into law that must be formed through the depth of knowledge and awareness beyond law.
    * This amalgam of actor and spectator conjoins through the interaction with the texts of law, of then and of now. Grotowski's spectator reacts, responds, is challenged, engaged.
    * The actor is the source of this response, who confronts the myths of law, the breaks into law's dramatic pretence.
- The poor theatre – as a law that neutralises game and strategy, as a law of response and responsibility.

Grotowski's work suffuses the theatrical antonyms, and some of the antonyms, particularly transgression, could only have emanated from Grotowski. Otherwise these five points are littered throughout this book. Some examples, such as the challenge to AI law and law as the TSST, which through Grotowski, become nothing other than 'those totally ordinary mechanisms governed by the laws of management and economics', reveal a law so dissociated from humanity that it's unaware of its consequences, and inevitably produces the loss of humanity in those who operationalise it. Bringing its dangers back to the present through the past is Grotowski's means by which we hold the mirror back up to ourselves. Transgression and confrontation have been deployed to reveal who the reasonable man really was, generated through montage bringing in the circumstances surrounding *Vaughan v Menlove* that bring that case from 1837 back to now, not only for the sake of restoring something of the past, but to turn this back to ourselves, to ask what we've lost in law through the elimination of prudence from law. And in Thomas Talfourd, we have all the features of the holy lawyer, turning back to the lifeworlds of this lawyer and judge whose life reveals something of the memory of

47 Kolankiewicz, *Rhizome*.

a denied place in the polity, which I'll turn to in Chapter 6. But you might have noticed something about his demeanour and manner already that speaks to the Grotowskian.

Bringing this all to bear, I now experiment through writing (as a poor proxy for a Grotowskian theatre), that breaks completely with the conventions of academic writing to offer a bridge to the final brief chapters of this book. These words are artless, written in 2016 or 2017, and more or less appear in the form in which they were generated when I first attempted to put something of theatrical jurisprudence onto paper (or screen), trying to workshop how Grotowski might be used to ground these concepts. The problem is that I can do these, show them, reveal them, bring them into a room with people, but its writing is something else again. That there've been so many interruptions along the way make this an artefact, of sorts, revealing that more or less after this book has been finished, I've not shifted too much from where this had begun, the five points listed above having already been in the text in one form or another. What the point of this is, is that without even remembering much of Grotowski's work when I first turned back to it, it had already written itself into my body as memory. I don't, now, try to explain what follows …

Times past

The slim book sits in a document holder, its pages akimbo, now marked and stained with age, its black spine broken and battered. A paperback, it has a slight tang to it, having spent decades hidden away in a box. It is a book I own, but its precise provenance is slightly hazy. It must have been purchased in 1985 or perhaps 1986, but its price tag, still firmly attached to its back cover, reveals that it was no small thing to acquire, costing the then princely sum for a book in Australia at the time, of $20.50. Each turn of the page is now a struggle, as it was then, for this book has been disintegrating from the time it was first used, all those years ago. Ordinarily, it would seem sensible to replace the book, but it's precious, for it holds orphan traces of its past in the form of annotations in pen on just a few pages – words like 'Artaud', 'myth', a few bracket marks – along with a few pages with corners upturned to remind and reiterate. The words are in a younger version of my hand, and were most likely triggered through promptings in a seminar, sometime in 1985 or 1986.

But away from these pages, in another part of the book, are other words, in a very different version of my hand, that are not from this time, and whose provenance is also hazy. These other annotations are located in an entirely different portion of the book, and their orthography eccentric. At the header are three words: 'Law insists on'. Further down the page are a set of words that are placed above and below two lines of print. An interview given in 1964 by Grotowski, 'The Theatre's New Testament', is now a series of pages dislodging rapidly from the disintegrating binding. In 1985 or 1986, these pages had remained unturned, but there is an annotation that presses onto the page differently. In my hand it says '*Law insists on … Text + Script … Loses The Actor/Spect/or*'. The first words head the page, but the second set surrounds a question that Grotowski is asked, of which part of his answer is reproduced above: 'Is the "holy actor" not a dream? The road to holiness is not open to everyone. Only the chosen few can follow it'.

At some point, this artefact will fail as a book.

It will be tempting to throw away the remnant pages with its orphan marks because it is perfectly possible to find its content through other means. Yet this particular artefact, my copy of the book, its disintegrating paper, it notes and marks and twisted marks on its edges matters; for now, the living artefact needs to speak, just a little longer.

The first time I opened it, I knew that this was an important book, and that its subject was revered. Its pages opened with some brief opening remarks by Peter Brook, one of the most famous theatre directors of all time, whose pathbreaking production of *A Midsummer Night's Dream* in 1970 stunningly rewrote the interplay between text and production. There was something of a strained compatriotism on my part, for the book recorded the work of a Polish theatre director. Poland mattered to me in ways that were irrelevant for most of us who now had this book, but otherwise the book remained closed, in more ways than one. There must have only been a scant ten pages that I know I read at the time, that would inevitably have been required reading. Whether I actually read the pages in advance of the seminar it was set for is anyone's guess, but there is a record that I opened the book and turned the pages of a an essay called 'Towards a Poor Theatre', a statement of principles, a manifesto and philosophy of theatre as conceived and practised by Jerzy Grotowski. The record in the form of the marks and annotations was most likely made in the seminar.

The turned ends of the pages are harder to place, and they, and some other marks in the pages matter, for the project that the book will trigger. Their instability is something that matters too, in ways that might seem surprising.

All those years ago, Grotowski was difficult, too Catholic, too mystical, and constantly changing his methods, techniques and practices. Read again as jurisprudent, in the process attempting to work through theatre theory as jurisprudence, Grotowski becomes something entirely different. This was a paradox: this book, published in 1968 and documenting work that had begun in the 1950s, marked an end to the first phase of his work, which he'd stopped pursuing nearly 20 years before I was first introduced to his work in this book, *Towards a Poor Theatre*, bearing the same name as the opening essay that recorded a significant point in the development of theatre theory, though this living theorist and practitioner had moved into new work.

What somehow hadn't registered at the time was that the collection was a friable remnant, literally and figuratively, and its publication in English in 1968 would mark the end of this phase of his work, which would only survive into the next year. Grotowski would move onto the next phase of his theatre experiments, a series of phases and stages of research, now mostly beyond a theatre space. What was both good and bad was that the collection could only be a trace of a practice that had evolved by the time I first encountered Grotowski, in 1985 or 1986. I recall, all these years later, that there was no lack of acknowledgment that Grotowski's work was ongoing, but this book, and more particularly the short 10-page essay, stood as essential. Reading this essay as part of a seminar in a postgraduate degree in theatre studies, the pull of the text, and the call to interpretation of words on the page was irresistible, and incongruous, for Grotowski resisted words, was wary of writing, of committing to paper, of recording his work in this way, preferring instead to pass on his work, physically, through his disciples and students, his collaborators and apprentices. It was as if the capture of an *oeuvre* would paralyse and fossilise a lived and living work; and the next year, in 1969, Grotowski put an end to this first phase of his work, later to be known as Theatre of Productions, a little over ten years after it began.

That I would ever think of his work again, or even more surprisingly, choose to hold onto my copy of this book, is serendipity. Theatre was put away in a box, literally and figuratively, when I began a law degree a few years after completing that postgrad theatre degree, but now my battered old copy, that falls to pieces at the barest movement, matters for a book that falls into a series interrogating law, space and materiality.

This brief fashioning of a time, place, encounter and, inevitably, a sense of disquiet that comes from a story disrupted, a formal textual expectation that remains unmet, offers a dumbshow of sorts that marks out the contours, such as they are, of a disruptive jurisprudence, one that requires of the jurisprudent an embodied responsibility.

My return to these mouldering papers, and the reveries they trigger, along with the personal nature of this encounter, is that which matters for a theatrical jurisprudence, a response and responsiveness, as responsibility – to law, and through the theatrical, to the self who is to live and operationalise that responsibility. It offers a means by which law might be rethought, returning law to an awareness of its humanity, and its responsibilities beyond time. As law shifts into the algorithmic and a relentless push to a base formalisation, Grotowski's work seems jurisprudential, reminding us that law is of time, place and self, and it's impossible for us to do law well without a formed awareness beyond the self in order to manifest that responsibility, to notice what's in law and beyond it, and how this affects our interpretative universe.

Strangely, the artefact and its story matters, a transformation effected through the passage of time when it had been hidden away between its first use and its later recovery, in a box marked 'theatre theory'. For anyone else it's neither here nor there that it is an original US edition, first published in 1968 by Simon and Schuster, but it matters for this work that it's this artefact and no other, even though the text was accessible in libraries or online. Though I'd perused, browsed, and scrolled through these other versions of my book when I began to think of the theatrical as jurisprudence, but they didn't look or feel right. I needed this *particular* artefact; I've now realised that it isn't a prop, but it's functioning as my interlocutor, not as a talisman, but as a means of interaction and response. My dissatisfaction with the English, Methuen edition, and the new second edition surprised me, a text being a text being a text, after all.

But returning to it so many years after it was first used in such a different way from its first use is a little strange, not least the near impossibility I've had in generating an understanding that theatre isn't a proxy for trials and that it could have something to say for jurisprudence. It hadn't quite happened yet in 2010, when I co-edited a special issue of *Law Text Culture* with Sophie Nield, called 'Law's Theatrical Presence', but started to form quite clearly two years later.

Sometime in the interim, between then and now, I've lifted the lid from the box the book lay in, not even daring to hope that I hadn't thrown it out or given it to someone else. My relief, and joy, was palpable, and not a little surprising and ironic. For in thinking a theatrical jurisprudence, there was no possibility that any other version or edition might conjure and shape the jurisprudential inspired by Grotowski. It had to come from a past, rather than from a present, it had to speak beyond its time and place. Now returning to a something from my past, and particularly the theatre theorist and practitioner, who I wasn't just ambivalent about but ignored as much as I could at the time, now offered something so much more to me now, as jurisprudent. Now, all those years later, a tiny flutter stirs the possibility, in spite of myself, that Grotowski, and the accounts of theatrical responsibility contained in *Towards a Poor Theatre*, might be the link, the theatre theory and practice that I needed to work with to ground a nascent theatrical jurisprudence.

And so my joy when my falling to pieces book was still there, in that box, so many years after it was put there, its pages ushering back into the view the people who shared that mosquito filled room in a Nissen hut in a hidden corner of UNSW, a building long since gone, and the MA in Theatre Studies, then brand new, also long gone. And then I remember something from that room, which is why the artefact mattered. We watched Grotowski at work with his actors, on film, on a screen pulled up to the side of the room. It was the bodies I'd remembered. In a sense now it wasn't surprising that I knew I needed to work with Grotowski for this jurisprudence. What had been etched into the score that would form the deeply inscribed impulse was the body. The work I did that I loved at the time was based in the body, from the Sydney Dance Company, to the Australian Dance Theatre, and back to the inspiration they obtained from Pina Bausch's dance theatre, Wuppertal Tanztheater. So this is why the artefact matters, because it restores this moment, generating encounter, now lucid and suffusing my being. This wasn't the written Grotowski I'd remembered but its bodily manifestation, albeit in black and white, albeit on a screen. This is what registered, the movements of the poor theatre revealing something much later as theatrical jurisprudence.

In returning to the book, it was now apparent why. Grotowski insisted that the body would speak. It is that speaking body, and what it must do for text and interpretation that held this jurisprudence.

You will have expected that these madeleine-like reveries, triggered by this disintegrating artefact, to have a point. They do, in law's refusal to countenance the possibility that these moments function only as they exist in any given point in time. Moments are required to become sensible, but in order to become so, they are written and rewritten through *an ex post facto* imposition of a *predetermined* narrative coherence, where they are filtered and framed by law's desire to see a beginning, middle and end. Word becomes law, which imprisons the random moments of human existence in a moment of creation.

So in Grotowski attempting to deal with the demons of the twentieth century, it now becomes clear that his work might offer something for a different kind of jurisprudence that also attempts to respond to the challenges law faces in the twenty-first century. In recovering a book 20 years after it was first entombed in 1989, there was no small irony that it mattered so much to find this artefact, and no less to acknowledge that this particular theatre theorist would offer the starting point of a theatrical jurisprudence. To recover this book with joy was an even greater surprise. I had already discarded the use of Brecht, Meyerhold, Stanislavsky and the canonical theatre practitioner theorists to shape thinking about theatrical jurisprudence. That left Grotowski, who I wanted to continue avoiding, until there was really no other choice, because if I wanted to think through theatrical jurisprudence, there was really no one else, including the more recent theatre practitioners like Augusto Boal. Grotowski's work spoke to this kind of jurisprudence of response and responsibility that mattered, and it was this early aspect of the work that would help. And that left Grotowski.

The short bursts of writing in *Towards a Poor Theatre* mean that concepts are compressed, but come to think of it, Aristotle doesn't deploy too much in the way of citation or depth of analysis. But it's the pages upon pages of photographs, more than 30 black-and-white photographs of the key productions that marked this first phase of his work, that speak through time, or more particularly, the bodies captured in those photographs that speak to us, and make us respond.

As remnants of being, a material presence captures the ineluctable embodiment that is Grotowski's work. But *Towards a Theatrical Jurisprudence* can't turn away from its bookness, though I will try to replicate those incredible images and the life they hold in them, albeit in black and white, and albeit through words.

Another leaf dislodges from my copy of the book.

The physical book was already falling to pieces then, in the rare moments that I turned its pages, its American glue holding American paper and card perishing and retreating.

Maybe it was meant to happen.

More than half the book is now in pieces, scattered and out of order. I've made a copy because there's no possibility of it holding together anymore, and before long, this new artefact is looking the worse for wear, those original markings and annotations, and the next ones now overwhelmed with more and more asterisks and underlinings, and highlighting pens of different hues, to revive what's in those pages, written somewhere else, that records work that I couldn't have known when it was taking shape, but which is present and palpable. I want to do this with law, out of time, too, and have already done some of this work, bringing then to now, as present. Grotowski has this covered too, and I realise I must have absorbed this also, all those years before.

Grotowski saw the actor's deepest calling as 'an emergence from oneself'; a discarding of the masks that we use in everyday life to reveal what it really means to be alive. Deeply influenced by Eastern philosophy, he viewed the theatre as a spiritual realm – a place where the body should be used to reveal the soul. Grotowski's importance is that we need to look at ourselves, who we are, how responsibility is shaped, and to offer to law a way to *notice*.

And this is why the theatrical is so important. It asks us to look up and outside ourselves, and our expectations, prejudices and presumptions. It asks us to pay attention to time and place, and through time and place, to notice what is wrong with the law we inherit, materially. This insistence on the material – the self, the world around us, the law that lives in the world – is far from unique, but it is how that is made manifest that matters. For the theatrical insists that we notice through being placed in a position where we not only notice but are forced to respond and react, to learn, to be traumatised, to be profoundly challenged, not intellectually or rationally (or solely so) but to acquire something of that imagination and experience needed to notice when law goes wrong. We simply can't notice what it is that we have never lived, either literally or by analogy. That isn't to say that having lived something will always work to make lawyers notice. That isn't the case at all. There has to also be a recognition beyond the self. That's why the claims that the broadening of law to individuals and groups previously unable to become lawyers doesn't always produce a linear, hypodermic corrective to injustice. For there is so much more to understanding how we notice and what makes us notice, and that is the formation of the self, and the interrogation of the self that is an essential component of shaping a theatrical jurisprudence, in particular one grounded in the work of Jerzy Grotowski, and his deeply grounded forms of training required of his actors, and too, through them, of his spectators.

It is not for nothing, then, that Grotowski's theatre makes demands, on its creators, on its audiences, and on the social order in which it functions. Theatre has, at least since the latter part of the nineteenth century, been at the forefront, the *avant garde*, at the cusp of change. Theatre of this kind hovers at the margins, and sits on the edge of danger, for theatre is able to ignite, challenge, and ask its audience to pay attention to, and notice when something, anything, has gone wrong. In turn, its participants find themselves endangered, for theatre functions as a site of bravery, and of challenge. It does this as a signal *par excellence* in times of danger and during periods of turmoil, and theatrical jurisprudence, too, must function at the edge, to ask lawyers to notice and pay attention and *to become aware*. And on yet another point of significant rupture, there is something else to be taken from his work – bravery in the face of tremendous and intense political pressure that is inevitably invested in a jurisprudence dependent on his insights.

This inchoate reminder of bravery adds something further to the original conception behind theatrical jurisprudence, which asks that lawyers to understand something of the lifeworld that inhabits law, and that asks that the legal self and its formation be developed beyond the limits of a bare law. To think of this, too, as a jurisprudence of bravery, is something that matters for law more than ever on the cusp of the third decade of the twenty-first century, and if dismissed and traduced as nostalgia, and hence treated as an irrelevancy, it opens the door wide to the repetition of the past and its inhumanity, over and over and over again.

5 The encounter

> The sight of the little madeleine had recalled nothing to my mind before I tasted it.
> (Proust, *À la recherche du temps perdu*)

Being there

Maks del Mar responds to the words I utter.[1] I'm not surprised, but then again, I am. I say 'You were too young, Maks', and move on.

It's June 2018, and we are in a room with thirty or so people in London, at a conference of contributors to a collection on Law and the Humanities, of which he, Maks, is editor, along with Bernie Meyler of Stanford and Simon Stern of Toronto. We are in Maks' home institution, Queen Mary College, University of London, though Maks is, like me, Australian. We also hail from the same state and city, though barely know one another. Maks is also many years younger than me, hence those words, 'You were too young, Maks'. The other participants must have wondered about this brief exchange, but I continued reading from my paper, leaving why I spoke those words to Maks unexplained and open.

This moment was triggered by my mention of a satirical musical that had opened in our home state in 2017, its subject an infamous right wing premier (the state's political leader) Johannes Bjelke-Petersen, who'd held power from the early 1970s until the late 1980s. A neat dramaturgical device brought 2017 into connection with the late 1970s in the shape of the then new president of the United States of America, whose similarities with this now long dead, unknown politician from the other side of the world were striking, at least for those of us who remembered, as this critic did:

> For Queenslanders of a certain age, there is so much about the rise of Donald Trump that seems eerily familiar. For 19 years, his prehistoric ancestor ruled the swamps of Australia's deep north – a hillbilly dictator who beat up protesters and confounded the media with complete gibberish while a dark web

1 Maks del Mar very generously agreed to my including an account of this encounter in this book and of the discussions afterwards, per email 27 November 2018.

> of corruption flourished behind him … These days, it's getting harder to convince people who weren't there that certain things actually happened, such as police being sent to university campuses on pre-dawn raids to rip condom-vending machines from toilet walls in 1987.[2]

While I was reading these words, Maks leant forward. He smiled. I said: 'You were too young, Maks'.

I asked Maks the next day if he knew why I had said these words to him. He had no idea that he'd responded like this, or that this was what had triggered my otherwise unfathomable interjection. It has to be said that there was very little in this presentation designed to generate responsiveness. My voice was flat, even in my retort to Maks, I spoke rapidly, my eye contact was sparse, and breaks from the words on the page were minimal, the whole thing barely differing from a private read, revealing just what is at stake in the presence or absence of experience.[3]

My retort was on display to everyone in the room, who must have wondered just what provoked it. For whatever stories Maks had heard, even from those close to the events, nothing could replace being there. Eventually, the Premier's own colleagues forced him from office in 1987 because of corruption, but this, along with a failed attempted prosecution for corruption in public office, and the condom vending machine bans,[4] would be retold for years. What had become more or less forgotten, though, was the banning of street march protests in the late 1970s, and the role of the later disbanded Special Branch, an arm of the police that had become actively engaged in political interventions;[5] law too was complicit in refusing to consider political interventions into police brutality.[6] The street march ban had earlier antecedents, but it began proper in 1977, prompting challenges to the law and its application in the form of street marches. An 18-year-old second year arts student at the University of Queensland, and a demi-participant at best, I found myself being photographed by a vast special branch officer, my threat to order evidenced by my sitting on the ground in the main square of the

2 Marett Leiboff, 'Challenging the Legal Self through Performance', in Simon Stern, Bernadette Meyler, and Maksymilian Del Mar (eds), *Oxford Handbook of Law and the Humanities* (Oxford: Oxford University Press 2019), Chapter 17, citing Andrew Stafford, 'By Joh, it could be Trump! Musical satire delves into Bjelke-Petersen's reign', *The Guardian*, 8 July 2017. https://www.theguardian.com/stage/2017/jul/08/by-joh-it-could-be-trump-musical-satire-delves-into-bjelke-petersens-reign

3 Leiboff, 'DITTO'.

4 A condom vending machine ripped from the University of Queensland Refectory is now held as an item in a collection in the State Museum. These were removed from other universities in Queensland as well: www.collections.qm.qld.gov.au/search.do?view=detail&page=1&id=1519258&db=object

5 Daniel Hurst, 'Inside Queensland's Spy Unit', *The Brisbane Times*, 7 April 2010. https://www.brisbanetimes.com.au/national/queensland/inside-queenslands-spy-unit-20100406-rpbg.html

6 *R v Bjelke-Petersen, Ex Parte Plunkett* [1978] QdR 305. See Frank Brennan, 'Case Note: *R v Bjelke-Petersen and Another, Ex Parte Plunkett*' (1979) 12 *Melbourne University Law Review* 284–291.

city, accompanied by a bag full of library books. Not wanting to miss my art history class, I took the bus into the city from the university, some kilometres away, watching the march as the bus passed by. On its arrival into the city, all hell broke loose, ushering in an era marked by the arrests of thousands over the next few years, the mere step or push onto the street into the so-called 'valley of death' from the safety of the main city square meaning certain arrest along with the application of unusual force, captured by television news crews,[7] until they too were threatened with the law to prevent the capture of evidence (remembering this was years before mobile phones).

University students and academics were a special target of the Premier.[8] Walter Sofronoff QC, who'd graduated from this same university in 1976, and was admitted to the Queensland Bar in 1977, was to remark to current day law students on the eve of his appointment as President of the Queensland Court of Appeal in 2017 that:

> In 1977 it was a law student (not me, although I wish it had been) who initiated a private prosecution against the Premier of Queensland alleging a conspiracy to pervert the course of justice. He lost the case, he could hardly have won it, but he won the point ...[9]

Maks could only know these things second hand, yet he held these events and their experience close enough to respond bodily, something that wasn't open to anyone else in the room, though curious and interested. Only he could, in this briefest of moments, register something of Grotowskian confrontation and transgression, told in the two physical responses he made: his movement forward and his smile. Maks' bodily response registered that he was able to *notice*, as impulses that preceded and initiated his physical actions,[10] and through them brought encounter, as a mode of responsiveness, into effect.[11] As Grotowski's actor Cieślak reminds us, as noted earlier, 'it is not that the body remembers, but that the *body itself is memory*'.[12]

7 Brennan, 'Case Note', 284–285.
8 'Bjelke Bitter Beer Ad – Queensland Uni Revue 1977' satirises the government and its overt fascist tendencies, using a song from then contemporary musical film about Nazi-era Germany, *Cabaret*, 'Tomorrow Belongs to Me': https://www.youtube.com/watch?v=dX9bwamb1Ls, accessed 14 January 2014. Because Australia's federal compact permits movement between jurisdictions freely, many individuals affected by the street march laws, which led to employment bans and the like, moved to other states in Australia. A considerable number returned at the end of the 1980s and early 1990s.
9 Walter Sofronoff, 'Law, Liberties and Rights: Foreword by Walter Sofronoff QC', *Justice and the Law Society (JATL) Blog*, 6 April 2017. www.jatl.org/blog/foreword. In 1995, I worked at the Litigation Reform Commission, Queensland. Sofronoff QC was a member of one of its committees, and I knew him in this context, by way of disclosure.
10 Salata, *Unwritten Grotowski*, 217.
11 Grotowski, *Poor Theatre*, 41.
12 Cited in Laster, 'Embodied Memory', 214.

So too Sofronoff QC, the son of Russian refugees, who turns to the body and to instinct to ground obligations and commitments to law, but using *law and its institutions as cypher*. Like most lawyers of the late twentieth century and early twenty-first, he is inured to the practices of positivism and the presumptions of the analytical to the point that the world aside from law *is reordered as law*. But like all lawyers who try to narrate or account for law within the confines and logics of law, he finds himself stepping outside of its strictures. He recounts a visit to Russia in 1991, where he was rebuked by friends for stepping onto grass, which puzzled him, given the absence of signs to the contrary:

> There, in a brief and otherwise inconsequential human interaction evoking the entirely spontaneous and otherwise mundane reactions of the people involved, is a demonstration of the visceral state of belief of two sets of people brought up within two distinct sets of culture, tradition and history. A lesson in constitutional law as a part of the make-up of a human being.[13]

The body holds law, viscerally, for Sofronoff; law must be protected and defended too, viscerally, in a call to arms against those who endanger it:

> People like these draw strength when they misbehave from the timidity and apathy of lawyers who seek a quiet life but who ought instead be reacting with zealous rage ... [and] for those of us whose lives are lived around or within the institutions of the law, particularly lawyers, *to react with loud outrage* whenever we sense any intrusion upon our precious ways of life.[14]
>
> (My emphasis)

As if regretting his failure to act in 1977, Sofronoff QC moved with what could only be read as zealous rage, loudly and with outrage, over the conduct of the political inheritors of the Bjelke-Petersen regime in 2014, when he resigned from the position of Solicitor-General,[15] which he'd held since 2005. After a series of incidents, the one that provoked him in the end was the young Attorney-General's defamation of the then President of the Court of Appeal and her husband. Sofronoff wrote an explosive letter to the local newspaper, denouncing this conduct concluding that: 'Queensland deserves much, much better from its first law officer. And, what is most unfortunate, his conduct has the hint of a nasty schoolboy's snicker in it.'[16] There were too many

13 Sofronoff, 'Law, Liberties and Rights'.

14 Ibid.

15 This is not a political position. The Solicitor-General is the second law officer of the jurisdiction, whose role is to appear as Counsel of that jurisdiction, and appears for that jurisdiction in appellate courts and on constitutional matters in the High Court. The Solicitor-General advices and is given instructions by the first law officer, the politician who is Attorney-General.

16 Walter Sofronoff, 'Opinion: Attorney-General Jarrod Bleijie's crisis of confidence' *The Courier-Mail*, 25 March 2014. https://www.couriermail.com.au/news/opinion/opinion-attorneygeneral-jarrod-bleijies-crisis-of-confidence/news-story/c56b6ffe68661a85e25109950a804d60

echoes of this government's antecedent of the 1970s and 1980s,[17] and it was ejected from office soon after, the memory remaining strong within the polity, of the kind that brought Maks to attention a few years later.

Aside from his the opening frolic on the Russian grass, Sofronoff QC otherwise omits anything of the detail or circumstances that ground the abstract forms of action he advocates or describes in this blog. Nothing connects his advice that 'any person who feels compelled merely to write a letter to a media outlet, by a sense that an important public principle has been violated,'[18] to his own spectacular letter (written to a media outlet) and its ripples way beyond its immediate target.[19] It is magisterially understated, but its bashful silence reveals nothing of the source of this suggestion. This is the positivist temperament in action, the abstract imagined as if, or law expressed as ideals completing its task. But despite this general tenor of the blog, he does include some description of past events, including the journalists whose work led to the creation of a commission of inquiry, colloquially known as the Fitzgerald Inquiry, that somehow managed to be instigated in the state, and of the work of the lawyers who helped reveal the corruption of the Bjelke-Petersen administration and electoral system, and certain of its highest ranking police officers, as if this wouldn't be known in any real sense by readers in 2017.

But curiously, Sofronoff is vigorous in his insistence that for people other than lawyers, something more is needed: 'In the case of people on the outside of the system, like politicians with power or influence in such matters, we can add as a potential source of harm a lack of proper education or relevant experience, an absent sense of history.'[20] For lawyers though, Sofronoff is silent, demanding nothing of history or education or experience, as if law is able to generate these conditions without more. Again, this is the positivist conceit in action, the imagined belief that somehow law holds within it everything that's needed for it to manifest right thinking and as if by osmosis, an account of all forms of human conduct. That the political first law officer who'd raised his ire was a law graduate and conveyancing practitioner would as a politician require training in history and the like almost begged the question that lawyers, too, don't simply acquire what law needs through it doctrines and principles.

This position conforms to the form of judgment that took shape in Australia from the mid-twentieth century, following in the position of 'strict and complete legalism' held by the then Chief Justice of the High Court, Sir Owen Dixon. Not only archly Austinian, strict and complete legalism turned judgment into algebraic and mathematical calculability, while holding to the structure of the Aristotelian

17 Sofronoff QC was appointed to the position of Solicitor-General and of President of the Court of Appeal by the Labor Party.

18 Sofronoff, 'Law, Liberties and Rights'.

19 Gabrielle Appleby, 'Politicising Advice: A Cautionary Tale for all Governments', *The Conversation*, 25 March 2014, https://theconversation.com/politicising-advice-a-cautionary-tale-for-all-governments-24773, who remarked that 'He has now revealed his outrage at the conduct of Queensland attorney-general Jarrod Bleijie.'

20 Sofronoff, 'Law, Liberties and Rights'.

well-made play. Judgments were now a closed package, made up of an array of citational and authorising materials in the forms of statutory provisions, case law, and legal principles, while the law report in which it nestled was reduced to headnote and keywords. Earlier in that century, the law reports would include the detail of or summary of the arguments of counsel, but these were now largely gone from the record as well.[21]

This style of case now bore little relationship with the judgments of the earlier part of the twentieth century and their Victorian antecedents, which were far less positivist and analytical than narrated in the textbooks and treatises of law, in which the judges would allow prejudice and presumption to slip into view and allow us to notice what animated their reasoning.[22] For instance, in the 1938 case of *Blum v Lipski*, Mann CJ in the Victorian Supreme Court managed to include this sentence in his judgment: ‘a man and his wife arrived from Europe entirely without means. It may be noticed in passing that the immigration laws apparently presented no obstacle.’ Mrs Blum had been killed a few months after arriving and the case had nothing to do with immigration. Even Dixon J, before moving to the position of strict and complete legalism, was happy to turn to the fictional Mikado, of Gilbert and Sullivan fame, to help guide him in reasoning.[23] Law had somehow belatedly adopted the precepts of Austinian positivism, presumed as the normative condition of law, again as if these had been the standard of law of the past, following a pedigree of seeming antiquity that was of recent creation. In part this meant turning to and replicating the law as generated by the textbook and treatise writers. If there was an authority, however inapt or irrelevant for the circumstances, it would be deployed in the name of principle, or if words were legally defined, they would be applied regardless of circumstance. This was the kind of law that suffused the legal consciousness in Australia, and the way law was learnt for generations of Australian lawyers. Critical legal interventions would arrive and then be seen off as quickly as possible, leaving Australian law wedded to the mathematical and algebraic as its normative universe, though Austin might have given way to Hart and Dworkin.

What this strictly legal disposition meant was that law would prefer to turn its face against law as lived, in favour of the abstract and calculable. This preference was on display in 1996, when Sofronoff QC appeared for the Wik Peoples from the Far North of Queensland before the High Court of

21 Marett Leiboff, ‘The Good Old Rule, the Catspaw and a Two-Headed Baby’, in Daniela Carpi and Marett Leiboff (eds), *Fables of the Law: Fairy Tales in a Legal Context* (Berlin: De Gruyter, 2016), 187–208, where the law report supplements in considerable detail what’s omitted from the judgment, in the early Australian High Court judgment in *Doodeward v Spence* (1908) 6 CLR 406.

22 *Blum v Lipski* [1938] VLR 247, 248–249. Also see Marett Leiboff, ‘Theatricalising Law in Three, 1929–1939 (Brisbane)’ (2016) 20 *Law Text Culture* 93–135.

23 Leiboff, ‘The Good Old Rule’, for judgments that include the text of uncited poem and fable in the case of *Doodeward v Spence* (1908) 6 CLR 406 in each of Griffith CJ and Higgins J; see also Dixon J and his development of the Mikado rule in *Thomas v R* (1937) 59 CLR 279, drawing on the principles derived from the characters and circumstances of a light operetta.

Australia,[24] in the second most significant native title case decided in Australia. The case proceeds knowing that doctrine is heavily weighted against the Wik Peoples' claim, despite the belated discovery in the common law in *Mabo (No 2)* in 1992 that Australia hadn't been terra nullius on the arrival of Europeans. How far this changed property rights in Australia was what was at stake, but that's not how the case was opened for the Wik Peoples. Michael Kirby, who was on the bench, recalled what happened when Sofronoff QC opened the case for them:

> A hush fell on the courtroom as he approached the central podium. He did not squander that historic moment. He opened his submissions in a most unusual way. He did so by talking in word pictures. His submissions commenced, as I recall, with a vivid description of the beauty of the Wik country in the northern part of Queensland. On 1 April 1915, in that country, he said, the Wik people were going about their daily lives as they and their ancestors had done for aeons. The men were getting their bark boats ready to fish because it was a clear day. The women were sitting with the children, teaching them about their traditions. Some older children were running off into the bush. At the very same moment, in the Land Titles Registry in Brisbane, the representatives of the Mitchelton Pastoral Holding were registering a pastoral lease under the Queensland Act. In the old measurements, it laid claim to an area of 535 square miles, approximately 1385 square kilometres. Sofronoff took our minds up to the Holroyd River district. The Wik people continued to live after their traditions. They went about their daily lives, untroubled and unconcerned by the happenings under white man's law in the Land Titles Office of which they had no knowledge. They rarely came into contact with the leaseholders. A vivid picture was painted of two communities, each with legitimacy according to its own perspective and laws.[25]

I recount these words in detail for two reasons. The first is that despite this detailed judicial memory, they don't appear in the transcript, or are referred to in any of the judgments.[26] The transcript records Sofronoff's prosaic legal argument,

24 *Wik Peoples v Queensland* (1996) 187 CLR 1.

25 The Hon Justice Michael Kirby AC CMG, 'Introduction', in *The Rise (And Fall?) of the Barrister Class by the Hon Michael McHugh AC*, 5–7. www.hcourt.gov.au/assets/publications/speeches/former-justices/kirbyj/kirbyj_aug07b.pdf. McHugh also refers to Sofronoff's word picture, though deciding against the arguments for the Wik people: Hon Michael McHugh AC QC, 'Preparing and Arguing an Appeal' (2010) *Bar News* 85–92, 91.

26 Gregory J Koppenol, President Land and Resources Tribunal, 'Recent Developments in Native Title in Australia with International Perspectives', Speech delivered at the Europe-Asia Legal Conference 2002, Lake Como, Italy, 2 July 2002 [17]. http://classic.austlii.edu.au/au/journals/QldJSchol/2002/30.pdf: 'I want to tell you about the opening arguments made by … Walter Sofronoff QC who led for the plaintiffs … He went on to say that even though the government parties did not suggest that there was any inconsistency between the native title rights and the pastoral activities, they

in which Sofronoff had taken the court to the Appeal Book, along with arguments containing something of the history of nineteenth-century law in colonial Australia, including the place of the pastoral lease. There are references to the discovery by historians of dispatches in 1848 from the Secretary of State in London, Earl Grey, to the Colonial Governor of New South Wales,[27] concerning the treatment of indigenous people and their land use in the face of the pastoral lease,[28] long before Australia became an independent nation in 1901. This wasn't what was expected of legal argument, either the use of history outside of law or the generation of Grotowskian encounter through the deployment of the word images that brought the court into the lifeworlds of the Wik Peoples, and the circumstances of law.

What was at issue was whether these pastoral leases extinguished native title. Four of the seven justices held that they didn't, of whom three turned to the history and circumstances surrounding the creation of pastoral leases in order to ground their reasoning. Gaudron J delved deep into land law in colonial Australia, holding that 'It is clear that pastoral leases are not the creations of the common law ... Even if pastoral leases were devised with common law concepts in mind, they were a novel concept and there is nothing to suggest that it was necessary or convenient for them to conform precisely to the common law.' Kirby J set out the reason for their creation – the conduct of 'squatters', who simply helped themselves to land outside of settled areas of the colony of New South Wales. Beginning in the 1820s, colonial administrators attempted to regulate this conduct, creating pastoral licences for an annual fee for grazing purposes. Noting that New South Wales became self-governing in 1855, in June 1859 Queensland became a separate colony, occupying a vast area of land in the northeast of the Australian landmass. As a self-governing entity, Queensland quickly adapted the pastoral lease for its own conditions and purposes, whilst still a colony.

These three justices brought to the fore long-standing concerns about the effects of the pastoral lease on indigenous peoples dating to at least to Earl Grey's dispatch of 1848. Toohey J observed that: 'The thrust of [then] contemporary documents, in particular communications by the Secretary of State, Earl Grey, to the Governor of New South Wales make it clear that Aborigines were not to be excluded from land under pastoral occupation.' These are indictors of sympathy and of care that continued to register concern on the cusp of Australian federation:

maintained that the Wik People's native title rights should nevertheless be regarded as extinguished. By that focussed approach, I think that Sofronoff QC may have captured a majority of the Court.'

27 Ann Curthoys, Ann Genovese and Alexander Reilly, *Rights and Redemption: History, Law and Indigenous People* (Sydney: UNSW Press, 2008) 48–50.

28 Wik Peoples v State of Queensland & Ors B8/1996 [1996] HCATrans 228 (11 June 1996). www.austlii.edu.au/cgi-bin/viewdoc/au/cases/cth/HCATrans/1996/228.html, or over the next two days of argument (12–13 June).

> The authorities in England expressed almost constant concern that the grant of pastoral leases should not be used to prevent Aborigines from using the land for subsistence purposes. And a similar concern was expressed within Australia. Thus in his 1900 Annual Report the Northern Protector of Aboriginals, Walter Roth, warned against the dispossession of blacks from their hunting-grounds and sources of water supply 'by their lands being rented for grazing rights at a nominal figure'. He added:
>
> 'Carrying the present practice (might against right) to a logical conclusion, it would simply mean that, were all the land in the north to be thus leased, all the blacks would be hunted into the sea.'

Kirby J, of all the justices, sought to work with encounter, through the bringing together of past and present. There are problems, he remarks, with engaging with law out of time, with

> legal materials written in a completely different legal environment of contrary understandings and beliefs. One of the founders of the Australian Constitution, Alfred Deakin, stated that the judicial method enabled 'the past to join the future, without undue collision and strife in the present'. In this case the present must revisit the past to produce a result, wholly unexpected at the time, which will not cause undue collision and strife in future.

The joining of present and past for the future couldn't have been possible without turning to the lives and conditions of being of the past. But the possibility of moving beyond law in its accepted guise was abjured by the other majority justice, Gummow J, who refused to accept the use of history, holding onto the presumptions of strict and complete legalism:

> There remains lacking, at least in Australia, any established taxonomy to regulate such uses of history in the formulation of legal norms. Rather, lawyers have 'been bemused by the apparent continuity of their heritage into a way of thinking which inhibits historical understanding' ... Even if any such taxonomy were to be devised, it might then be said of it that it was but *a rhetorical device devised to render past reality into a form useful to legally principled resolution of present conflicts* ... The better guide must be 'the time-honoured methodology of the common law' whereby principle is developed from the issues in one case to those which arise in the next.
>
> (References omitted, my emphasis)

Law in this register is absent history because law exists as if out of time, as an imagined continuity of principle. As the instances of law recounted in this book reveal, this is an imagined narrative of law. And this is the second reason for recording the word picture recounted by Michael Kirby. As well as animating the lifeworlds of the Wik People of the past for the present, as an instance of Grotowskian encounter, Sofronoff is asking us to notice the effect of the law on the

Wik Peoples at a time they were denied agency within the polity. In doing so the law is asked to bring itself into the warm breath of connection with those lives, of the past and of now, and in doing so turns law away from the calculable into the human.[29] The practices of rhetoric, as the 'historical and practical-human character of reason and of knowledge',[30] are also the mirror that Grotowski demands of the encounter, as that action of stepping over as transgression.

The influence and effect of Sofronoff's opening submission, and what they represent would continue to reverberate, years after he made those remarks, but not all with an eye to the benefit they generated. High Court Justice Virginia Bell in 2012 turned to them to criticise the place of rhetoric in law. But unlike Gummow J she used rhetoric in the colloquial sense, as meaningless show, turning to Sofronoff's word picture in a speech to women lawyers, to whom she said that 'none of the decisions of the justices were in the least bit influenced by the poetry by which the proceedings had been outlined'.[31] Sofronoff QC wasn't the target of this statement *per se*, but rather Michael McHugh, the former High Court Justice who dissented in *Wik*, who'd published a book arguing for the return of rhetoric in advocacy: 'He bemoaned that by the 1960s the bar no longer comprised the colourful individuals that had once populated it.'[32] It was here, in his introduction to McHugh's book, that Michael Kirby recounted the word picture, along with his observation that it involved a good use of rhetoric. Conjoining rhetoric and style with legal ineptitude, and a means by which talented women were denied a place in advocacy, rhetoric was an irrelevancy in modern litigation: 'judges today prefer reason, rather than style of delivery, to dominate court proceedings. The true test of a talented barrister is their ability to distil legal principle … a skill she believes women who outperform men academically tend to exhibit.'[33]

The (re)turn to reason by and large must deny the place of life and lifeworld, bringing these remarks in line with conundrum faced by the judges in the Scottish Feminist Judgments Project, involving the dissonance between the lifeworlds of lawyers and the practices of law and its method of reasoning.[34] Whether she was aware of doing this or not, these remarks turned against the possibility of the social or historical that she had, in other speeches,[35] recognised, and that she observed, in the slightest way possible, in a case decided in 2017, to which I'll turn at the end of the chapter.

29 Sofronoff QC appears as an interviewee in *Wik vs Queensland: The Day Wik Won the Battle but Lost the War* in 2018. The film is available through some sites. https://www.wikvsqueensland.com/WIKvsQUEENSLAND_PressKit.pdf

30 Goodrich, *Legal Discourse*, 98.

31 Leanne Mezrani, 'Judge Says Bar Is No Place for Rhetoric', *Lawyers Weekly*, 13 August 2012. https://www.lawyersweekly.com.au/news/10570-judge-says-bar-is-no-place-for-rhetoric

32 Ibid.

33 Ibid.

34 Chapter 1.

35 Virginia Bell AC, 'By the Skin of Our Teeth: The Passing of the *Women's Legal Status Act* 1918', *Francis Forbes Lecture*, 30 May 2018. www.hcourt.gov.au/assets/publications/speeches/current-justices/bellj/bellj30May2018.pdf

The warm breath of connection

The Wik advocacy, along with loudly naming bad conduct in his letter to the media, and in his advice to law students, reveals something in Sofronoff apart from the circumstances of law which he so loves. His advocacy and attention to the concerns of law is grounded in 'warm openness',[36] based on 'human interest … on a feeling of sympathy, a feeling of acceptance',[37] and at the same time, bringing to bear Grotowski's ideal spectator who 'undergoes an endless process of self-development, whose unrest is not general but directed towards a search for the truth about himself and his mission in life'.[38] His interventions and sympathies evoke Grotowski's call to legibility between the bodies of actor and spectator, becoming perceptible by speaking *to* the now as an act of transgression.[39] Its language speaks of law, but it speaks to a deep concern for the human condition, expressed through law. The small slips of worlds beyond its confines are the site of encounter, brought into being through a deeply held humanity.

The strongest indication of this slip is revealed in his remarks at the ceremony welcoming him as a Justice of and President of the Court of Appeal of Queensland in 2017. Some of the remarks about law in the blog are repeated, such as his intense adherence to the rule of law, but now there's something more about the role of the barrister, and what's really a love of the bar. In the manner of these things, his peers make much of his love of very fast cars, music, flying, but there's also a chiding of from those at the bar who disagreed with his stance against the Attorney-General. But there's now autobiographical detail that he's clearly been shy of acknowledging before. Recounting the circumstances of his refugee Russian parents, including his father's escape from Russia in 1930, he was born in Australia, but along with his family, moved at a tender age to Hong Kong in 1955. His first language was Russian, which he spoke at home, and then Cantonese his second, only learning English at school. He returned to Australia in 1966, as a 13-year-old living with his late brother and his family.[40] Though attending one of Brisbane's privileged private boy's schools, Churchie, he countered the position that judges and senior lawyers 'are drawn from some Australian aristocracy or elite stratum … if that were true, I wouldn't be sitting here today'.[41] This is, after all, the son of a refugee whose first language rendered him apart from his peers, whose experience enables him to notice what's not necessarily apparent to his peers who've never been marked by their difference. He says nothing of this but

36 Grotowski, *Poor Theatre*, 47.
37 Ibid.
38 Ibid, 40.
39 Ibid, 19.
40 The President, 'In The Matter of a Welcome Ceremony to Mark The Appointment of the Honourable Justice Walter Sofronoff as a Judge of the Supreme Court of Queensland to Sit as President', *Supreme Court of Queensland, Court Of Appeal Division*, Thursday 6 April 2017, 1–13. https://archive.sclqld.org.au/judgepub/2017/holmes06042017.pdf
41 Ibid., 1–15.

inklings remain that something burns in him because of what he uniquely notices, largely through his adherence to law, but as an instance of humanity.

Theatricalisation, rendered bodily and dramaturgically, takes us into the circumstances of law, revealing how law functions with and through the life and lifeworlds beyond law. Sofronoff is able to *notice* when law is about to go wrong because the ideals of law he adheres to, like autonomy and so on, aren't rendered only in the abstract but are brought to bear by images of his freedom-loving Cossack father, riding away from Russia forever, recounted in his welcome speech. This is how he notices, as encounter, reminding us of the lives of the Wik Peoples, and the action triggered by officials who act badly. Maks del Mar was baffled that he'd responded physically, and that *my* intervention was prompted by *his* bodily response. These small movements were triggered by impulse, as response, but in Walter Sofronoff we're brought into Ryszard Cieślak's orbit, the merest move, in the form of a few words, bringing us deep into encounter. This is law that burns deep with history, time and place, and life that brings the past back to us. It's as if Sofronoff begins to manifest something of Grotowski's holy actor as holy lawyer, 'who, through his art, climbs upon the stake and performs an act of self-sacrifice'.[42]

Counter-encounter

This is now a long way away from where it started but I now turn back to where I ended my talk at the conference in 2018. I've used a decision of the Australian High Court of late 2017 as a case study of the place of training and experience, as performance, but its place here, now is different. The case dealt with a Constitutional question concerning the laws of another Australian state that confined and curtailed protest,[43] 40 years after the Queensland street march ban. This was a majority judgment of six, with one judge dissenting; the majority found that these laws impermissibly burdened an implied Constitutional protection of political communication, now extended to protest. Some of the justices are Sofronoff's contemporaries, and it was possible to find something of the same responsiveness in the justices who'd lived through, or more correctly, sat to one side of protest. Justice Bell was part of a judgment bloc with two justices from Queensland, Chief Justice Kiefel, and Justice Keane. She had had strong experiences of dealing with the effects of protest in a different state of Australia at much the same time as the Queensland street march bans. In the barest of traces of remarks in their joint judgment, we hear the call to history and/or experience, of the past into the present:

> the powers exercised by police officers under the Protesters Act have important *consequences for protesters and for protests generally and experience suggests* that their exercise will not always be based upon a correct appreciation of

42 Grotowski, *Poor Theatre*, 43.
43 *Brown v Tasmania* [2017] HCA 43 (18 October 2017).

> whether the land in which a protester is situated is forestry land to which the Protesters Act applies. In its practical operation, the Protesters Act may bring protest activity to an end upon the mistaken, albeit reasonable, belief of a police officer, unless the protesters are disposed to resist a direction, and thereby risk a breach of the peace, in order to test the issue.[44]
>
> (My emphasis)

There is something syntactically slippery in the grammar in this sentence. Experience here could simply mean the operation of this act as already applied to those who were arrested under its aegis. Or it could also turn back to these and other protests and their legal consequences of which all three justices were aware, albeit in very different ways. To speak of history and experience invokes rhetoric, as already noted, as the 'historical and practical-human character of reason and of knowledge'.[45] Law as reason simply couldn't address the problem of protest without the call to history and experience, again marked in two of the other judgments.

But these points of connection were absent from the judgments of the two youngest justices. One of the justices instead turned to abstract rights and principles to ground her judgment, agreeing with the majority. But the youngest justice, who was born just a few years before the 1977 street march bans, saw nothing in the circumstances of the law and its application that seemed so alive to most of the other justices, and dissented.[46] This young, brilliant justice saw legislation that was unwieldy, a matter of order and politics rather than the denial of political communication.

There was no encounter.

44 *Brown* [73].
45 Goodrich, *Legal Discourse*, 98.
46 Leiboff, 'Challenging the Legal Self'.

6 Reclaiming the holy lawyer

> I am interested in the actor because he is a fellow human being … which means my encounter with a person other than myself, the feeling, the contact, the sense of mutual comprehension created by the fact that we are both opening ourselves to another human being, that we are trying to understand him and thus overcome our solitude.[1]
>
> Whatever may be the judgment of legal critics on the rank he should hold, as lawyer, advocate, and judge, there is but one judgment that in each he strove through a long career with spotless honour, and died as nobly as ever [sic] warrior died in the battle field, proclaiming great truths of public justice and social duty, with all the power and fervour of his great intellect and still greater heart.[2]

What follows is a story of a holy lawyer.[3] To try to reclaim the holy lawyer, as a model or as a type for the rest of us, say, through a set of instructions and commands, would countermand and deny the encounter and the responsiveness manifested through the warm breath of connection. In the story that follows, there are no to-do lists or prescriptions or rules. Through the life and practice recounted there, with a few prompts, we find all we need to know of the holy lawyer. This story serves to remind that holy lawyers have been part of law for a long time. But it also shows how legal antitheatricality will kill off holy lawyers, figuratively, and perhaps literally, leaving us with a history that has stripped these lawyers from the narrative, and so revives a story that shouldn't have been lost.

1 Jerzy Grotowski, 1967, cited by James Kirkup, in Paul Allain, 'Obituary: Jerzy Grotowski', *The Independent*, Thursday 19 January 1999. https://www.independent.co.uk/arts-entertainment/obituary-jerzy-grotowski-1074849.html

2 Anonymous, 'ART. VIII.-The Late Mr. Justice Talfourd' (1854) 20.2 *The Law Magazine Or, Quarterly Review of Jurisprudence* 298–326, 322. Reprinted in book form as *A Memoir of Mr. Justice Talfourd: By a Member of the Oxford Circuit* (London: Butterworths, 1854). A copy of this rare book is held in the National Library of Australia.

3 In the account that follows, a limited set of sources has been used. Unless there is a specific point to be identified, sources won't be cited but will have been drawn from the materials contained in the chapter.

The sacrifice

A judge, about to preside over the hearing of 150 criminal cases whilst on circuit in Stafford, begins by making lengthy opening remarks to the grand jury. Its topics range widely, with something of criminality, but with far more care and attention of its source:

> I cannot help thinking that it may, in no small degree, be attributed to that separation between class and class which is the great curse of British society, and for which we all, in our respective spheres, are in some degree, more or less, responsible … that reciprocation of kind words and gentle affections, those gracious admonitions and kind inquiries, which, often more than any book education, tend to the cultivation of the affections of the heart and the elevation of the character of those of whom we are the trustees … And if I were asked what is the great want of English society, I would say, that it is the mingling of class with class I would say, in one word, that that want is the want of sympathy.[4]

He continued for much longer, moving through even more topics before remarking: 'the story may be perfectly true which the prosecutor in this case tells – although it may be vividly felt by him – yet he is obliged to confess …'[5] His demeanour suddenly changed, his face flushed, his voice thick and inarticulate, suddenly falling forward and swaying to one side, before being caught by his clerk and his son, who was his marshal. He was immediately attended by two doctors present, but nothing could be done. He was dead within minutes; the more prurient newspapers reported that he 'was literally carried out a corpse'.[6] Tended by senior doctors at the judge's lodgings, life was declared extinct. Mr Justice Thomas Noon Talfourd was dead at the age of 58.

Thomas Talfourd's death on 13 March 1854 was as extraordinary as the life that had preceded it. *The Law Magazine*'s memorialist(s) remarked that: 'The death of no judge ever caused so profound a sensation as that of Justice Talfourd. He was the first who ever died whilst on the Bench, and in the act of discharging his judicial functions.'[7] *The American Law Register* transformed his death into the sacrificial: 'in fit keeping with his life: an *euthanasia*, such as has been often asked but rarely found. He was struck down suddenly, and without pain … his warning for eternity came, and he passed tranquilly and instantly from his own judgment seat to that of his Maker'.[8] *The*

4 Anonymous, 'ART. VIII', 323, reporting the words of Justice Talfourd.
5 Ibid., 324.
6 For example, 'Sudden Death of Mr. Justice Talfourd,' *Empire*, Tuesday 20 June 1854, 2. That's not to say that the versions squared, some gratuitous in their detail like the former, and others creating an account of a gentle death, seemingly to spare the sensibilities of delicate readers: 'Judge Talfourd's Last Address', *Adelaide Times*, Saturday 15 July 1854, 4.
7 Anonymous, 'ART. VIII', 298.
8 Anonymous, 'The Late Mr Justice Talfourd' (1854) 2.9 *The American Law Register* 513–517, 516.

Law Magazine's memorialist(s) acknowledged that to say 'that no judge ever left a more deep and glowing sense of his worth behind him, or was ever more heartily and honestly beloved while living, is to give but feeble expression to the universal sorrow at his death'.[9] The former Serjeant Talfourd's fame, along with his very public death whilst doing law and justice, produced an outpouring of grief and sympathy around the world. Charles Dickens' lament for his friend appeared widely,[10] spreading as far as the colonies, along with a range of reports and literary tributes originally published in England, including an heroic elegy, *Talfourd*, published in *Punch* and reproduced as far away as Sydney and Hobart.[11]

For far away colonial Australia, this wasn't just an abstract human interest story. Talfourd was well known in the Australian colonies, with stories and reports of him regularly appearing in the colonial press, as lawyer, as judge, as politician, as writer and editor, and through his plays and theatre. Some of its denizens may have had first-hand experience of him, not least those transported to the Australian penal settlements for lengthy periods for crimes committed in England, many of whom remained in the Australian colonies after their sentences ended. Some new convicts were still serving their sentences, but transportation had just ceased to the east coast colonies.[12] Edward Menlove, who'd arrived in Melbourne in 1853, must have paid some attention to the death of the advocate who represented Vaughan against his father years before.[13]

Australian colonial readers would have had a range of responses to the accounts of Talfourd's death, from the muscular sentimentality of most of the panegyrics where Talfourd's death signified something of a sacrifice for the higher purpose of law and justice in society. *The Law Magazine*, on the other hand, considered its role very different from the sentiments expressed in other publications, its anonymous memoir stating that its purpose was to remember him as lawyer, though it hoped that its approach just and generous.[14] Reading as the work of several unedited hands, and later published anonymously as the work of a member of the Oxford Circuit,[15] this extraordinary ranging piece, more than 12,000 words long, mixes lavish and sentimental tribute with spite and jealousy, kindness and generosity, sometimes in double doses of repetition, in its memoir of this 'sound, rather than a first-rate lawyer':[16]

9 Anonymous, 'ART. VIII', 324.
10 For example, 'The Late Mr. Justice Talfourd', *Adelaide Times*, Saturday 1 July 1854, 4.
11 For example, *The Sydney Morning Herald* on Monday 3 July 1854, and *The Courier*, Hobart, on Thursday 6 July1854, the tributes sometimes preceding the news of his passing.
12 Transportation ended in the eastern seaboard colony of New South Wales in 1850, encompassing what would become the colonies of Victoria (1851) and Queensland (1859). It ceased in the island colony of Tasmania in 1853. Former convicts were welcomed in free settler South Australia. Originally a free settlement, Western Australia became a penal colony in 1849, with transportation occurring there between 1850 and 1868.
13 Chapter 3.
14 Anonymous, 'ART. VIII', 306.
15 Note 1 above.
16 Anonymous, 'ART. VIII', 306.

> His unquestioned success at the Bar will always remain a marvel to those who thoroughly know not only what are the impediments and aids to victory in that arena, but what are the mental and moral requisites of success. One of the most necessary conditions is an intellectual aptitude as well as a natural taste for the work.[17] It is sufficiently obvious that Talfourd pursued his profession from no natural love for its avocations, or from any notion that it would afford him a fitting means of gratifying the aspirations of his soul, or giving scope to the exercise of the high and peculiar powers of his mind. It is no derogation of the man to affirm that it never did so. The whole calibre of his moral being was ill attuned for the work.[18]

That's not to say that praise wasn't strewn generously in fits and start throughout the piece, and is contradictory, suggesting its multi-authorship. We see an image of a man whose key interests were literary, and whose victories in law were based on interests that suited Serjeant Talfourd. Certain passages are carefully crafted with counterclaim, so that each sting comes with its own justification, and each moment of praise with its own complaint, illustrated in this passage that I've marked to signify the swings between one and the other:

> As an advocate at the Bar his powers were far more suited to appeals in behalf of noble impulses and great principles *than to the ordinary duties of advocacy.* His intellectual as well as moral being sympathised so intensely with all that was high, noble, generous, or virtuous in our nature, *that he had little power of evoking that artificial fervour in indifferent causes which has no other stimulus than a high fee or forensic fame. Thus he occasionally fell below par in the common arena of Nisi Prius. Nor was this observable alone where he had causes in hand which were obnoxious to his high moral sense. He required the incentive of high emprise for high efforts.* Wherever appeals were to be made to the genial sympathies and better feelings of human nature; – wherever justice was in peril from force, falsehood, or intrigue, – wherever treachery was to be denounced, tyranny in high places fearlessly assailed, hypocrisy unmasked, the liberties or the welfare of the people to be upheld, – the fervour of his soul found utterance, and his great heart spoke out in the glowing words in which his rich imagination so gorgeously clothed his thoughts.[19]
>
> (My emphases)

It's possible to read this seeing nothing in the way of opprobrium, but that would be too benevolent. His peers do see the good in Talfourd, but it's just not as a lawyer; but as a lawyer, his personal qualities mean that he's able to notice injustice; but that makes him care-less of the everyday of law; but then again he's also the lawyer who will eschew the lure of high fees and ordinary work to bring more

17 Ibid., 303.
18 Ibid., 304.
19 Ibid., 305–306.

difficult cases to light for the betterment of everyone. His peers acknowledge and marvel at his deeply held ethic (as opposed to the rules of ethics), who wouldn't tolerate bad behaviour or the gaming of cases, of using cross-examination against those who were truthful and deserving, saving a fury for those of his peers and juniors who played the system. His American tribute writer, on the other hand, is unstinting in her or his praise:

> the combination of his talents was so rare, and *his private character so pure and noble*, that we cannot refrain from adding our small tribute of respect to the memory of one who has been in many ways and *in the highest degree an honor and an example to our profession.*[20] He was upright and honorable to a marked degree; most generous and kindly in his feelings; strong and constant in his attachments; and, what is unfortunately a rare quality among lawyers, *extremely liberal and charitable.*[21]
>
> (My emphases)

Whether or not they are rebuking their English brothers, whose article was a source of their own piece, is anyone's guess, and what caused Talfourd's peers to damn with faint praise and criticise, albeit tempered with high praise and valorisation, has to be guessed at, but there are a number of possibilities, ranging from jealousy of his success and his popularity and successes outside of law, his intensely good character and nature, his kindness, his politics, his famous friends, his sense of justice and fairness, his deployment of rhetoric through the use of topics and imagination rather than bare black letter law, his demands that law be administered fairly; and as the Americans were to attest and as found in the Australian publications, that Talfourd, usually as Serjeant Talfourd, was incredibly well known. Even *The Law Magazine* owned that he'd been the target of vendettas,[22] despite his own exemplary conduct towards his peers, perhaps because of his intolerance of poor practice.[23] But if there'd been anything at all, given that it was universally acknowledged that he made his own way at the bar, its most likely derived from exceptional benefits afforded him as Serjeant through the agency of Lord Brougham, just as the rank was in decline, granting Talfourd precedence by warrant in 1834, confirmed by patent in 1840,[24] and who was then appointed the high rank of Queen's Serjeant six years later, and almost immediately elevated to the most senior rank of all, as Queen's Ancient Serjeant, making him head of the English Bar.[25] This meant, all the years after Francis Bacon was appointed the first King's Counsel to obtain some precedence over the Serjeants, that he had priority over King's, then Queen's, Counsel who would otherwise have

20 Anonymous, 'The Late Mr Justice Talfourd', 513.
21 Ibid., 516.
22 Anonymous, 'ART. VIII', 316.
23 Ibid.
24 David Pugsley, 'Mr Justice Talfourd and the Western Circuit' (2007) 39 *Bracton Law Journal* 35–51, 35.
25 Ibid., 38.

had precedence.[26] All this given that he'd been overlooked for silk and then awarded the consolation of the coif, of the rank of Serjeant, instead.[27]

Whatever prompted these complaints, one thing is clear. All in all, Thomas Noon Talfourd was unlike any of his peers. Through everything written about him, he appears as the archetypal holy lawyer, in the sympathy he embodies and practices, the responsiveness and responsibility to law beyond the black letter, and the concerns he manifests for law in its social and individual life. He is broadly educated, and brings that breadth into his law, from his youthful first publications that would bring him to the attention of the world, writing of everything from politics to literature to history, and eventually writing his own successful play *Ion*, for which he turns to those in theatre for advice before offering it for production. Through his own natural sentiments and concerns, along with the conditions that formed him, as well as this depth of interaction in worlds beyond law, Talfourd holds within him the sympathies that enable him to *notice.* He is that legal self in whom consciousness and instinct is united, bringing the warm breath of connection into law, who confronts the myths of law, and neutralises game and strategy, in order to generate response, responsiveness and responsibility in law.[28] And just as Jerzy Grotowski reminds us not to mistake the 'holy' actor with holiness in the religious sense, the holy lawyer isn't holy in the religious sense either, but nor is she or he an actor. It's in the self and her or his formation, the conditions through which he or she notices, which makes the holy lawyer. We've seen how close Walter Sofronoff QC moved towards Grotowski's image of the holy actor as 'a person who, through his art, climbs upon the stake and performs an act of self-sacrifice'.[29] This is Talfourd's fate too, because the holy lawyer is inevitably challenged, teetering on the brink of sacrifice against the general position of law, their concerns labelling them as outsider, and who challenges the assumptions and expectations of law. They are driven by principles (not principle) and virtues that challenge complacency. And in the topic and sentiment of his final speech, it's not surprising that contemporary writers were pulled to the image of Talfourd's death as that of noble sacrifice.[30] But it's through his life, as formation and through the scars and marks of difference that he bore, that we see just how the future Serjeant Talfourd would become the archetypal holy lawyer.

Being Thomas Noon Talfourd

In 1837, the year *Vaughan v Menlove* was heard and *Ion*'s success had added to Talfourd's fame,[31] *The New Monthly Magazine and Humourist* devoted several of its pages to a 'Memoir of Mr. Serjeant Talfourd, M.P.'[32] This profile piece did something more than just paint a picture of this lawyer, politician and litterateur.

26 Chapter 3.
27 Chapter 3.
28 Chapter 4.
29 Grotowski, *Poor Theatre*, 43.
30 See note 2 above.
31 Chapter 3.
32 LB, 'Memoir of Mr. Serjeant Talfourd, M.P.' (1837) *The New Monthly Magazine and Humourist* 213–220, 214.

It did this too, until it began a curious accounting, a rhetorical balance sheet of sorts, seemingly written to answer unstated assertions. Talfourd had written for this periodical for twelve years from 1820 so it's more than apparent that he was well known to the profile writer. The piece opened by observing that Talfourd was both true to himself and to his profession, along with the 'still higher purposes' that nature had meant him to serve.[33] As a lawyer, though his 'larger apprehension and sympathy may take in both Shakespeare and Blackstone', this didn't change the quality of his lawyering. Moreover, 'he may feel and comprehend not merely the laws themselves *but the objects for which they were made, the interests which they embrace, and the humanities they vindicate and protect*' (my emphasis).[34] The writer is dealing with something very particular, as if to correct the record in a generalist, not a legal, publication, weighing in with a series of retorts that must have come from somewhere:

> It is preposterous to suppose that he would more imperfectly understand the motives, actions, and position of an individual, because he perfectly understands all qualities of human dealing; that he should be less qualified to do justice to a client, because he can fathom the injustice that is done to humanity; that he cannot weigh facts because he can estimate fiction; or that he is disqualified from mastering the immediate by his sympathy with the remote. It is easier to count the stones in the street than the stars in heaven; and the eye of imagination that can achieve the more difficult triumph need not allow matter-of-fact to monopolise the glory of the easier task.[35]

It seems that the same pot-shots that were directed against Talfourd in death were fired at him during his career from within the small world of the Oxford Circuit and Westminster Hall, but not without, as his fame and popularity grew, though other publications were keen to suggest that he was as much a favourite of the bar as the public.[36] Looking back over his life, it looks like this was nothing new for Thomas Noon Talfourd, as if almost from the very beginning. 'The boy, in Mr. Talfourd's case, is father to the man',[37] the 1837 profile writer remarks, and a quick traverse of his childhood and adolescence reveals significant events that would shape Talfourd and put him on the outer at the Bar. What it also seemed to do was supercharge his nature and bring him towards broader humanistic attitudes in law, but so too what would be a recognition of law as the theatrical.

Talfourd, as his *Law Magazine* memorialist remarked sniffily, wasn't born into the established church, a detail that mattered a great deal. What mattered too to this memorialist was that he had been born in Stafford, but all other accounts say that he was born at Reading in May 1795, to a brewer father and a mother whose

33 Ibid.
34 Ibid.
35 Ibid., 214.
36 Note 44 below.
37 Ibid.

own father was the minister of the dissenting chapel.[38] What must have caused intense consternation was his choice in late adolescence to move to the established Church of England. He attended the Reverend Dr Valpy's Reading Grammar School for the final two years of his schooling, leaving in 1812 at the age of 17. These short years provided Talfourd with a mentor and a source of refuge, and a hand that would guide and fan his sympathies and talents. Writing in 1837 of Dr Valpy sometime after his death, Talfourd remarked that:

> His system of education was animated by a portion of his own spirit: it was framed to enkindle and to quicken the best affections … [it] resembled nothing less than the imagination of the greatest of our poets, embracing every thing human; shedding its light upon the just and the unjust,[39]

characteristics later attributed to himself. But there was practical help too:

> The hold which the Reading-school boy had upon it could not be forfeited, not even 'by slights, the worst of injuries;' and when broken in fortune, deserted by relatives, and frowned on by the world, he had only to seek the hospitable roof of his old master – 'claim kindred there, and have his claims allow'd.'[40]

In these cryptic words we're brought into Thomas Talfourd's move to the Church of England, the distress this caused his family of dissenters, and of the bullying that he appears to have endured. His liberal, radical politics appeared when he was young,[41] and he published his own first piece of writing as a 16-year-old, and finding a love of theatre – Shakespeare particularly – denied to him in his home.[42] We hear its echoes in what he writes of theatre's uplifting character in the preface to the 4th edition of *Ion*, speaking to dissenters and others for whom theatre held everything evil, remarking on the work Macready had done to ensure the creation of an uplifting, national theatre. Yet despite his abilities, qualities and early fame, and that he was already a published author, his contemporaries at Dr Valpy's school were to recall of Talfourd that he was a dull, stupid boy.[43] It is an impossible charge.

For all his brilliance, Thomas Talfourd wouldn't attend university. A series of possibilities would explain why, but his origins in a dissenting family would seem

38 DEX1410 – 'Legal and Personal Papers of Thomas Noon Talfourd (1795–1854), Judge and Writer.' *The Berkshire Record Office*. http://ww2.berkshirenclosure.org.uk

39 Thomas Noon Talfourd, 'Notice, Instead Of Dedication', *Ion: A Tragedy in Five Acts*, 4th edition (London: Edward Moxon, 1837), iii–vi, v.

40 Talfourd, 'Notice, Instead Of Dedication', vi.

41 LB, 'Memoir', 215.

42 Anonymous, 'Mr. Sergeant Talfourd, M.P.' (1838) 31 *The Mirror of Literature, Amusement, and Instruction* v–viii, v.

43 D/EX 1432/1/5 noted in the annotations accompanying the Talfourd papers, *The Berkshire Record Office*. http://ww2.berkshirenclosure.org.uk

to hold the key. University College was still years away when he received introductions that would lead him to his chosen field of law – despite what his critics asserted, he had chosen law as a field. What brought him this opportunity were his literary achievements, and a series of introductions took him to the future Lord Chancellor, who would later be his champion as Serjeant, the then Mr Brougham. He gave Talfourd an introduction to Joseph Chitty, with whom Talfourd undertook at a pupillage that commenced just after he finished school, from 1813 to 1817, remembering that there was no other form of legal education available at the time other than that privately arranged. Brougham also encouraged him to continue his writing career during the pupillage. Chitty was a special pleader, and Talfourd also followed this path, working as a special pleader, and eventually being called to the bar in 1821, four years later. All the while he continued to write, from political pamphlets and tracts to poetry, to literary and dramatic criticism, contributing to periodicals and encyclopaedia, from law writing to literary editing. Amongst his law writing was a task carried out by most at the bar – that of reporter – as the legal reporter on the Oxford Circuit for *The Times*, something which he disclosed, unlike his peers who did this work anonymously.

One of his memorialists did own of Talfourd's career at the bar that 'He made way by perseverance, and in some measure by the aid of friends, steadily as a junior, and in twelve years from his call took the coif.'[44] In 1838 it was reported in the general periodicals that Talfourd's practice at the bar was lucrative, and steadily increasing, quoting a writer of the day that he ranks high as a lawyer, chiefly as an advocate, and his amiable deportment has rendered him 'as great a favourite with the bar as he is with the public'.[45] As if he wasn't busy enough, Talfourd was elected as a Liberal MP for his home city of Reading in 1835 and 1837 and again in 1847, leaving Parliament on his elevation to the Bench in 1849. The last was something he'd wanted for some time, as we find in Dickens' lamentation. This movement between Parliament and Bench might seem odd to an early twenty-first-century mind, but it was par for the course in the nineteenth and early twentieth centuries, with some continuation of this practice late into the twentieth century. His parliamentary years saw him introduce a copyright bill in 1837, kindling his friendship with Dickens, though it would take years for it to be passed. Dickens wasn't his only famous literary friend. He was Charles Lamb's executor and edited his letters and other writings for publication, and had numerous friends in the theatre, including Macready. By 1847, another profile writer would remark that 'The name of Serjeant Talfourd is well known in Westminster Hall, in the House of Commons, and in the Republic of Letters. It would be difficult to say in which of these three spheres he is best known.'[46]

Curiously again for a twenty-first-century lawyer, considerable attention was paid to Talfourd's physical characteristics and demeanour. One remarked that

44 Anonymous, 'ART. VIII', 304–305.
45 Anonymous, 'Mr. Sergeant Talfourd, M.P.' (1838), vii.
46 Anonymous, 'Serjeant Talfourd', *The London Journal: and Weekly Record of Literature, Science and Art* (1847) 6.146, 11 December 1847, 233–234.

'Mr. Talfourd's manner is little like that of a popular advocate, or an actor of any public rank on the great stage of life for upwards of twenty years; it is the manner of a retired, sensitive, and amiable scholar,'[47] while there was a general consensus that he wasn't physically imposing or muscular, and barely of average height, with 'an oval face, a copper-coloured complexion, regular and agreeable features, and dark, lustrous eyes; his countenance has a highly intellectual expression, and his eyes are indicative of the kindness of his nature'.[48] His eyes were given even the greatest of attention from the writers: 'Soft and touching, and almost bewitching in their expression, they have an irresistible charm; and one might almost fancy that the learned gentleman achieves as much by them as by the beauty of his sentiments and the poetry of his diction.'[49] On the other hand, his voice was wanting, with some huskiness, limited modulation because of his engrossment with his subject, and an inability to pronounce the letter r. He only made slight physical actions, mostly as a gentle movement of the right arm 'without having any theatrical gesture'.[50] Rather, the writers intimate, it's his eyes that reach into his character, as the window of the soul, where we see instantly that he's goodly and kind, as a quietly minimal Ryszard Cieślak, whose eyes reveal the impulses that burn within him, out of which law is animated.

Reclaiming the holy lawyer

The eyes have it, and no less Talfourd in his last words that reveal his impulses creating the score – the terminology Grotowski uses to mark up a script, so to speak – through which he generates his law. He wants us to look up from our books and look around us, bodily attending to others in order to generate and manifest a physically grounded response and responsibility, out of which law follows: 'the reciprocation of kind words and gentle affections, those gracious admonitions and kind inquiries, which, often *more than any book education, tend to the cultivation of the affections of the heart and the elevation of the character*' (my emphases).[51] And so too his call for sympathy, not that mawkish and cloying pity which attends a twenty-first-century image of the word (drowned out by the later creation of the word empathy, a word that holds a different meaning entirely), as understanding, compassion, kindness and awareness of the needs of others. Grotowski too turned to sympathy as that which invokes 'warm openness',[52] based on 'human interest … on a feeling of sympathy, a feeling of acceptance',[53] grounding the connection between actor and spectator. Talfourd, in his recognition that *book education* is unable to generate this same kind of responsiveness that's produced by noticing physically, draws on the same concerns of Grotowski: of warm

47 LB, 'Memoir', 220.
48 Anonymous, 'Serjeant Talfourd', v.
49 Ibid.
50 Ibid.
51 Anonymous, 'ART. VIII', 324.
52 Grotowski, *Poor Theatre*, 47.
53 Ibid.

openness, of human interest, on sympathy and acceptance. The vitality of being and presence is paramount to correct the ills that he's trying to fix, to make the lives of people better, which is ultimately the point of law. In his own preface to the 4th edition of the play *Ion*, we hear exactly these same points in the last words he utters at the end of his life, expressed then in his pleas to those for whom theatre is evil, as if talking to his own dissenting family who withheld the theatrical from him. But these words are a cloak, at least when viewed through the perfect vision of retrospect where the sentiments are repeated, for he is taking us to law, and what it should be. He's writing of theatre, but he is as much writing of law:

> I firmly believe that its maintenance is most important to *the expansion of all that is social*, and to the *nurture of all that is great within us*; because I deem it – not as an instructor in the way of direct moral invitation or purpose – but as *dissolving the crust of selfishness* which daily cares and labours gradually form about the kindest hearts; as *softening the pride* of conventional virtue, and *bringing the outcasts of humanity within its sphere*; and as combining all the picturesque varieties which external distinctions present with the *sense of the noble equality* which lies beneath them.[54]
>
> (My emphases)

His call to the theatrical as a proxy for law is, as I remind, not based in the drama but in the liveliness that comprehends the theatrical. His American tribute writer was able to see something of this to make what was an over-hopeful claim based on Talfourd's example – that through him it was now recognised that a broader rather than narrower mindset produced better law – that he was a 'conspicuous illustration of this altered sentiment, and of the abandonment of ancient prejudices on this subject'.[55] Observing that literary eminence or even literary tastes that had been assumed dangerous for lawyers had been overcome, meaning that the 'arrogant dullness of black letter students, content to know only the crude and barren learning of their books and despising all beyond, has been fortunately succeeded by a much higher and more liberal tone of feeling.'[56] Remarking that those who excelled at the bar were now also eminent in science, history and general literature and writing for the press, had changed the field of those who were 'once thought too abstruse and scholastic to take part in the affairs of ordinary life'.[57] So too, they turned to him to show that

> the rugged paths of legal science may be made beautiful by the graces of literature and humanity, at no sacrifice of practical usefulness and skill … Talfourd … [is] illustrious proof that the practice of the law need neither blunt the feelings nor narrow the intellect.[58]

54 Thomas Noon Talfourd, 'Preface to the Fourth Published Edition', vii–xxii, xxii.
55 Anonymous 'The Late Mr Justice Talfourd', 513.
56 Ibid.
57 Ibid.
58 Anonymous, 'The Late Mr Justice Talfourd', 517–518.

His legal memorialists observed that 'he was neither a mere lawyer, nor a mere poet, nor a mere orator, nor a mere litterateur, nor a mere lover of all that was good in man and beautiful in nature' but the in these combinations 'stood alone'.[59] Put another way, Talfourd was no instance of a general rule but the exception that proves nothing. His 1847 profile remarked on the rarity of his abilities: 'The annals of our civil jurisprudence furnish but few precedents of the same happy union of law and literature.'[60] But then again, maybe he is the exemplar, for, returning to the memorial (its odd structure revealing itself in full blast) another portion suggests that he has something more to offer:

> It has been often said that no one can be a lawyer who does not exclusively devote himself to law. We not only believe, but know this to be an error. The isolated pursuit of any one single branch of knowledge or mental labour is, on the contrary, detrimental to perfection in it … of educational aptitude and general knowledge. The more a man has of these, the better lawyer and advocate he is likely to be … [for] another pursuit is another mental exercise, and therefore additional mental power. No man can possibly require the devotion of his entire time and attention to law … If he does so, to a certainty he injures his intellectual power, and instead of increasing his professional ability, materially lessens it.[61]

But what Talfourd was doing was something different. He took what he saw from theatre, and brought it back to law. Though he's most visible to us through his appearances in court, for obvious reasons, we have to remember he spent years as a special pleader where he did nothing but undertake law as process. The writer of the 1847 profile was to show us something of Talfourd's abilities as speechmaker, but the text reveals how Talfourd turns to encounter and impulse, as total act, as theatre that speaks to us, now and in the future, again echoing his position in law. The speech wasn't recent, but was made, extempore, in 1836, at an event in support of the Covent Garden Fund,[62] in aid of retired actors. Talfourd picked up on the remarks of the publisher, Sir George Murray, who had rather oddly compared the theatrical to the military profession Talfourd agreed that it was apt to 'compare the glorious *impulses* of a soldier to those of the stage' (my emphasis).[63] His speech has begun by reminding us that drama and theatre aren't the same thing. A momentous trial, though, is like drama:

> restrained, bounded and dignified by solemnities and forms which defined it as a thing set apart from the common succession of human affairs … closed by a catastrophe which was anticipated with quivering expectation, with

59 Anonymous, 'ART. VIII', 299.
60 Anonymous, 'Serjeant Talfourd', 234.
61 Anonymous, 'ART. VIII', 321–322.
62 Ibid.
63 Ibid.

> sometimes a background of public interest, where the struggle of principles and the fate of the parties might be discerned in the intellectual perspective.[64]

He carefully confined what he means by drama to the Aristotelean, as tragedy. And then he turned his attention to theatre, or the 'art of acting', which can't 'make a cold appeal to posterity, but receives its immediate reward from present affection ... as lustre ... which makes the successes of the past live in the comforts and the gratitude of the present'. In remarking of the then presumption that 'the drama is dying among us', he turned to a production of *Virginius*, in which 'the old forms of Roman austerity were animated with present life'. The brilliant actors of his day, he said, were able to produce something in those in their presence – even in an auditorium with 3,000 people, as he'd remarked elsewhere, you would be brought into the world generated by the bodies of the actors. What he's drawn to, in bringing the mirror of being into the present, are precisely the practices of the Grotowskian. He takes us further, for though the speech honours 'The Patrons of the Drama', he extends these patrons beyond 'the high or even the middle rank of society' to 'the honest-hearted frequenters of the pit and the galleries, without the aid of whose sympathy it would, indeed, languish and expire'.[65] It's these participants at the theatre in whom response and responsiveness is found, and expanding on this social and political point, he added his hope that one day:

> the tradesman, the artisan and the mechanic will learn to appreciate a scene of greatness and of beauty beyond their ordinary sphere, but akin to their natures; and that then the *distinction of rank will shed grace upon the stage*, while *the noble equality of the human heart* will be vindicated in the union of all ranks, and the melting down of all distinctions in one pervading emotion – *one convulsive throb of sympathy* – one burst of generous pleasure.[66]

That, of course, is the whole point of theatre, of which Talfourd was keenly aware, in its liveliness, its capacity to generate response and responsibility, and to change people through its interactions. This is what Talfourd the lawyer wants too, as if normalising what are called the theatrical antonyms expressed against the narrow and confined register of legal antitheatricality. But even then his memorialists couldn't let this be. Turning to the success of *Ion*, they accepted that drama had a function, but not theatre. They did remark that its 1836 production was really very good, but this 'was scarcely an acting play', for it was missing 'stage claptrap' needed for the 'vitiated taste of a London audience'. And as if countermanding everything that Talfourd asserted about theatre, a field that he knew exceeding well, and for his realisation that law needed theatre in order to move into the deeper forms of understanding needed to really engage with law, the memorialists

64 Ibid.
65 Ibid.
66 Ibid.

brought us back to the lifelessness and indifference embedded deep into the logics of legal antitheatricality: 'The truth, if it were honestly told, we suspect being, that people intellectual enough to enjoy the higher order of the drama do not frequent theatres, and they who do, have a taste only for coarser excitement.'[67]

The memorialists, of course, have engaged in a campaign of disinformation and canard. If Talfourd is to be stripped of his validity immediately, it will staunch sentiment for his kind of lawyering, before he can become a martyr. His memorialists write him into a corner, as unique and as a one off, and who can be followed up to a point, but not too far. We have to remember that this kind of campaign won't take long to have effect, especially as law is turning to John Austin's ideas, and the normalisation of law had already begun with the creation of a formal curriculum for the bar, while changes like the new authorised law reports would begin the next decade. Talfourd's image of law as sympathy needs to be written out of the picture if this new technocratic law is to succeed. What is clear is that his memorialists, as Bacon's inheritors, are merely replaying a dispute that has gone on at least since the sixteenth century, when Bacon does his best to deny a place in law for Plowden.

As if

It's easy to think of a life completed as functioning as a kind of fiction. I've hoped to prevent this happening through the mode in which this story is written, just as Talfourd wanted to hold onto the liveliness of theatre and through the same sympathy and liveliness, law. Through his alter ego, Tommy Traddles in Dickens' *Great Expectations*, Talfourd's life is partly rewritten as fiction. Fiction can't replicate the messiness of real life. And this troubled Talfourd, as early as 1836: 'I trust the day will never arrive with the prevalence of mere scientific pursuits, or even of our literary tastes, will cause our old stores of pleasure to be forsaken.'[68]

By that he means theatre, and all the warmth and liveliness it entails, something that matters to him in life and on the cusp of death. Talfourd's ability to notice is in part grounded in the harms and slights etched in him and written into his body. From the bullying he endured, to the sadness of losing people close to him because of his choices, the difficulties he faced getting to the bar, the clever barrister defamed and backstabbed by his colleagues – all this means he's able to notice what will be missed by others. As one of the legal memorialists was good enough to notice, it was his 'kindness of disposition and warm sympathy with humanity which distinguished him so eminently above the throng of his profession. A more social, genial, frank, generous, or liberal man never lived.'[69]

67 Anonymous, 'ART. VIII', 307.
68 Anonymous, 'Serjeant Talfourd', 234.
69 Anonymous, 'ART. VIII', 308.

7 Towards a theatrical jurisprudence

Transgression

Hans-Thies Lehmann makes the startling claim, for law at least, that theatre is obliged to hold law to account:

> The theatre affords the exemplary site, to paraphrase Stephen Greenblatt, *for subjecting to interrogation the social energies that circulate* – instead of reinforcing them with image-laden storytelling. Therefore, the theatre has the task of presenting revenge within the law, the failure of the law, what proves unjustifiable in its foundations, and the exclusions and acts of deception that constitute it – *over and over, for such work can never be done once and for all.* It is to be *repeated, remembered and performed anew day by day and moment by moment.*[1]
>
> (My emphases)

His observations speak in much the same terms as the Grotowskian practices of transgression, through confrontation. Confrontation, it's recalled, brings together the deep bonds of myth and archetype that have been lost, in the absence of a common belief system, through which actor and spectator share bodily in either holding or challenging 'some universal truth'.[2] These truths are simply those things bound up in the human condition and the stories that need to be retold, because they matter. The challenge is how to bring this to the core of being, rather than as bare display. This is beyond difficult, but when it's realised, it's transformative. As Lehmann rightly observes, as a mark of antitheatrical legality bound up in law's dramatic pretence: 'Theatre does not concern the law itself so much as what is 'wrapped up' and 'bound' in or by it; this general truth holds for theatrical tradition and tragic drama since the Renaissance'.[3] Read literally, Lehmann's charge is that law only thinks of theatre as a practice demanding control, such as its display. But what he's also pointed to is that law, and those in whom

1 Lehmann, *Tragedy*, 109.
2 Chapter 4.
3 Lehmann, *Tragedy*, 109.

law is entrusted, treat law as rules on display, which have lost their connection with life.

That it is theatre's role to point out what's missing from law might seem an impertinence for those of us deeply immersed in law and its practices. But when we think of these most basic of theatre practices, grounded in dramaturgy and in bringing to bear Grotowski's techniques in order to generate the conditions through which we are able to *notice* in law, then there is nothing left of law but display. Put another way, law finds it next to impossible, except in the most unusual circumstances, to generate the kind of depth of responsiveness to deeply held facets of the human condition that theatre, of the kind worked with in this book, presumes as a matter of course. Liveliness, in the Baconian register, is to be rendered nugatory, as law's commitment to abstraction and the ideal, as calculation, and as algorithm is rendered as signs that display, but have next to no possibility of working with the humanity it holds in its hands. This is in large part because of its reshaping as technocratic through the filtering of being as calculable abstraction. In this mode, law prides itself on its ahistoricity, happily losing touch with the conditions that shaped it, or pulling the shutters down and obliterating it from view. When its pasts are displayed, it is to reinforce the perfection of its practices, regardless of its veracity.

This mix of calculability and the ideal means that law has to engage in extraordinary stratagems of avoidance designed to avoid conditions of the liveliness of humanity, and to appear to function with signs as display. Take the case of Dr Fredrick Toben who brought a defamation action against *The Australian* newspaper and Greens Party politicians,[4] who, on realising that they had invited a Holocaust denier to an event, withdrew the invitation. This was reported in the newspaper in more or less those terms. Dr Toben, who was born in Germany in 1944, moved to Australia as a child, where he established an organisation called The Adelaide Institute, through which he worked to dispute the existence of the Holocaust or its extent. Though Holocaust denial isn't unlawful in Australia, forms of speech that offend, insult, humiliate or intimidate another person or a group of people on the basis of their race or ethnicity, subject to a range of permissible contexts, are proscribed.[5] After a series of incidents, Dr Toben was, by order of the Federal Court of Australia, prevented from publishing certain material because this material breached those laws. He spent time in prison for contempt of court for disobeying a court order preventing publication that breached that law.

In this case, the publisher of *The Australian* and the other defendants sought to have the case brought by Dr Toben struck out as an abuse of process in part because of those other orders. At first instance, McCallum J in the New South Wales Supreme Court, agreed:

4 *Toben v Nationwide News Pty Ltd; Toben v Mathieson* [2015] NSWSC 1784 McCallum J (*Toben); Toben v Nationwide News Pty Ltd* [2016] NSWCA 296 Meagher JA; Ward JA; Payne JA (*Toben CA*).

5 *Racial Discrimination Act 1975* (Cth) ss 18C and 18D.

> Dr Toben seeks by these proceedings to manipulate the process of the court to create a forum in which to assert the very views by the attribution with which he claims to have been defamed. Those are the very views his expression of which is otherwise prohibited by the orders of Branson J. That is a cynical misuse of the process of the court which must be stopped.[6]

But to get to that point, the court had to engage in an extraordinary set of manoeuvres, not least because it was unclear what was grounding the defamation case itself. The Court allowed counsel for the defence to cross-examine Dr Toben on what counsel had called 'the epistemological loop',[7] in which 'the pleadings and the proceedings are being treated as "some sort of parlour game"'.[8] Unusually, McCallum J allowed Mr Toben to submit his own pleadings, along with those of his counsel, a practice that would normally be rejected but which then formed the basis of cross-examination by counsel for the defendants. His own counsel's pleadings were based in the straightforward claim that Dr Toben was a Holocaust denier, on the basis of accepted terms, so that the Holocaust was '"the systematic murder of Jews and others by the Nazis during the war" and that the term "Holocaust denier" means a person who denies that the Holocaust occurred'.[9] His octogenarian counsel, Clive Evatt, the brother-in-law of the modernist architect, Harry Seidler, who had to flee Vienna because of his Jewish background, would inevitably have thought the claim enough. But Dr Toben's lengthy pleadings had a different purpose, as a series of claims that contained details of his position about the Holocaust and about what he called Holocaust narratives,[10] which challenged and countermanded the limited basis of what was contained in the pleadings of his own counsel. This became a strategic lightning rod for counsel for the defendants, as these alternate pleadings helped ground his cross-examination. It helped win the case, but the strategy, designed to pull at the threads of the veracity of the defamation claim provided a forum for Dr Toben's views, turned the case into a vehicle through which Dr Toben would assert his views about the Holocaust.

This inevitably confounded the case, and what the court was having to decide. As the New South Wales Court of Appeal held, through Ward JA: 'He cannot possibly find it offensive to be called something that he has seemingly been happy to label himself as. Rather, what he denies (or now wishes merely to call into question) is that particular aspects of the historical record of or writings about the Holocaust in fact occurred.'[11] He'd also made it public that he wanted to use court proceedings to obtain a legitimation of his views:

6 *Toben* [105].
7 *Toben* [32].
8 *Toben* [50].
9 *Toben* [32].
10 *Toben* [35]–[40].
11 *Toben CA* [106].

> Dr Toben, in his own writings (see [26] above), has expressed the opinion that it matters not whether he wins or loses court proceedings ... [his] predominant purpose in the defamation proceedings is not to vindicate his reputation but to have an otherwise unavailable public forum to express his views and that, but for his desire to use the proceedings as an opportunity to air his views, the proceedings would not have been commenced. In the defamation proceedings now brought, Dr Toben has denied seeking to use the court process as a platform for historical polemic ... this denial should not be believed.[12]

But this is where the courts were brought into a diabolical problem grounded in the demands of rationality and reason in law. The courts were caught by the same epistemological loop and parlour game which demanded that they 'not mention the war', a catch phrase repeated in an episode of the 1970s English television comedy, *Fawlty Towers*, entitled 'The Germans', in which the key character, hotelier Basil Fawlty, continues to mention the war, repeatedly, to the distress of his German guests.[13] Thus Ward JA observed that any case on the matter would require 'an extensive inquiry into the events of World War II and that the costs and court resources that would have to be expended to determine those issues'.[14] This exercise had already been carried out in a significant UK defamation case of a Holocaust denier, a case not cited in either judgment.[15] Instead, the judgments involved a judicial struggle to find a conceptual means to deal with this case precisely because of the broad liberal rights attending it, though finally reaching a conclusion that stayed the case as an abuse of process. But what happened along the way was that the courts were forced to move into the strictures of abstraction, meaning everything is open to contestation. Whether it means to or not, law becomes on agent of fragmentation that fractures Grotowskian confrontation. So law invites this: Dr Toben complained on appeal that McCallum J used her own understanding of the Holocaust, as well as saying that he was an anti-Semite. This was held to not be so on appeal, but in one passage, Ward JA's rebuke reads very strangely:

> In my opinion, there was no finding by her Honour as to the 'commonly understood' meaning of the Holocaust, nor did her Honour impermissibly apply her own knowledge or understanding of historical events. What her Honour clearly identified, when referring to the denial of an 'obvious truth', was that a statement that someone is a Holocaust denier (as, for that matter, would be a statement that someone denies any other historical or world event) can only convey a defamatory imputation if it would be perceived as discreditable so to deny such an event. That must be correct.[16]

12 *Toben CA* [124].
13 'The Germans'. https://en.wikipedia.org/wiki/The_Germans, accessed 12 November 2014.
14 *Toben CA* [18].
15 *Irving v Penguin Books Limited* [2000] EWHC QB 115.
16 *Toben CA* [82].

Maybe, but Ward JA is more or less caught in the parlour game that requires an evacuation and fragmentation of common knowledge, or of the concept of judicial notice, where notorious facts or knowledge can be accepted by the court without the need for proof or evidence. Rather, there is a demand of absence, when it is presence that's needed, remembering that this is a case involving the ability of a court to strike out a claim as an abuse of process. After all, this was a defamation action and not a case about Holocaust denial – but law's abstractions and the demands of reason and rationality turned it into a case about Holocaust denial.

This was precisely the warning of Szajna and Flaszen, in reminding that Auschwitz would be overborne by the technocratic over humanity.[17] Law imagines that ideals which govern its practices and processes, along with those that imbue doctrine and principle, can function as a form of practised humanity in the absence of the realities and liveness of being. But this doesn't happen just because. Without a self who can notice (not the formal legal concept of judicial notice), as holy lawyer through an awareness of self and beyond self, law has the potential to be used for any purpose. Practised humanity is required in order to make law's ideals function, which they can only do through that which is lived rather than that which is analysed. Practised humanity is the work of theatre. Law, as Lehmann makes clear, could do with much more of it.

Theatrical jurisprudence

If theatre's work of interrogating law is 'never done once and for all',[18] this needs to be law's practice too, to remind, through repetition and renewal, of the instances of injustice and of failure of law, and their circumstances. This means finding the means through which it can notice how injustice manifests, and when this must be attended to, in cases like *Wik*.[19] But law also needs to reiterate and remember, to not lose sight of injustice past, especially where challenges are wrought through remanifestations in different guises and through new means. And this is where the theatrical antonyms come into play. Transgression, through stepping over and as Grotowskian confrontation, as antonymic of ethics, reveals what's at stake when law is brought into the realities of being, as opposed to rules that function as display. Instinct, as antonymic of thinking, is that 'step before' that helps us notice because no amount of thinking can bring liveliness and life-world into play. Instinct is what's needed to respond to the liveliness of being or the possibility of noticing as sympathy. Disruption, as antonymic of order, offers a means through which we manifest what it is we notice, while liveliness and courage, as antonymic of morality, asks us to act and respond rather than deferring to ideals and abstractions. Finally, imagination as antonymic of propriety/belief, enables us to conjure a life or a world or a past into being, rather than thinking that bare analysis will enable us to understand lives and times beyond our own.

17 Chapter 4.
18 Lehmann, *Tragedy*, 109.
19 Chapter 5.

But it requires a being who's able to make this happen, in order to register something beyond the self. Thus the antonyms don't overbear their opposite number, but operate to help us notice and to stop pretending that law is somehow able to be actualise in the abstract.

This is what constitutes theatrical jurisprudence. As Peter Brook remarks, as noted at the outset of the book, theatre: 'always asserts itself in the present. This is what can make it more real than the normal stream of consciousness. This is also what can make it so disturbing.'[20] So let me take you, in the absence of any harms you might have lived through, into a place of confrontation, to bring you into something of the lifeworlds of those in whom terror and trauma is etched, literally and figuratively. Not as trauma in the psychoanalytic or the abstract, but as real and as present.

So some words follow. Words on their own do nothing, produce nothing, are an absence that has to be made present. So take these words. Try them on people whom you've brought into a room for some purpose. Give them no warning so they have no idea what's going to hit them. What happens next is what makes this present and disturbing.

> *You are sitting comfortably at your seat, waiting to be entertained.*
>
> **Get up. Now. NOW. Move. HURRY UP.**
> **Do you think I'm joking?**
> **Get in front of that screen.**
> **Look straight ahead.**
> **Keep your eyes open.**
> **I don't care if the light's blinding you.**
> **STOP TWITCHING.**
> **Don't get out of line.**
> **Now move. MOVE. MOVE.**
>
> *In nothing more than a heartbeat you catch your breath and wonder if this is real, or if you slip your mind to one side, think you're in a game, that it'll go away. It won't. It's real, ever so real. Your blood runs cold. You look around, and wonder if you can slip away without be noticed, or if you might try to reason your way out of whatever's happening to you and the other people in the room. Try it. None of it works. You realise there's no before and no after, only now. Ice rushes through your veins. You have nowhere to run.*

And then some respite. Images begin to flow as you're standing there. Grotowski didn't have too much time for images, wanting bodies to produce confrontation to generate the conditions of transgression, just as Peter Brook knew that presence and liveliness disturb, but images as trigger can also produce confrontation, presence and liveness. That's what these images do. They make

20 Brook, *Empty Space*, 11.

demands of you, bringing the words and phrases you've already been subjected to into being, compounding the uncertainty of what's happening to you, and generating their own liveness. Otherwise there's nothing in these words and we bring our world to them. We see terrorism, or riots, or demands of respectability, or the conduct of others rather than of us. We bring to words what we know, or what we don't, and that means that even when we think we're simply applying words, we've brought ourselves into them.

> *The images you'll see will attenuate and modify these words, and you will be brought into a theatrical presence as the images are played. You are forced to stand there knowing why you have nowhere to run, then and now and now and then, as you read your fate through the images. They're now not of others, but of you.*

You see a black-and-white image of men in uniforms, with tanks moving towards Les Invalides in Paris, followed by another image of a group of men, walking in front of the Tour Eiffel in Paris, including Adolph Hitler. Then a colour photograph of SS soldiers marching through the streets of Paris. If you didn't know before you know now that you're in Nazi occupied Paris. This isn't a fiction film. It's real life, as a colour photograph of Paris street signs displayed in German, with ordinary people standing nearby, rolls past, then a colour image of the Rue de Rivoli in Paris, adorned with Nazi flags.

And then, in case you're still wondering why you're standing there, you see a copy of the ordinance in relation to the control of Jews, in French, issued by the Prefecture of Police, as displayed on the street, followed by an ordinary photograph, in black-and-white, of a group of men huddled together at what looks like a train station. You're wondering why they've turned up. They're waiting to be deported by the French police to Drancy camp, en route to Auschwitz, where they await certain murder. You can't tell why they're being deported, this ordinary looking group of men, though one man who wears plus fours stands out. You have to be told why they're being deported. They're Jewish, like one of the women in a colour image of two women walking down the street. The older woman is wearing a yellow star emblazoned with the word 'Juif', French for Jew, to mark her out, because no one would know otherwise, and besides, it's the law.

> *You are presented with a yellow star and you are told to put it on. If you refuse you'll be taken away immediately. You are lined up, wearing your yellow star that marks you, whoever and whatever you are. You want to remove it but you can't.*

Now you see a series of black-and-white photographs. Buses are lined up outside a building. The building is the Vel d'Hiv, the winter velodrome. Paris police rounded up thousands of French Jews and took them there as a holding prison, before they were speedily deported from France, sending them to inevitable murder at Auschwitz. In the meanwhile, the lavatories are closed to prevent escapes. If you want to go to the toilet, you have nowhere to go other than the place you're standing.

You are lined up. You are marched ahead, around and around in the room you've been kept in. You don't know what will happen next.

Now there are two black-and-white photographs of police officers and men with bicycles having their identities checked. You can't tell a thing, but the men are Jewish and will be arrested and sent to Auschwitz. They aren't wearing yellow stars, but their identity cards give them away. A black-and-white photograph of a sign on the door of a shop appears next, announcing in French and German that it's a Jewish business. Shoppers mustn't enter. The business doesn't survive. The owners try to leave France but must leave all their property behind, which is then taken by the government, obviously without compensation.

Then a juxtaposed photograph of a present day location in Paris in colour, with a black-and-white overlay of the location at the end of fighting in Paris at the end of World War II, with children playing in a burnt out German car. Their fate was different from other children, and the next photograph is in colour, of a plaque in French, which reads 'Remembering the 12,000 Jewish children deported from France between 1942 and 1944, arrested in the schools, in their homes and in the streets who died at Auschwitz or elsewhere, their sacrifice will never be forgotten.' They weren't sacrificed. They were murdered.

And then some more juxtaposed colour photographs, now of the Place de la République and the Rue de Rivoli, with black-and-white images of fighting by the Resistance at the end of the European war in 1944, followed by a single black-and-white image of Resistance fighters on the streets of Paris.

You are now allowed to sit.

A series of black-and-white images follows of disturbances on the streets of Paris. Careful attention to the clothing of those on the streets reveals that whatever had been has now passed.

You can remove your yellow stars.

It's the 1960s, or to be precise, May 1968 but it's hard to tell. A black-and-white image of a woman screaming in the street is followed by image after image of streets filled with rubble and damaged cars, of people fighting on the streets before they join hands around burnt out cars, obviously dancing, and sitting in the gutters, people are singing, with others playing guitars. It's followed by a black-and-white image of ruins in the street, with a flag of surrender on display.

You might now want to get to your feet. It's your choice.

A series of colour images begins to flow, of a young man and woman comforting each other, of a sign saying 'Nous sommes Charlie' surrounded by candles, of the army guarding the Tour Eiffel, of an Hasidic Jewish man walking on the street, surrounding by police and army, a demonstration passing by with a banner saying 'Not afraid', of two older women walking past a masked soldier, then a worried and harried man walking hurriedly, holding the hands of children, their darker colouring suggesting their difference, and clearly deeply distressed. There are now images of police, alert and tense, some masked, about to move into action, followed by a colour image of people running, terrified, and at its centre, a man, distressed and alert, his colouring suggesting his difference, pulling two screaming girls along with him, followed by an image of French Muslims marching in solidarity with France.

> *Impulse is on display and we can barely ignore the fear and distress. You think you might need to run too.*

And now, two images at the Place de la République, of a young woman contemplating the candles on display and of the sign, 'Je suis Paris'.

> *You recognise these images. They mean something to you even if you originally saw nothing in the other images, when you thought they had nothing to do with you. You may go now, or you can stay. It's up to you.*

Now if you have a chance, read the judgments in *Toben*, at both first instance and in the Court of Appeal. Or cases about refugees or about terror. Of about rights to protest or of free speech. Or the circumstances of *Wik*. Or Walter Sofronoff's blog. They'll look different now.

> *What you see now might be very different from what you saw before your own ordeal. What you experienced wasn't display. It was done to you.*

Of course, the words and the actions applied to you could have involved any setting, any scenario. There's nothing in the words except fear and demand. They are as applicable to the force applied to indigenous people stripped of their lands or taken from their families, to police brutality against protestors, to bureaucratic demands, to the treatment of refugees. Whatever the situation, to lose the possibility of agency and undergo the institution of fear can't have been experienced by most of us, yet this is what law has to animate through the abstract words and ideals of law.

Imagine now how this plays out if we've never had to live through this ourselves. Most of us will never be the people who live these lives, but now, with something written into our bodies, we will have cultivated the conditions of sympathy that take us beyond our own lives and experiences into something beyond what we might think about into what we might have lived.

Bibliography

Books and articles

Alexander Isabella, *Copyright Law and the Public Interest in the Nineteenth Century* (Oxford and Portland, OR: Hart Publishing, 2010).

Allain Paul and Ziółkowski Grzegorz (eds), *Voices from Within: Grotowski's Polish Collaborators* (London: Polish Theatre Perspectives/TAPAC, Theatre and Performance Across Cultures, 2015).

Allen Andrew P, Kennedy Paul J, Dockray Samantha, Cryan John F, Dinan Timothy G, Clarke Gerard, 'The Trier Social Stress Test: Principles and practice' (2017) 6 *Neurobiology of Stress* 113–126.

Anonymous, 'ART. VIII. – The Late Mr. Justice Talfourd' (1854) 20. 2 *The Law Magazine Or, Quarterly Review of Jurisprudence* 298–326.

Anonymous, *A Memoir of Mr. Justice Talfourd: By a Member of the Oxford Circuit* (London: Butterworths, 1854).

Anonymous, 'The Late Mr Justice Talfourd' (1854) 2. 9 *The American Law Register* 513–517.

Appleby Gabrielle and Dixon Rosalind (eds), *The Critical Judgments Project: Rereading Monis v The Queen* (Leichhardt, Sydney: Federation Press, 2016).

Antaki Mark, 'The Turn to Imagination in Legal Theory: The Re-Enchantment of the World?' (2012) 23 *Law and Critique* 1–20.

Archer Jayne Elisabeth, Goldring Elizabeth and Knight Sarah (eds), *The Intellectual and Cultural World of the Early Modern Inns of Court* (Manchester: Manchester University Press, 2011).

Aristodemou Maria, 'The Seduction of Mimesis: Theatre as Woman and the Play of Difference and Excess in Aeschylus's Oresteia' (1999) 11 *Cardozo Studies in Law and Literature* 1–33.

Aristodemou Maria, *Law and Literature: Journeys from Her to Eternity* (Oxford: Oxford University Press, 2000).

Aristotle, *Aristotle in 23 Volumes, Vol. 23* [trans. WH Fyfe] (Cambridge, MA: Harvard University Press; London: William Heinemann, 1932).

Artaud Antonin, *The Theater and Its Double* [trans. Mary Caroline Richards] (New York: Grove Press) 1958.

Artaud Antonin, *Antonin Artaud: Collected Works* [trans. Victor Corti] (London: Calder & Boyars, 1974).

Bacon Francis, *Elements of the Common Lawes of England* (London: J More Esq., 1636).

Bacon Francis, *The Works of Francis Bacon, Volume the Sixth Containing De Augmentis Scientiarum Vol. 1* (London: M Jones, 1815).

Bacon Francis, *The New Organon, or True Directions Concerning the interpretation of Nature* (1863) [trans. James Spedding, Robert Leslie Ellis and Douglas Denon Heath] (eBooks@Adelaide, 2014). https://ebooks.adelaide.edu.au/b/bacon/francis/organon.html.

Bacon Francis, *The Advancement of Learning* [1893], ed. Henry Morley (Project Gutenberg ebook), Book 2, Aphorism V.

Bakhtin Mikhail, *Rabelais and His World* [trans. Hélène Iswolsky] (Bloomington: Indiana University Press, 1984).

Bańkowski Zenon and Del Mar Maksymilian (eds), *The Moral Imagination and the Legal Life: Beyond Text in Legal Education* (Farnham, Surrey: Ashgate, 2013).

Barba Eugenio, *The Paper Canoe: A Guide to Theatre Anthropology* (London and New York: Routledge, 1995).

Barba Eugenio and Flaszen Ludwik, 'A Theatre of Magic and Sacrilege', trans Simone Sanzenbach (1965) 9. 3 *The Tulane Drama Review* 166–189.

Barish Jonas, *The Antitheatrical Prejudice* (Berkeley: University of California Press, 1981).

Barr Olivia, *A Jurisprudence of Movement: Common Law, Walking, Unsettling Place* (Abingdon: Routledge, 2016).

Bell Virginia AC, 'By the Skin of Our Teeth: The Passing of the Women's Legal Status Act 1918', Francis Forbes Lecture, 30 May 2018www.hcourt.gov.au/assets/publications/speeches/current-justices/bellj/bellj30May2018.pdf

Birkett Melissa A, 'The Trier Social Stress Test Protocol for Inducing Psychological Stress' (2011) 56 *Journal of Visualized Experiments: JoVE*3238 .

Bix Brian, 'John Austin', *The Stanford Encyclopedia of Philosophy* (Winter 2016 edition), ed. Edward N Zalta . https://plato.stanford.edu/archives/win2016/entries/austin-john/.

Blackstone William, 'On the Study of Law', *Introduction to the First Volume of the Commentaries on the Laws of England* 1765–1769, http://avalon.law.yale.edu/subject_menus/blackstone.asp

Blair Rhonda, *The Actor, Image, and Action: Acting and Cognitive Neuroscience* (New York: Routledge, 2008).

Blair Rhonda, 'Cognitive Neuroscience and Acting: Imagination, Conceptual Blending, and Empathy' (2009) 53. 4 *TDR* 92–103.

Blair Rhonda and Cook Amy (eds), *Theatre, Performance and Cognition: Languages, Bodies and Ecologies* (London: Methuen, 2016).

Boal Augusto, *Legislative Theatre: Using Performance to Make Politics* [trans. Adrian Jackson] (London: Routledge, 1999).

Boal Augusto, *Games For Actors and Non-Actors*, 2nd edn [trans. Adrian Jackson] (London: Routledge, 2002).

Boal Augusto, *Theatre of the Oppressed* [trans. Charles A McBride, Maria-Odilia Leal McBride and Emily Fryer, updated edition] (London: Pluto Press, 2008).

Botting Fred (ed.) *The Gothic* (Cambridge: DS Brewer, 2001).

Brennan Frank, 'Case Note: *R v Bjelke-Petersen and Another, Ex Parte Plunkett*' (1979) 12 *Melbourne University Law Review* 284–291.

Brewer John and Staves Susan (eds), *Early Modern Conceptions of Property* (Abingdon and New York: Routledge, 1995).

Brook Peter, *The Empty Space* [orig. McGibbon & Kee, 1968] (Harmondsworth: Penguin Books, 1968).

Brooks Christopher W, 'Plowden, Edmund (c.1518–1585)' *Oxford Dictionary of National Biography* (Oxford: Oxford University Press, 2004).

Brooks Peter, *The Melodramatic Imagination: Balzac, Henry James, Melodrama and the Mode of Excess* (New Haven CT and London: Yale University Press, 1976 and 1995).

Brooks Peter and Gewirtz Paul (eds), *Law's Stories: Narrative and Rhetoric in the Law* (New Haven: Yale University Press, 1996).

Bryan Michael, 'Early English Law Reporting' (2009) 4 *University of Melbourne Collections* 45–50.

Burwick Frederick, *British Drama of the Industrial Revolution* (Cambridge: Cambridge University Press, 2015).

Cairns Adrian, 'Zen and the Art of Acting' (2006) 2. 5 *New Theatre Quarterly* 26–28.

Calder Gillian, 'Embodied Law: Theatre of the Oppressed in the Law School Classroom' (2009) 1 *Masks: An Online Journal for Law and Theatre* 11–35.

Carpi Daniela and Leiboff Marett (eds), *Fables of the Law: Fairy Tales in a Legal Context* (Berlin: De Gruyter, 2016) .

Carpi Daniela and Ost François (eds), *As You Law It: Negotiating Shakespeare* (Berlin: De Gruyter, 2018).

Castejon Vanessa, Cole Anna, Haag Oliver and Hughes Karen (eds), *Ngapartji Ngapartji, In Turn, In Turn: Ego-histoire, Europe and Indigenous Australia* (Canberra, Australia: ANU Press, 2014).

Chadwick Henry, *Augustine: A Very Short Introduction* (Oxford: Oxford University Press 2001).

Cheah Pheng, Fraser David and Grbich Judith, *Thinking Through the Body of Law* (St. Leonards, Australia: Allen and Unwin, 1996).

Corcoran Suzanne, 'Theories of Statutory Interpretation', in Suzanne Corcoran and Stephen Bottomley (eds), *Interpreting Statutes* (Leichhardt, Australia: Federation Press, 2005), 8–30.

Corcoran Suzanne and Bottomley Stephen (eds), *Interpreting Statutes* (Leichhardt, Australia: Federation Press, 2005).

Crofts Penny, *Wickedness and Crime: Laws of Homicide and Malice* (Abingdon: Routledge, 2013).

Curran Kevin, *Shakespeare's Legal Ecologies: Law and Distributed Selfhood* (Evanston, IL: Northwestern University Press, 2017).

Curran Kevin (ed.), *Shakespeare and Judgment* (Edinburgh: Edinburgh University Press, 2017).

Curthoys Ann, Genovese Ann and Reilly Alexander, *Rights and Redemption: History, Law and Indigenous People* (Sydney: UNSW Press, 2008).

Damasio Antonio, *Descartes' Error: Emotion, Reason and the Human Brain* (London: Vintage, 2006).

Damasio Antonio, *The Feeling of What Happens: Body, Emotion and the Making of Consciousness* (London: Vintage, 2000).

Damasio Antonio, *Looking for Spinoza: Joy, Sorrow and the Feeling Brain* (London: Vintage, 2004).

Del Mar Maksymilian, 'The education of attention and encounter in the legal academy', in Zenon Bańkowski and Maksymilian Del Mar (eds), *The Moral Imagination and the Legal Life: Beyond Text in Legal Education*, 33–63.

Derrida Jacques, 'The Theater of Cruelty and the Closure of Representation' (1978) 9. 3 *Theater* 6–19.

Dershowitz Alan M, 'Life Is not a Dramatic Narrative', in Peter Brooks and Paul Gewirtz (eds), *Law's Stories: Narrative and Rhetoric in the Law* (New Haven CT: Yale University Press, 1996), 99–105.

Desautels-Stein Justin and Tomlins Christopher (eds), *Searching for Contemporary Legal Thought* (Cambridge: Cambridge University Press, 2017).

Docker John, 'Of Pearls and Coral: Jurisography and Ego History' (2016) 20 *Law Text Culture*, 18–32.

Douglas Heather, Bartlett Francesca, Luker Trish, Hunter Rosemary (eds), *Australian Feminist Judgments: Righting and Rewriting Law* (Oxford: Hart Publishing, 2015).

Dryden John, *An Essay of Dramatick Poesie* (London: Herringman, 1668).

Dutton Richard (ed.), *The Oxford Handbook of Early Modern Theatre* (Oxford: Oxford University Press, 2011).

Edelman Justice, 'Understanding Causation and Attribution of Responsibility', presented at the Commercial Conference of the Supreme Court of Victoria, University of Melbourne, Banco Court, 7 September 2015. www.fedcourt.gov.au/digital-law-library/judges-speeches/speeches-former-judges/justice-edelman/edelman-j-20150907

Etxabe Julen, *The Experience of Tragic Judgment* (Abingdon: Routledge, 2013).

Falletti Clelia, Sofia Gabriele and Jacono Victor (eds), *Theatre and Cognitive Neuroscience* (London: Bloomsbury Methuen, 2016).

Feldshuh David, 'Zen and the Actor' (1976) 20. 1 *The Drama Review: TDR* 79–89.

Fischer-Lichte Erika, *The Transformative Power of Performance* [trans. Saskya Iris Jain] (Abingdon: Routledge, 2008).

Fitzpatrick Peter, *The Mythology of Modem Law* (London: Routledge, 1992).

Forell Caroline, 'Reasonable Woman Standard of Care' (1992) 11 *University of Tasmania Law Review* 1–16.

Foulkes Richard, 'Macready, William Charles (1793–1873)' *Oxford Dictionary of National Biography*. https://doi.org/10.1093/ref:odnb/17741: www.oxforddnb.com/view/10.1093/ref:odnb/9780198614128.001.0001/odnb-9780198614128-e-17741

Gaakeer Jeanne, 'Reverent Rites of Legal Theory: Unity-Diversity-Interdisciplinarity' (2012) 36 *Australian Feminist Law Journal* 19–43.

Gaakeer Jeanne, 'Configuring Justice' (2012) 9 *No Foundations: An Interdisciplinary Journal of Law and Justice* 20–44.

Gaakeer Jeanne, '"*Sua cuique persona*"? A Note on the Fiction of Legal Personhood and a Reflection on Interdisciplinary Consequences' (2016) 28. 3 *Law and Literature* 287–317.

Gale CJ and Whatley TD, *Treatise on the Law of Easements* (London: S Sweet, 1839).

Gamow George, *Thirty Years That Shook Physics: The Story of Quantum Theory* (New York: Doubleday, 1966).

Gardner John, 'Equality, Responsibility and the Law by Arthur Ripstein' (2001) 51. 3 *University of Toronto Law Journal* 273–308.

Gardner John, 'The Many Faces of the Reasonable Person' (2015) 13. 1 *Law Quarterly Review* 563–584.

Genovese Ann and McVeigh Shaun, 'Nineteen Eighty Three: A Jurisographic Report on *Commonwealth v Tasmania*' (2015) 24. 1 *Griffith Law Review* 68–88.

Genovese Ann, McVeigh Shaun and Rush Peter D, 'Lives Lived with Law: An Introduction' (2017) 20 *Law Text Culture* 1–13.

Getzler Joshua, 'Brian Simpson's Empiricism' (2012) 3. 2 *Transnational Legal Theory* 127–139.

Goffman Erving, *The Presentation of Self in Everyday Life* (Harmondsworth: Penguin, 1990).

Goodrich Peter, 'Rhetoric as Jurisprudence: An Introduction to the Politics of Legal Language' (1984) 4. 1 *Oxford Journal of Legal Studies* 88–122.

Goodrich Peter, 'Law and Language: An Historical and Critical Introduction' (1984) 11 *Journal of Law and Society* 173–206.

Goodrich Peter, *Legal Discourse: Studies in Linguistics, Rhetoric and Legal Analysis* (London: Macmillan, 1987).

Goodrich Peter, 'Poor Illiterate Reason: History, Nationalism and Common Law' (1992) 1. 1 *Social and Legal Studies* 7–28.

Goodrich Peter, *Law in the Courts of Love: Literature and Other Minor Jurisprudences* (Abingdon: Routledge, 1996).

Goodrich Peter, 'Rhetoric and Somatics: Training the Body to Do the Work of Law' (2001) 5 *Law Text Culture* 241–270.

Goodrich Peter, 'The New Casuistry' (2007) 33 *Critical Inquiry* 673–709.

Goodrich Peter, 'Theatres of the Book: Covering, Flaunting, Marketing, Author and Text' (2010) 14 *Law Text Culture* 357–383.

Goodrich Peter, 'Specters of Law: Why the History of the Legal Spectacle Has not Been Written' (2011) 1. 3 *UC Irvine Law Review* 773–812.

Goodrich Peter, 'The Theatre of Emblems: On the Optical Apparatus and the Investiture of Persons' (2012) 8 *Law, Culture and the Humanities* 47–67.

Goodrich Peter, 'Rhetoric and Law', in Michael J. MacDonald (ed.), *The Oxford Handbook of Rhetorical Studies* (Oxford: Oxford University Press, 2017), 613–624.

Goodrich Peter, 'How Strange the Change from Major to Minor' (2017) 21 *Law Text Culture* 30–53.

Gordon Craig Edward, 'The Actor and the Übermarionette' (1908) 1. 2 *Mask* 3–15.

Grbich Judith, 'The Body in Legal Theory' (1992) 11 *University of Tasmania Law Review* 26–58.

Grochala Sarah, *The Contemporary Political Play: Rethinking Dramaturgical Structure* (London: Bloomsbury Methuen Drama, 2017).

Grotowski Jerzy, *Towards a Poor Theatre* (New York: Simon and Schuster, 1968).

Grotowski Jerzy, 'On the Genesis of Apocalypsis', trans. Kris Salata (2008) 52. 2 *TDR: The Drama Review* 40–51.

Gurnham David, *Memory, Imagination, Justice: Intersections of Law and Literature* (Aldershot: Ashgate, 2009.)

Hadley Elaine, *Melodramatic Tactics: Theatricalized Dissent in the English Marketplace, 1800–1885* (Stanford CA: Stanford University Press, 1995).

Hanly Conor, 'The Decline of Civil Jury Trial in Nineteenth-century England' (2005) 26. 3 *The Journal of Legal History* 253–278.

Hanne Michael and Weisberg Robert (eds), *Narrative and Metaphor in the Law* (Cambridge: Cambridge University Press, 2018).

Hansen Pil and Bläsing Bettina, *Performing the Remembered Present: The Cognition of Memory in Dance, Theatre and Music* (London: Methuen, 2017).

Hariman Robert, 'Theory without Modernity', in Robert Hariman (ed.), *Prudence: Classical Virtue, Postmodern Practice* (University Park, PA: Penn State University Press, 2003) 1–32.

Hariman Robert (ed.), *Prudence: Classical Virtue, Postmodern Practice* (University Park, PA: Penn State University Press, 2003).

Harp Richard and Stewart Stanley (eds), *The Cambridge Companion to Ben Jonson* (Cambridge: Cambridge University Press, 2000).

Harvey David J, *The Law Emprynted and Englysshed: The Printing Press as an Agent of Change in Law and Legal Culture 1475–1642* (Oxford: Hart Publishing, 2015).

Herman Didi, '"I Do not Attach Great Significance to It": Taking Note of "The Holocaust" in English Case Law' (2008) 17 *Social and Legal Studies* 427–452.

Herman Didi, 'David Seymour, Law, Antisemitism and the Holocaust' (2009) 18 *Social and Legal Studies* 423–425.

Herman Didi, *An Unfortunate Coincidence: Jews, Jewishness and English Law* (Oxford: Oxford University Press, 2011).

Hildebrandt Mireille, *Smart Technologies and the End(s) of Law: Novel Entanglements of Law and Technology* (Cheltenham: Edward Elgar 2015).

Hildebrand Mireille and Jeanne Gaakeer (eds), *Human Law and Computer Law: Comparative Perspectives* (Dordrecht: Springer Netherlands, 2013).

Hobsbawm Eric, 'Introduction: Inventing Traditions', in Eric Hobsbawm and Terence Ranger (eds), *The Invention of Tradition* (Cambridge: Cambridge University Press, 2003) 1–14.

Hobsbawm Eric and Ranger Terence (eds), *The Invention of Tradition* (Cambridge: Cambridge University Press, 2003).

Hobsbawn Eric and Rudé George, *Captain Swing* (London: Phoenix Press, 2001) (first published 1969 by Lawrence and Wishart).

Hodges William, 'Vaughan v Menlove', *Court of Common Pleas Vol. III: From Hilary Term, Seventh Will. IV to Michaelmas Term, First Vict. 1837* (London: Henry Butterworth, 1839), 51–55.

Hobgood Allison P, *Passionate Playgoing in Early Modern England* (Cambridge: Cambridge University Press, 2014).

Hobgood Allison P, 'God's Game of Hide-and-Seek: Bacon and Allegory', in Howard Marchitello and Evelyn Tribble (eds), *The Palgrave Handbook of Early Modern Literature and Science* (London: Palgrave Macmillan, 2017), 115–138.

Hogan-Doran Dominique SC, 'Computer Says "No": Automation, Algorithms and Artificial Intelligence in Government Decision-making' (2017) 13 *The Judicial Review* 1–39.

Holdsworth WS, 'The Disappearance of the Educational System of the Inns of Court' (1921) 69. 3 *University of Pennsylvania Law Review* 201–222.

Holdsworth WS, 'Case Law' (1934) 50 *Law Quarterly Review* 180–195.

Hughes Robert, *The Fatal Shore: A History of the Transportation of Convicts to Australia 1787–1868* (London: Vintage Books, 2003).

Hunter Rosemary, 'More than Just a Different Face? Judicial Diversity and Decision-making' (2015) 68. 1 *Current Legal Problems* 119–141.

Hunter Rosemary, McGlynn Clare, Rackley Erika (eds), *Feminist Judgments: From Theory to Practice* (Oxford: Hart Publishing, 2010).

Hutson Lorna (ed.), *The Oxford Handbook of Law and Literature, 1500–1700* (Oxford: Oxford University Press, 2017).

Hyde Alan, *Bodies of Law* (Princeton, NJ: Princeton University Press, 1997).

Johnson Mark, 'Mind Incarnate: from Dewey to Damasio' (2006) 135 *Daedalus* 46–54.

Jones David, *Crime, Protest, Community, and Police in Nineteenth-century Britain* (London: Routledge and Kegan Paul, 1982).

Jonson Ben, '(On) Lord Francis Bacon' (1625) https://sourcebooks.fordham.edu/mod/1625jonson-bacon.asp

Jonson Ben, 'On Lord Bacon's Birth-Day', in *The Works of Ben Jonson* (Boston: Phillips, Sampson, and Co., 1853).

Kaspiew Rae, 'Rape Law: Legal Narrative and Sexual Violence' (1995) 20 *Melbourne University Law Review* 350–392.

Kayman Martin A, 'Corpus Juris, Habeas Corpus, and the "Corporeal Turn" in the Humanities' (2016) 28. 3 *Law and Literature* 355–378.

Kempin, JrFrederick G, 'Precedent and Stare Decisis: The Critical Years, 1800 to 1850' (1959) 3 *American Journal of Legal History* 28–54.

Kirby Hon JusticeMichaelAC CMG, 'Introduction', in *The Rise (and Fall?) of the Barrister Class by the Hon Michael McHugh AC*, 5–7. www.hcourt.gov.au/assets/publications/speeches/former-justices/kirbyj/kirbyj_aug07b.pdf

Koppenol Gregory J, President, Land and Resources Tribunal, 'Recent Developments in Native Title in Australia with International Perspectives'. Speech delivered at the Europe-Asia Legal Conference 2002, Lake Como, Italy, 2 July 2002http://classic.austlii.edu.au/au/journals/QldJSchol/2002/30.pdf

Kuharski Allen J, '*Voices from Within: Grotowski's Polish Collaborators*, edited by Paul Allain and Grzegorz Ziółkowski; and *Acting with Grotowski: Theatre as a Field for Experiencing Life* by Zbigniew Cynkutis' (2017) 61:4 (T236) *TDR: The Drama Review* 180–183.

Kuhlken Robert, 'Settin' The Woods on Fire: Rural Incendiarism as Protest' (1999) 89. 3 *The Geographical Review* 343–363.

Laster Dominika, 'Embodied Memory: Body-Memory in the Performance Research of Jerzy Grotowski' (2012) 28. 3 *New Theatre Quarterly* 211–229.

Lazarus Micha, 'Aristotelian Criticism in Sixteenth-Century England', *Oxford Handbooks Online* (Oxford University Press, 2016) doi:10.1093/oxfordhb/9780199935338.013.148.

Lehmann Hans-Thies, 'From Logos to Landscape: Text in Contemporary Dramaturgy' (1997) *Performance Research* 55–60, 57.

Lehmann Hans-Thies, *Postdramatic Theatre* [trans. Karen Jürs-Munby] (Abingdon: Routledge, 2006).

Lehmann Hans-Thies, *Tragedy and Dramatic Theatre* [trans. Erik Butler] (Abingdon: Routledge, 2016).

Leiboff Marett, 'Law, Muteness and the Theatrical' (2010) 14 *Law Text Culture* 384–391.

Leiboff Marett, 'Ghosts of Law and Humanities (Past, Present, Future)' (2012) 36 *Australian Feminist Law Journal* 3–17.

Leiboff Marett, '"DITTO": Law, Pop Culture and Humanities and the Impact of Intergenerational Interpretative Dissonance' (2012) 36 *The Australian Feminist Law Journal* 145–163.

Leiboff Marett, 'Towards a Jurisprudence of the Embodied Mind: Sarah Lund, Forbrydelsen and the Mindful Body' (2015) 6. 2 *Naveiñ Reet: Nordic Journal of Law and Social Research* 77–91.

Leiboff Marett, 'The Good Old Rule, the Catspaw and a Two-headed Baby', in Daniela Carpi and Marett Leiboff (eds), *Fables of the Law: Fairy Tales in a Legal Context* (Berlin: De Gruyter, 2016), 187–208.

Leiboff Marett, 'Cultural Legal Studies as Law's Extraversion', in Cassandra Sharp and Marett Leiboff (eds), *Cultural Legal Studies: Law's Popular Cultures and the Metamorphosis of Law* (Abingdon: Routledge, 2016), 29–49.

Leiboff Marett, 'Theatricalising Law in Three, 1929–1939 (Brisbane)' (2016) 20 *Law Text Culture* 93–135.

Leiboff Marett, '"Stir Up the Australian Youth to Merriment": A Midsummer Night's Dream, Summer 1989–1990 (Sydney, Australia) and the Theatrical Transmutability of Law's Texts', in Daniela Carpi and François Ost (eds), *As You Law It: Negotiating Shakespeare* (Berlin: De Gruyter, 2018), 247–268.

Leiboff Marett, 'Theatricalizing Law' (2018) 30. 2 *Law and Literature* 351–367 doi:10.1080/1535685X.2017.1415051

Leiboff Marett, 'Challenging the Legal Self through Performance', in Simon Stern Bernadette Meyler, and Maksymilian Del Mar (eds), *Oxford Handbook of Law and the Humanities* (Oxford: Oxford University Press, 2019), Chapter 17.

Leiboff Marett and Nield Sophie, 'Law's Theatrical Presence: Special Issue' (2010) 14 *Law Text Culture* 1–2.

MacDonald Michael J (ed.), *The Oxford Handbook of Rhetorical Studies* (Oxford: Oxford University Press, 2017).

MacNeil William P, *Novel Judgements: Legal Theory as Fiction* (London: Routledge, 2012).

Manderson Desmond, 'Statuta v. Acts: Interpretation, Music, and Early English Legislation' (1995) 7. 2 *Yale Journal of Law and the Humanities* 317–366.

Manderson Desmond, *Songs Without Music: Aesthetic Dimensions of Law and Justice* (Berkeley: University of California Press, 2000).

Manderson Desmond, 'Apocryphal Jurisprudence' (2001) 26 *Australian Journal of Legal Philosophy* 27–59.

Manderson Desmond, 'Fission & Fusion: From Improvisation to Formalism in Law and Music' (2010) 6. 1 *Critical Studies in Improvisation* 1–10.

Manderson Desmond and Martinez Cristina S, 'Justice and Art, Face to Face' (2016) 28. 2 *Yale Journal of Law and the Humanities* 241–263.

Marchitello Howard and Tribble Evelyn (eds), *The Palgrave Handbook of Early Modern Literature and Science* (London: Palgrave Macmillan, 2017).

Maxwell-Fyfe David, 'The Inns of Court and the Impact on the Legal Profession in England' (1950) 4 *Southwestern Law Journal* 391–397.

McBain James, '"Attentive Mindes and Serious Wits"', in Lorna Hutson (ed.), *The Oxford Handbook of Law and Literature, 1500–1700* (Oxford: Oxford University Press, 2017), 80–96.

McDonald Elisabeth, Powell Rhonda, Stephens M⊠mari, Hunter Rosemary (eds), *Feminist Judgments of Aotearoa New Zealand – Te Rino: A Two-Stranded Rope* (Oxford: Hart Publishing, 2017).

McGlynn Margaret, 'Idiosyncratic Books and Common Learning: Readings on Statutes at the Inns of Court', in Lorna Hutson (ed.), *The Oxford Handbook of Law and Literature, 1500–1700* (Oxford: Oxford University Press, 2017), 41–60.

McHugh Hon. Michael AC QC 'Preparing and Arguing an Appeal' (2010) *Bar News* 85–92.

McKenzie Jon, *Perform or Else: From Discipline to Performance* (London: Routledge, 2001).

McVeigh Shaun, 'Office and Persona of the Critical Jurist: Peripheral Legal Thought (Australia)', in Justin Desautels-Stein and Christopher Tomlins (eds), *Searching for Contemporary Legal Thought* (Cambridge: Cambridge University Press, 2017), 386–405.

Meehan Michael, 'The Good, the Bad and the Ugly: Judicial Literacy and Australian Cultural Cringe' (1990) 12 *Adelaide Law Review* 431–448.

Meehan Michael, 'Blackstone's Commentaries: England's Legal Georgic?', in Wilfrid Prest (ed.), *Re-Interpreting Blackstone's Commentaries: A Seminal Text in National and International Contexts* (Oxford: Hart Publishing, 2014), 59–71.

Minkkinen Panu, 'The Radiance of Justice: On the Minor Jurisprudence of Franz Kafka' (1994) 3 *Social and Legal Studies* 349–363.

Mohr Richard and Contini Francesco, 'Reassembling the Legal: The Wonders of Modern Science in Court-Related Proceedings' (2011) 20 *Griffith Law Review* 994–1019.

Moran Leslie J, 'Law and the Gothic Imagination', in Fred Botting (ed.), *The Gothic* (2001: Cambridge: DS Brewer, 2001), 87–109.

Nelson Alan H, 'The Universities and the Inns of Court', in Richard Dutton (ed.), *The Oxford Handbook of Early Modern Theatre* (Oxford: Oxford University Press, 2011), 280–291.

Nicoll Allardyce, *A History of English Drama 1660–1900, Volume 4: Early Nineteenth Century Drama 1800–1850* (2nd edn, Cambridge: Cambridge University Press, 1955).

Nora Pierre, 'Between Memory and History: *Les Lieux de Mémoire*' (1989) 26 *Representations* 7–24.

Nora Pierre, '"Introduction" from *Essais d'Ego-Histoire*' [trans. Stephen Muecke], in Vanessa Castejon , Anna Cole , Oliver Haag and Karen Hughes (eds), *Ngapartji Ngapartji, in Turn, in Turn: Ego-histoire, Europe and Indigenous Australia* (Canberra, Australia: ANU Press, 2014), 21–22.

North Roger, *A Discourse on the Study of the Laws, with Notes and Illustrations* (London: Published by a Member of the Inner Temple, 1824).

Nussbaum Martha C, *Poetic Justice: The Literary Imagination and Public Life* (Boston: Beacon, 1995).

Nussbaum Martha C, *Cultivating Humanity: A Classical Defense of Reform in Liberal Education* (Cambridge, MA: Harvard University Press, 1997).

Nussbaum Martha C, *Political Emotions: Why Love Matters for Justice* (Cambridge, MA: Belknap Press, 2013).

Olson Greta, 'Law Is not Turgid and Literature not Soft and Fleshy: Gendering and Heteronormativity in Law and Literature Scholarship' (2012) 36 *Australian Feminist Law Journal* 65–86.

Olson Greta, 'The Turn to Passion: Has Law and Literature Become Law and Affect?' (2016) 28. 3 *Law and Literature* 335–353.

O'Sullivan Richard, 'Edmund Plowden, Master Treasurer of the Middle Temple' (1957) 3 *The Catholic Lawyer* 44–58.

Parker James EK, *Acoustic Jurisprudence: Listening to the Trial of Simon Bikindi* (Oxford: Oxford University Press, 2015).

Parsley Connal, 'The Mask and Agamben: The Transitional Juridical Technics of Legal Relation' (2010) 14 *Law Text Culture* 12–39.

Pearson Ashley and Tranter Kieran, 'Code, Nintendo's Super Mario and Digital Legality' (2015) 28. 4 *International Journal for the Semiotics of Law* 825–842.

Philippopoulos-Mihalopoulos Andreas, *Spatial Justice: Body, Lawscape, Atmosphere* (Abingdon: Routledge, 2015).

Philippopoulos-Mihalopoulos Andreas, 'The Funambulist Atmosphere'. *The Funambulist Papers* 29 https://thefunambulist.net/philosophy/guest-writers-essays-29-the-funambulist-atmosphere-by-andreas-philippopoulos-mihalopoulos

Philippopoulos-Mihalopoulos Andreas, 'Withdrawing from Atmosphere: An Ontology of Air Partitioning and Affective Engineering' (2016) 34. 1 *Environment and Planning D: Society and Space* 150–167.

Poole Steve, '"A Lasting and Salutary Warning": Incendiarism, Rural Order and England's Last Scene of Crime Execution' (2008) 19. 2 *Rural History* 163–177.

Plowden Edmund, *The Commentaries, or Reports of Edmund Plowden* (Oxford: Blackwell, 2015).

Porter Roy, *Enlightenment: Britain and the Creation of the Modern World* (London: Penguin, 2000).

Prest Wilfred, *The Inns of Court under Elizabeth I and the Early Stuarts, 1590–1640* (London: Longman, 1972).

Prest Wilfred, *The Rise of the Barristers: A Social History of the English Bar 1590–1640* (Oxford: Clarendon Press, 1986).

Prest Wilfrid (ed.), *Re-Interpreting Blackstone's Commentaries: A Seminal Text in National and International Contexts* (Oxford: Hart Publishing, 2014).

Puchner Martin, *Stage Fright: Modernism, Anti-Theatricality, and Drama* (Baltimore, MD: Johns Hopkins University Press, 2002).

Pugsley David, 'Mr Justice Talfourd and the Western Circuit' (2007) 39 *Bracton Law Journal* 35–51.

Raffield Paul, *Shakespeare's Imaginary Constitution: Late-Elizabethan Politics and the Theatre of Law* (Oxford: Hart Publishing, 2010).

Raffield Paul, 'The Dramatic Imagination and the Dream of Law', in Marco Wan (ed.), *Reading The Legal Case: Cross-Currents between Law and the Humanities* (Abingdon: Routledge, 2012), 175–189.

Raffield Paul, *The Art of Law in Shakespeare* (Oxford: Hart Publishing, 2017).

Ramshaw Sara, *Justice as Improvisation: The Law of the Extempore* (Abingdon: Routledge, 2013).

Rancière Jacques, *The Emancipated Spectator* [trans. Gregory Elliott] (London and New York: Verso, 2009).

Rancière Jacques, *The Lost Thread: The Democracy of Modern Fiction* [trans. Steven Corcoran] (London: Bloomsbury, 2017).

Read Alan, *Theatre and Law* (Basingstoke: Palgrave Macmillan, 2016).

Richards Eric, '"Captain Swing" in the West Midlands' (1974) 19. 1 *International Review of Social History* 86–99.

Rogers Nicole, 'The Play of Law: Comparing Performance in Law and Theatre' (2008) 8. 2 *QUT Law Review* 429–443.

Rogers Nicole, 'Performance and Pedagogy in the Wild Law Judgment Project' (2017) 27 *Legal Education Review* Article 3, 8–11.

Rogers Nicole and Maloney Michelle (eds), *Law as if Earth Really Mattered: The Wild Law Judgment Project* (Abingdon: Routledge, 2017).

Ross Richard J, 'The Memorial Culture of Early Modern English Lawyers: Memory as Keyword, Shelter, and Identity, 1560–1640' (1998) 10 *Yale Journal of Law and the Humanities* 229–326.

Rush Peter, 'Killing Me Softly with His Words: Hunting the Law Student' (1990) 1 *Law and Critique* 21–37.

Salata Kris, *The Unwritten Grotowski: Theory and Practice of the Encounter* (New York: Routledge, 2013).

Sammons Jack L, 'Justice as Play' (2010) 61 *Mercer Law Review* 517–550.

Sammons Jack L, 'The Law's Melody' (2011) 55 *Villanova Law Review* 1143–1160.

Sarrazac Jean-Pierre, 'The Invention of "Theatricality": Rereading Bernard Dort and Roland Barthes' [trans. Virginie Magnat] (2002) 31. 2/3 *SubStance* 57–72.

Seymour David, *Law, Antisemitism and the Holocaust* (London: Routledge Cavendish, 2007).

Shapiro Barbara J, 'Law and Science in Seventeenth-Century England' (1969) 4 *Stanford Law Review* 727–766.

Shapiro Barbara J, *A Culture of Fact: England, 1550–1720* (Ithaca, NY: Cornell University Press, 2000).

Sharp Cassandra and Leiboff Marett (eds), *Cultural Legal Studies: Law's Popular Cultures and the Metamorphosis of Law* (Abingdon: Routledge, 2016).

Simpson AWB, 'Legal Liability for Bursting Reservoirs: The Historical Context of 'Rylands v. Fletcher'' (1984) 13. 2 *The Journal of Legal Studies* 209–264.

Slowiak James and Custo Jairo, *Jerzy Grotowski* (London and New York: Routledge, 2007).

Smith Joseph, 'The Sword and Shield of Perseus: Some Mythological Dimensions of the Law' (1983) 6. 3–4 *International Journal of Law and Psychiatry* 235–261.

Sofronoff Walter, 'Law, Liberties and Rights: Foreword by Walter Sofronoff QC'. *Justice and the Law Society (JATL) Blog*, 6 April 2017. www.jatl.org/blog/foreword

Stalford Helen, Hollingsworth Kathryn, Gilmore Stephen (eds), *Rewriting Children's Rights Judgments: From Academic Vision to New Practice* (Oxford: Hart Publishing, 2017).

Stallybrass Peter and White Allon, *The Politics and Poetics of Transgression* (Ithaca, NY: Cornell University Press, 1986).

Steel H Spenden, 'Origin and History of English Inns of Chancery' (1907) 13. 8 *The Virginia Law Register* 585–593.

Stern Simon, 'Narrative in the Legal Text: Judicial Opinions and Their Narratives', in Michael Hanne and Robert Weisberg (eds), *Narrative and Metaphor in the Law* (Cambridge: Cambridge University Press, 2018), 121–139.

Stewart Stanley, 'Jonson's Criticism', in Richard Harp and Stanley Stewart (eds), *The Cambridge Companion to Ben Jonson* (Cambridge: Cambridge University Press, 2000), 175–187.

Stone Peters Julie, 'Legal Performance Good and Bad' (2008) 4. 2 *Law, Culture and the Humanities* 179–200.

Sugarman David, 'Legal Theory, the Common Law Mind and the Making of the Textbook Tradition', in William Twining (ed.), *Legal Theory and Common Law* (Oxford: Blackwell, 1986) 26–62.

Sugarman David, 'Promoting Dialogue between History and Socio-legal Studies: The Contribution of Christopher W. Brooks and the 'Legal Turn' in Early Modern English History' (2017) 44. S1 *Journal of Law and Society* S37–S60.

Sugarman David and Warrington Ronnie, 'Land Law, Citizenship and the Invention of Englishness: The Strange World of the Equity of Redemption', in John Brewer and Susan Staves (eds), *Early Modern Conceptions of Property* (Abingdon and New York: Routledge, 1995), 112–143.

Talfourd Thomas Noon, 'Notice, Instead Of Dedication', in *Ion: A Tragedy in Five Acts* (4th edn) (London: Edward Moxon, 1837), iii–vi.

Talfourd Thomas Noon, 'Preface to the Fourth Published Edition', in *Ion: A Tragedy in Five Acts* (4th edn) (London: Edward Moxon, 1837), vii–xxii.

Tamanaha Brian, 'The Third Pillar of Jurisprudence: Social Legal Theory' (2015) 56 *William and Mary Law Review* 2235–2277.

Taxidou Olga, *Tragedy, Modernity and Mourning* (Edinburgh: Edinburgh University Press, 2004).

Temple Kathryn, 'Blackstone's "Stutter": The (Anti)Performance of the Commentaries', in Wilfrid Prest (ed.), *Re-Interpreting Blackstone's Commentaries: A Seminal Text in National and International Contexts* (London: Bloomsbury, 2014) 3–20.

Tomlins Christopher, 'Re-Interpreting Blackstone's Commentaries: A Seminal Text in National and International Contexts' (2015) 36 *Adelaide Law Review* 599–621.

Tranter Kieran, 'Disrupting Technology Disrupting Law' (2017) *Law, Culture and the Humanities*, 10–11. https://doi.org/10.1177/1743872117704925

Twining William (ed.), *Legal Theory and Common Law* (Oxford: Blackwell, 1986).

Upton Andrew, 'A Message from Andrew Upton', in *Program: A Midsummer Night's Dream* (Sydney: Sydney Theatre Company, 2016).

van Rijswijk Honni, 'Interventions into the feeling of popular justice: Australia's Stolen Generations, the problem of sentimentality, and re-encountering the testimonial form', in Cassandra Sharp and Marett Leiboff (eds), *Cultural Legal Studies: Law's Popular Cultures and the Metamorphosis of Law* (Abingdon: Routledge, 2016), 71–94.

Veeder Van Vechten, 'The English Reports, 1292–1865' (1901) 15 *Harvard Law Review* 1–25.

Veitch Scott, *Law and Irresponsibility: On the Legitimation of Human Suffering* (London: Routledge Cavendish, 2007).

Wan Marco (ed.), *Reading the Legal Case: Cross-Currents between Law and the Humanities* (Abingdon: Routledge, 2012).

Watt Gary, *Dress, Law and Naked Truth: A Cultural Study of Fashion and Form* (London: Bloomsbury, 2013).

Watt Gary and Raffield Paul (eds), *Shakespeare and the Law* (Oxford: Hart Publishing, 2008).

Winfield Percy H, *The Chief Sources of English Legal History* (Cambridge, MA: Harvard University Press, 1925).

Wolford Lisa, *Grotowski's Objective Drama Research* (Jackson: University of Mississippi Press, 1996).

Yelle Robert A, 'Bentham's Fictions: Canon and Idolatry in the Genealogy of Law' (2005) 17 *Yale Journal of Law and the Humanities* 151–179.

Young Alison, 'The Waste Land of the Law, the Wordless Song of the Rape Victim' (1998) 22. 2 *Melbourne University Law Review* 442–465.

Zagorin Perez, *Francis Bacon* (Princeton, NJ: Princeton University Press, 1999).

Zurcher Andrew, *Shakespeare and Law*. Arden Critical Companions (London: Methuen, 2010).

Media

Allain Paul, 'Obituary: Jerzy Grotowski', *The Independent*, Thursday 19 January 1999. https://www.independent.co.uk/arts-entertainment/obituary-jerzy-grotowski-1074849.html

Anonymous, 'Death of Mr Edward Menlove', *Oamaru Mail*, XXVIII. 8243 , 27 July 1903. https://paperspast.natlib.govt.nz/newspapers/OAM19030727.2.5

Anonymous, 'Judge Talfourd's Last Address', *Adelaide Times*, Saturday 15 July 1854, 4.

Anonymous, 'Mr. Sergeant Talfourd, M.P.' (1838) 31 *The Mirror of Literature, Amusement, and Instruction* v–viii.

Anonymous, 'Popular English Drama – The Mystery Plays', Harvard's Geoffrey Chaucer Website, undated, https://chaucer.fas.harvard.edu/pages/popular-english-drama-mystery-plays

Anonymous, 'Serjeant Talfourd', *The London Journal: and Weekly Record of Literature, Science and Art* (1847) 6. 146 , 11 December 1847, 233–234.

Anonymous, 'Sudden Death of Mr. Justice Talfourd', *Empire*, Tuesday 20 June 1854, 2.

Anonymous, 'Talfourd', *The Sydney Morning Herald*, Monday 3 July 1854.

Anonymous, *The Courier*, Hobart, on Thursday 6 July 1854.

Anonymous, 'The Late Mr. Justice Talfourd', *Adelaide Times*, Saturday 1 July 1854, 4.

Appleby Gabrielle, 'Politicising Advice: A Cautionary Tale for All Governments', *The Conversation*, 25 March 2014. https://theconversation.com/politicising-advice-a-cautionary-tale-for-all-governments-24773

'Applications of Artificial Intelligence to Legal Informatics'. *Wikipedia*. https://en.wikipedia.org/wiki/Applications_of_artificial_intelligence_to_legal_informatics

'Bjelke Bitter Beer Ad – Queensland Uni Revue 1977', https://www.youtube.com/watch?v=dX9bwamb1Ls

'Burlton Hall, a Grade II Listed Building in Loppington, Shropshire'. https://britishlistedbuildings.co.uk/101212510-burlton-hall-loppington#.XDbillwzaUk

Carr Shanann, 'Remembering Edward Menlove'. https://culturewaitaki.org.nz/epitaph/remembering-edward-menlove-2009-2010

'Constable, John, 1776–1837'. https://www.tate.org.uk/art/artists/john-constable-108

'Constable John, *The Hay Wain*, 1821'. London: The National Gallery. https://www.nationalgallery.org.uk/paintings/john-constable-the-hay-wain

Croxford Rianna, 'Exeter University Suspends Five Law Students in Racism Scandal', *Financial Times*, 21 March 2018. https://www.ft.com/content/807db2b0-2c42-11e8-a34a-7e7563b0b0f4

Culture Poland, *Artists: Jerzy Grotowski*, 'Laboratory Theatre'. https://culture.pl/en/artist/jerzy-grotowski

Flaszen Ludwik, 'Photograph, Andyzan, Uzbekistan'. United States Holocaust Museum. https://www.ushmm.org/search/results/?q=ludwik+flaszen.

Fret Jarosław and Kolankiewicz Leszek, *Rhizome* (Film), Theatre Olympics 2016. http://www.theatreolympics2016.pl/en/calendar/rhizome

Hook Thomas and Colburn Henry (eds), *The New Monthly Magazine and Humourist*, Part 3 (London, 1837) 213–220.

Howes Hetta Elizabeth, 'Medieval Drama and the Mystery Plays', British Library, 31 January 2018. https://www.bl.uk/medieval-literature/articles/medieval-drama-and-the-mystery-plays

Hunt Elle, 'Judge Compares Offensive Facebook Posts to Football in Sentencing Sydney Man', *The Guardian*, 29 July 2016. https://www.theguardian.com/australia-news/2016/jul/29/court-sentences-sydney-man-for-sexually-explicit-facebook-comments

Hurst Daniel, 'Inside Queensland's Spy Unit', *The Brisbane Times*, 7 April 2010. https://www.brisbanetimes.com.au/national/queensland/inside-queenslands-spy-unit-20100406-rpbg.html

'Hymns Ancient and Modern'. *Wikipedia*. https://en.wikipedia.org/wiki/Hymns_Ancient_and_Modern

Interview with Paul Allain , 'Grotowski's Influence: Barba, Brook And Beyond', *Essential Drama*, 19 November 2017. http://essentialdrama.com/tag/paul-allain/

'Justice of the Common Pleas'. *Wikipedia*. https://en.wikipedia.org/wiki/Justice_of_the_Common_Pleas

Kembrey Melanie, 'Sydney Labourer Zane Alchin Sentenced for Harassing Women on Facebook', *The Sydney Morning Herald*, 29 July 2016. https://www.smh.com.au/national/nsw/sydney-man-zane-alchin-sentenced-for-harassing-women-on-facebook-20160729-gqg8l8.html

King Katie, 'Racism at Exeter Law School: Students Expelled and Suspended as Investigation Concludes', *Legal Cheek*, 1 May 2018. https://www.legalcheek.com/2018/05/racism-at-exeter-law-school-students-expelled-and-suspended-as-investigation-concludes/

Kirkup James, in Allain Paul , 'Obituary: Jerzy Grotowski', *The Independent*, Thursday 19 January 1999. https://www.independent.co.uk/arts-entertainment/obituary-jerzy-grotowski-1074849.html

LB, 'Memoir of Mr. Serjeant Talfourd, M.P.' (1837) *The New Monthly Magazine and Humourist*, 213–220.

Lee Daniel, 'Legal Science and Legal Reform in the Juridical Thought of Sir Francis Bacon' (University of California, Berkeley, 2014), 1–13. http://rems.berkeley.edu/files/2012/03/Daniel-Lee-Legal-Science-and-Legal-Reform-in-the-Juridical-Thought-of-Sir-Francis-Bacon.pdf

Marks Lucy, 'Artificial Intelligence Law Firm Aims to Roll Out in Remote, Low Socio-Economic Communities', Australian Broadcasting Corporation, 14 November 2017.

Menlove, Thomas, https://www.rootschat.com/forum/index.php?topic=435224.0

Mezrani Leanne, 'Judge Says Bar Is No Place for Rhetoric', *Lawyers Weekly*, 13 August 2012. https://www.lawyersweekly.com.au/news/10570-judge-says-bar-is-no-place-for-rhetoric.

'Notice: Creditor's Petition, "Thomas Menlove"", *The London Gazette*, Saturday 6 April 1844, 392.

'Notice: Insolvent Debtor No 64–872 (Thomas Menlove)' *The Jurist* (1844) 123.

'Old Colonists: Mr Edward Menlove'. *The Cyclopedia of New Zealand* [*Otago & Southland Provincial Districts*]. http://nzetc.victoria.ac.nz/tm/scholarly/tei-Cyc04Cycl-t1-body1-d4-d28.html

'Red Barn Murder'. *Wikipedia*. https://en.wikipedia.org/wiki/Red_Barn_Murder

Scottish Feminist Judgments Project, Theatre Workshop, www.sfjp.law.ed.ac.uk/2017/10/16/hello-world/

Sofronoff Walter, 'Opinion: Attorney–General Jarrod Bleijie's crisis of confidence', *The Courier-Mail*, 25 March 2014. https://www.couriermail.com.au/news/opinion/opinion-attorneygeneral-jarrod-bleijies-crisis-of-confidence/news-story/c56b6ffe68661a85e25109950a804d60

Stafford Andrew, 'By Joh, It Could Be Trump! Musical Satire Delves into Bjelke-Petersen's Reign', *The Guardian*, 8 July 2017. https://www.theguardian.com/stage/2017/jul/08/by-joh-it-could-be-trump-musical-satire-delves-into-bjelke-petersens-reign

Sutton Candace, 'Tinder Shamer in Prison Charged with Slicing Girl's Underwear'. https://www.news.com.au/national/nsw-act/courts-law/tinder-slut-shamer-in-prison-charged-with-slicing-girls-underwear/news-story/f06933aeaad51c90e265d636cf7e4eac

'The Dress'. *Wikipedia*. https://en.wikipedia.org/wiki/The_dress

'The Germans'. *Wikipedia*. https://en.wikipedia.org/wiki/The_Germans

Weekly Bill for the Theatre Royal, Covent Garden for Friday 28 April1837, Theatre Royal. https://ubir.buffalo.edu/xmlui/handle/10477/2734

'Vaughan, of Burlton Hall', in *Burke's Genealogical and Heraldic History of the Commoners of Great Britain and Ireland*, 2 (1837) 238–242.

Walter Steve, 'Aristotle Didn't Know Anything about Theatre: Why Do Playwrights Still Adhere to the Philosopher's Over-Simplistic View of Drama? It's a Greek Tragedy', *The Guardian*, 4 October 2010. https://www.theguardian.com/stage/theatreblog/2010/oct/04/aristotle-poetics-theatre-sophocles-euripides4.

Widener Michael, 'Landmarks of Law Reporting 4 – Plowden: The First Modern Law Reports'. https://library.law.yale.edu/news/landmarks-law-reporting-4-plowden-first-modern-law-reports, 4 May 2009.

Winick Erin, 'Lawyer-Bots Are Shaking Up Jobs', *MIT Technology Review*, 12 December 2017. https://www.technologyreview.com/s/609556/lawyer-bots-are-shaking-up-jobs/

Wik vs Queensland: The Day Wik Won the Battle but Lost the War, Film, 2018.

'*Wik vs Queensland*: The Day Wik Won the Battle but Lost the War'. Film Press Kit, 2018. https://www.wikvsqueensland.com/WIKvsQUEENSLAND_PressKit.pdf

Archives

Berkshire Record Office, DEX1410 – 'Legal and personal papers of Thomas Noon Talfourd (1795–1854), judge and writer'. http://ww2.berkshirenclosure.org.uk

Berkshire Record Office, D/EX 1432/1/5, Talfourd papers. http://ww2.berkshirenclosure.org.uk

Queensland Museum, Condom vending machine, University of Queensland Refectory. www.collections.qm.qld.gov.au/search.do?view=detail&page=1&id=1519258&db=object

Shropshire Archives, XD3651/D/5/773: 'Draft agreement: George Wycherly with Thomas Menlove (Jan 1835) Shropshire Archives box 481 Jan 1835 Description: re sale and purchase of farm and lands at Burlton (Two copies)'.

Shropshire Archives, XD3651/D/5/774: 'Draft agreement: Thomas Menlove with John Cheshire (Jan 1835) Shropshire Archives, box 481, Jan 1835 Description: Agreement for sale and purchase of land at Burlton. Related People: Menlove, Thomas, Cheshire, John,'

Cases

Blum v Lipski [1938] VLR 247.

Blyth v The Company of Proprietors of The Birmingham Waterworks (1856) 11 Exch 781, 156 ER 1047.

Brown v Tasmania [2017] HCA 43 (18 October 2017).

Doodeward v Spence (1908) 6 CLR 406.

Irving v Penguin Books Limited [2000] EWHC QB 115.

Millar v Taylor (1769) 98 ER 201.

Mirehouse v Rennell (1833) 1 Cl. & F. 527, 546, 6 ER 1015.

R v Bjelke-Petersen, Ex Parte Plunkett [1978] QdR 305.

R v Saunders and Archer (1573) 2 *Plowden* 473; 75 ER 706.

R v Stanbrook (Supreme Court of Victoria, 10 November 1992).

R v Stanbrook (Court of Criminal Appeal, 16 March 1993).

The President , 'In The Matter of a Welcome Ceremony to Mark The Appointment of the Honourable Justice Walter Sofronoff as a Judge of the Supreme Court of Queensland to sit as President'Supreme Court of Queensland, Court Of Appeal Division, Thursday 6 April 2017, 1–13. https://archive.sclqld.org.au/judgepub/2017/holmes06042017.pdf

Thomas v R (1937) 59 CLR 279.

Toben v Nationwide News Pty Ltd; Toben v Mathieson [2015] NSWSC 1784

Toben v Nationwide News Pty Ltd [2016] NSWCA 296

Tonson v Collins (1760) 96 ER 180

Vaughan (or Vaughn) v Menlove (Nisi Prius) (1837) 7 Car. & P. 525.1, 173 *English Reports* 232

Vaughan (or Vaughn) v Menlove (1837) 3 Bing (NC) 467, 132 *Eng Rep* 490

Vaughan (or Vaughn) v Menlove S. C. 4 Scott, 244

Vaughan (or Vaughn) v Menlove 3 Hodges, 51

Vaughan (or Vaughn) v Menlove G L. J. Q P. 92

Vaughan (or Vaughn) v Menlove 1. Jur, 215

Walton Stores (Interstate) Ltd v Maher (1988) 164 CLR 387.

Wik Peoples v Queensland (1996) 187 CLR 1.

Wik Peoples v State of Queensland & Ors B8/1996 [1996] HCATrans 228 (11 June 1996). www.austlii.edu.au/cgi-bin/viewdoc/au/cases/cth/HCATrans/1996/228.html

Legislation

Racial Discrimination Act 1975 (Cth) ss 18C and 18D (Australia).

*Stage Licensing Act*1737 (10 Geo 2 C28).

*Supreme Court of Judicature Act*1873.

*Theatre Acts*1843 (6 & 7 Vict c.88).

*Theatres Act*1968 (UK).

Vagabonds Act 1572 (14 Eliz.I, c. 5).

Index

For Product Safety Concerns and Information please contact our EU
representative GPSR@taylorandfrancis.com
Taylor & Francis Verlag GmbH, Kaufingerstraße 24, 80331 München, Germany

www.ingramcontent.com/pod-product-compliance
Ingram Content Group UK Ltd.
Pitfield, Milton Keynes, MK11 3LW, UK
UKHW011016180926
475701UK00004B/770

* 9 7 8 0 3 6 7 7 8 4 6 9 0 *